The Time-Life Gardener's Guide

LAWNS AND GROUND COVERS

A

REDEFINITION
BOOK

TIME® LIFE BOOKS

The Time-Life Gardener's Guide

LAWNS AND GROUND COVERS

TIME-LIFE BOOKS, ALEXANDRIA, VIRGINIA

CONTENTS

A yard is more than an array of flowers, shrubs and trees. It is a complete environment that is unified by one underlying element—the lush green expanse of a lawn or a ground cover. Grasses and ground covers are more than functional; they come in a broad variety of forms, textures and colors, and are worthy of display in their own right. Whether you use a neatly shaped lawn to surround your house, a flowering ground cover to enliven a slope, or the billowing foliage of an ornamental grass to soften the edges of your property, these plants will serve to unify your yard.

This volume describes the types of turfgrasses (grasses used for lawns), ornamental grasses and ground covers that are widely available and tells how to select, plant and maintain them. At the end of the volume is a dictionary with photographs accompanying more than 135 entries. Each entry describes the areas, climates and conditions in which the grass or ground cover will flourish.

4

MAKING THE MOST OF NATURE

5

DICTIONARY OF GRASSES AND GROUND COVERS

1
OFF TO
A GOOD START

Grasses and ground covers, unlike most garden plants, are actively encouraged to spread well beyond their point of origin, blanketing a wide area as quickly as possible in an expanse of green. To accomplish this goal they use whatever means nature gave them. Most of the popular ground covers—pachysandra, periwinkle, cotoneaster, ivy, juniper—are either vines, creeping plants whose long stems put down new roots wherever a leaf node touches the ground; or perennials that grow by spreading on underground stems called rhizomes; or prostrate shrubs that have wide-spreading branches. Lawn grasses spread either by rhizomes, by aboveground stems called stolons or by an ever-widening crown that continues to expand until it meets its neighbor. Ryegrass and hard fescue are of this last type; zoysia and St. Augustine grass spread outward by means of stolons or rhizomes.

Aiding and abetting these natural inclinations are a variety of planting techniques, explained on the following pages. Many are used by professionals in charge of such high-profile surfaces as golf courses, the gardens of stately homes and highway medians. Among them are a method for planting grass in the form of plugs, or chunks of sod, in a grid established by a homemade grid-forming rake, and an alternative method that tills rooted sprigs of grass into the soil. One method is shown for distributing grass seed by means of a mechanical spreader, and a section on ground covers explains not only how to plant them but how to position them so that they will grow in the desired direction.

Before you embark on any of these procedures, the soil should be thoroughly prepared—weeded, fertilized, tilled and, if necessary, treated with soil amendments. And some young plants need to be protected with moisture-conserving mulch. This information is provided in this section.

FILLING IN
THE BARE SPOTS

A reseeded patch of lawn lies ready for a light covering of straw mulch. Given proper watering, the bare spot will start showing new green shoots within one to three weeks; about a month later, the patch will have become indistinguishable from the surrounding lawn.

Bare spots can mar even the best-kept lawns. The most common cause is excessive foot traffic, which compacts soil and prevents grass roots from getting the air, water and nutrients they need. Grass may also die in places where you have accidentally spilled too much herbicide, too much fertilizer or some of the gasoline intended for your power mower.

Bare spots are easily repaired by reseeding. But simply spreading seed and raking it into the soil will waste a good deal of seed. For the best chance of its germinating, seed should be spread on bare spots only after the soil underneath has been reconditioned.

If a bare spot was caused by compacted soil, first break up the soil to a depth of 3 to 6 inches; then lighten the soil texture and add important nutrients by working in a few inches of peat moss and some fertilizer. Rake the patch until it is level with the surrounding lawn. Then scatter seed by the handful over the patch.

If the bare spot was caused by spilled chemicals, dig up and discard the contaminated soil and replace it with fresh, amended soil. Rake the area level with the surrounding lawn and spread seed over it.

Seed for the repair should match the seed you used to start the lawn. Planting different kinds of grasses side by side will result in a permanently unkempt look. If you don't have some of the original seed on hand, buy the same (or a similar) mix at a garden supply center.

After planting, keep the patch watered and exclude foot traffic until the grass is well established. If necessary, fence off the patch with stakes and string.

1 With a trowel, a shovel or a garden fork, loosen the top 3 to 6 inches of soil in the bare spot. Into the loosened soil, work 2 inches of peat moss and a sprinkling of lawn fertilizer. Level the patch. (For bare spots caused by spilled chemicals, dig up and discard the top 3 to 6 inches of soil, and substitute uncontaminated, amended soil.)

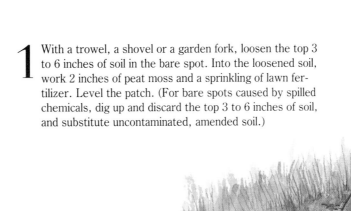

2 Spread seeds thinly and evenly on the surface of the prepared soil *(left)*. Then scratch them into the soil with the teeth of a rake, lightly tamp them down with the flat side of the rake and smooth out the soil.

3 Scatter a very thin layer of clean straw over the newly seeded area *(right);* this mulch will help retain moisture in the soil. Water the patch well. Keep it moist and protect it from use until the new grass is well established. □

TILLING THE SOIL AND ENRICHING IT

There is only one sure way to grow velvety grass or green and vigorous ground cover plants and that is to prepare the soil for them carefully and ahead of time, before any planting is done. Most soils need some enriching; all can benefit from the sort of tilling, clearing and smoothing pictured opposite and on the following pages. It is also a good idea to test the quality of the existing soil before tilling it, to find out exactly what sort of enriching and amending it needs.

First of all, test the soil's acid-alkaline balance, called the pH level. A level of 7.0 is neutral; below that the soil tends toward acidity. Turfgrasses prefer slightly acid surroundings in the 6.5 to 6.9 range, ground covers a more acidic 6.0 to 6.5. Take some samples of earth from several parts of the area to be planted, put the samples in small plastic bags, label them, and then send them to the nearest county extension office or state university. The laboratory report that comes back will indicate whether the various soil areas need to be made more alkaline by mixing in crushed limestone or more acidic by the addition of sulfur.

The lab report should also include measurements of vital minerals: calcium, potassium, phosphorus and magnesium. If there are deficiencies, purchase a fertilizer that contains the needed nutrients (garden supply centers will help select the right type and amount).

Then evaluate the soil's texture. Ideally the soil should be a crumbly loam—firm enough to hold moisture, but neither dense and clayey nor too loose and sandy. To improve the soil's structure, add organic matter: rotted leaves, compost, peat moss. Even good soil can benefit from enrichment with some organic matter. Spread it over the area being planted and work it into the soil with a rotary tiller, along with the fertilizer and any other needed amendments. For the anatomy of a rotary tiller, see page 13.

Growing thick and lush and bright green, a recently planted stretch of turfgrass has the look of a long-established lawn. Careful preparation of the ground before planting makes possible this sort of satisfying and speedy growth.

1 Start preparing your soil by churning it up with a rotary tiller, with the blades set to dig down 6 inches. If the site already has grass on it, make a preliminary run with the blades set for a 2- to 3-inch-deep surface till. Rake up and discard the cut-up grass before doing the regular 6-inch-deep tilling. Make sure the ground is moist before using the tiller; dry soil is hard to till properly.

2 Rake the tilled soil carefully, breaking up any clods and removing rocks, weeds, remaining bits of uprooted grass and all miscellaneous debris. For growing turfgrass especially, the soil should be as smooth and fine-textured as you can make it.

3 Spread a layer of peat moss or other organic matter over the tilled area. The layer should be 2 to 4 inches thick; less than that will not much improve the soil's richness or texture. If your soil test indicated a need for lime, sulfur or fertilizers, add them now.

4 Using the rotary tiller again, churn all the amendments into the soil thoroughly. Then smooth the plot once more with a rake *(right)*. Fill in any depressions where excess water might gather, and level off any mounds.

5 As a final finishing touch before planting, firm the tilled and amended soil with a light lawn roller. (Rollers are available by the day from tool rental agencies.) Rolling gets rid of air pockets as well as providing the smooth surface that lawns especially need. □

HOW A ROTARY TILLER WORKS

Motor-driven rotary tillers make working the soil a lot easier than doing it by hand, and they do it more efficiently. They can be rented from tool and garden centers—or you can buy one if the amount of gardening you do warrants the expense. The smaller and less costly sort—front-tine tillers with the rotary blades up front—are useful for tilling soil that has been worked before. Larger and more expensive rear-tine tillers, like the one shown here, have the power to break up earth that has never been tilled before and is likely to be compacted. Both sorts are essentially the same, though, and share the features detailed below.

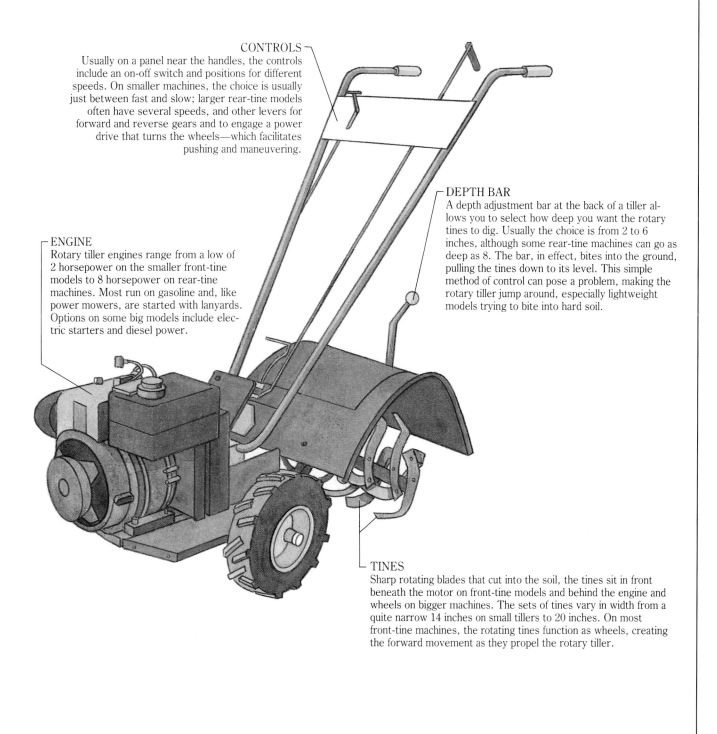

CONTROLS
Usually on a panel near the handles, the controls include an on-off switch and positions for different speeds. On smaller machines, the choice is usually just between fast and slow; larger rear-tine models often have several speeds, and other levers for forward and reverse gears and to engage a power drive that turns the wheels—which facilitates pushing and maneuvering.

DEPTH BAR
A depth adjustment bar at the back of a tiller allows you to select how deep you want the rotary tines to dig. Usually the choice is from 2 to 6 inches, although some rear-tine machines can go as deep as 8. The bar, in effect, bites into the ground, pulling the tines down to its level. This simple method of control can pose a problem, making the rotary tiller jump around, especially lightweight models trying to bite into hard soil.

ENGINE
Rotary tiller engines range from a low of 2 horsepower on the smaller front-tine models to 8 horsepower on rear-tine machines. Most run on gasoline and, like power mowers, are started with lanyards. Options on some big models include electric starters and diesel power.

TINES
Sharp rotating blades that cut into the soil, the tines sit in front beneath the motor on front-tine models and behind the engine and wheels on bigger machines. The sets of tines vary in width from a quite narrow 14 inches on small tillers to 20 inches. On most front-tine machines, the rotating tines function as wheels, creating the forward movement as they propel the rotary tiller.

GRASSES, GROUND COVERS AND THEIR USES

Massed lilies-of-the-valley, showing scores of tiny, fragrant white flowers, crowd between two rocks in a sunny, secluded part of a landscape. Perennials that clump thickly and retain their vivid green foliage all summer, as these low-growing lilies-of-the-valley do, make fine ground covers.

Turfgrasses and ground cover plants do essentially the same job. They carpet the land around a house and set off the rest of the landscaping—the trees and shrubs and flower beds. There are two large differences, though, between them. Grass can be walked and played on, and a smooth lawn of it has a neat and manicured look matched by nothing else. Ground covers are looser and, like flower beds, are distinctly unsuited to foot traffic.

But ground covers have their advantages. For one, they do not have to be mowed and, once established, need only a minimum of other maintenance. For another, a number of ground covers will flourish where grass refuses to grow—in areas densely shaded by house or trees, in dry hot spots, in cool and wet ones. They are also ideal for narrow and odd-shaped places that, planted with grass, would be virtually impossible to mow.

Ground covers come in many shapes, sizes, textures and even colors. They range from small shrubs—low-growing but woody—to creeping vines to a host of spreading perennial plants. And a number of ornamental grasses can be used as ground covers. Ornamental grasses, which may or may not be relatives of the turfgrasses and are usually tall, shoot up in dense clumps of wonderfully varied shape and color. All of these types of ground covers are pictured on pages 16-17.

The turfgrasses themselves are also varied. They can be divided, though, into the two main classes shown opposite—the so-called bunching grasses, which grow well only in cooler northern regions, and the creepers, which are usually suited to hot climates.

Grasses and ground covers need not be thought of as mutually exclusive. Most homes have lawns around them, but there is every reason to include ground covers in the landscape—to clothe difficult spots, to add variety or beauty, and to lighten the yard-keeping chores.

TWO KINDS OF TURFGRASSES

On turfgrass, each grass blade grows from the base upward instead of from the tip, as most plants do; that is why turfgrasses are the most durable of ground covers and why they thrive despite traffic and regular close mowing. The base of each blade is partially below the soil surface and protected from damage. This is true of both bunching grasses, so called since they grow in clumps or bunches, and the quite different creepers that spread by sending out lateral stems.

BUNCHING GRASSES
The classic cool-season lawn grasses—handsome but delicate fescue, ryegrass and others—generally grow upright in clumps from deep roots. Once planted, they spread by putting out new shoots called tillers. The more the tillers are encouraged to grow by proper fertilizing, mowing and watering, the denser a lawn will be.

CREEPING GRASSES
All the grasses that are known as warm-season grasses and that grow best in hot climates—the Bermudas, zoysia, St. Augustine and centipedegrass— spread by means of stems that grow sideways. The stems are called stolons if they creep along the surface of the soil *(below)*, rhizomes if they tunnel beneath it *(right)*. In either case, these grasses spread far faster than the bunching grasses with their upright growth habit.

GROUND COVERS

The plants that make up the three main groups of ground covers *(below)* are remarkably diverse in texture, shape and growing habits. But they all form relatively low-growing and close-knit blankets of green—qualities that good ground covers should have. Most spread quickly, conserve moisture in the ground (and thus need little watering) and by growing densely keep out weeds. Among them, species can be found that will flourish in almost any soil and in the coolest shade or the hottest sun.

SHRUBS
Several sorts of woody shrubs—creeping juniper *(above)*, dwarf yew, dwarf azalea and cotoneaster among others—make good ground covers since their branches grow horizontally, so that the plants remain low and close to the soil. A number of these small shrubs are evergreens; such plants provide foliage through the year, and some of them put forth delicate but decorative blooms at various times during the growing season.

VINES
English ivy *(below)* and other vines are the quintessential ground covers because their stems root as they grow and spread very swiftly. This rooting habit also makes them excellent for anchoring soil and stopping erosion. Some of them flourish in shaded areas where grass will not survive.

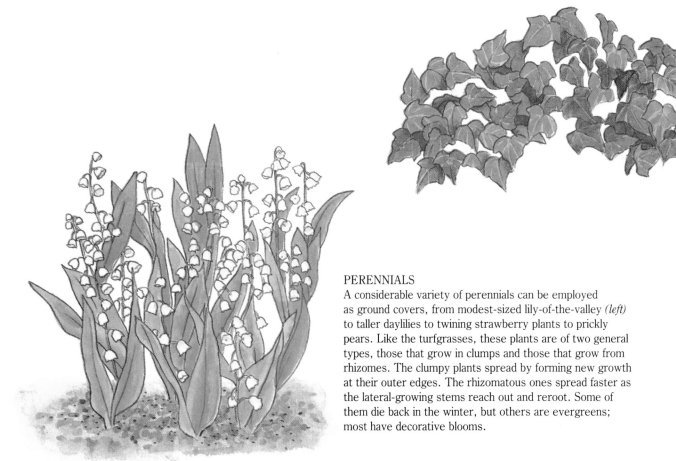

PERENNIALS
A considerable variety of perennials can be employed as ground covers, from modest-sized lily-of-the-valley *(left)* to taller daylilies to twining strawberry plants to prickly pears. Like the turfgrasses, these plants are of two general types, those that grow in clumps and those that grow from rhizomes. The clumpy plants spread by forming new growth at their outer edges. The rhizomatous ones spread faster as the lateral-growing stems reach out and reroot. Some of them die back in the winter, but others are evergreens; most have decorative blooms.

ORNAMENTAL GRASSES

Grasses and grasslike sedges and rushes are increasingly used as ground covers, for the decorative qualities of their long leaf blades and for their ability to grow fast over large areas. Two or three species, of different shades and varying heights, can be banked one behind another for a wild billowing effect at the far borders of a landscape.

GRASSES

The ornamental grasses that are properly called "ornamental grasses" are true grasses; their stems are round and jointed. Some of them, such as fountain grass *(left),* grow 3 feet high and some are taller still. Planted in a mass, they make effective wind screens as well as handsome backgrounds for other plantings. Many grow feathery seed heads, which add to their decorative effect, and they generally stay erect through the winter, waving in the wind and lending interest to the landscape when virtually all growing things are dead or dormant.

SEDGES

Looking like grasses but belonging to a different botanical family—the stem structures of sedges are triangular and unjointed —various sedges make good ground covers in damp areas, where they thrive. You can mass them in a boggy part of the garden, or use them as accents near the margin of a pond or a small pool.

RUSHES

Similar to sedges but having rounded, unjointed stem structures, the rushes are also marsh plants and share the same preference for wet soil conditions. They are especially useful as ground covers where a property falls off toward a lake or the shore of a coastal inlet. □

ONE WAY TO START A LAWN: WITH PLUGS OF GRASS

A lawn of heat-tolerant St. Augustine grass thrives in Florida, where the hot weather favors palm trees and other tropical plants. Like other warm-season grasses, St. Augustine can be started from chunks of sod, or plugs, which grow together to form a rugged lawn.

Growing a lawn in the South and the Southwest takes special thought. Only the so-called warm-season grasses—those that withstand blistering sun and high temperatures—will survive the torrid summers of Florida and Arizona. A couple of them, centipedegrass and St. Augustine grass, are rather coarse, but they are very rugged and can tolerate great heat. Another pair, the finer-textured hybrid Bermudas and zoysia, produce dense, hardy carpets so lush that they look like well-tended fairways. (By no accident, these grasses are widely used on Southern golf courses.) And zoysia grows so thick that it chokes off all weeds, including crabgrass.

The trick is planting these grasses. Some do not grow well from seed; others refuse to grow at all from seed. However, most of the warm-season strains are what experts call stoloniferous, which means they grow by spreading. They have lateral stems, or stolons, that creep and root and creep some more, sending up grassy shoots as they go. The answer, then, is to start a lawn by planting plugs—little chunks of sod—at regular intervals and letting them grow together. The result will be patchy at first, but these grasses spread so fast that in less than a year a lawn will fill in.

The plugs can be round or square and 2 to 4 inches across. They are generally available by mail order and from turf farms. They come variously by the piece and by the hundred. Or you can buy a strip of sod and cut it up yourself. As a rule of thumb, 324 two-inch plugs, or 81 four-inch plugs of Bermuda or zoysia, can be cut from 1 square yard of lawn; spread out at 1-foot intervals they will cover 324 square feet, or 36 square yards.

As with any sort of planting, the soil should be prepared and enriched ahead of time *(pages 10-13)*. The best season to put in plugs is the spring, and preferably on a cool, cloudy day. The proper way to do the actual planting is shown at right and on the following two pages.

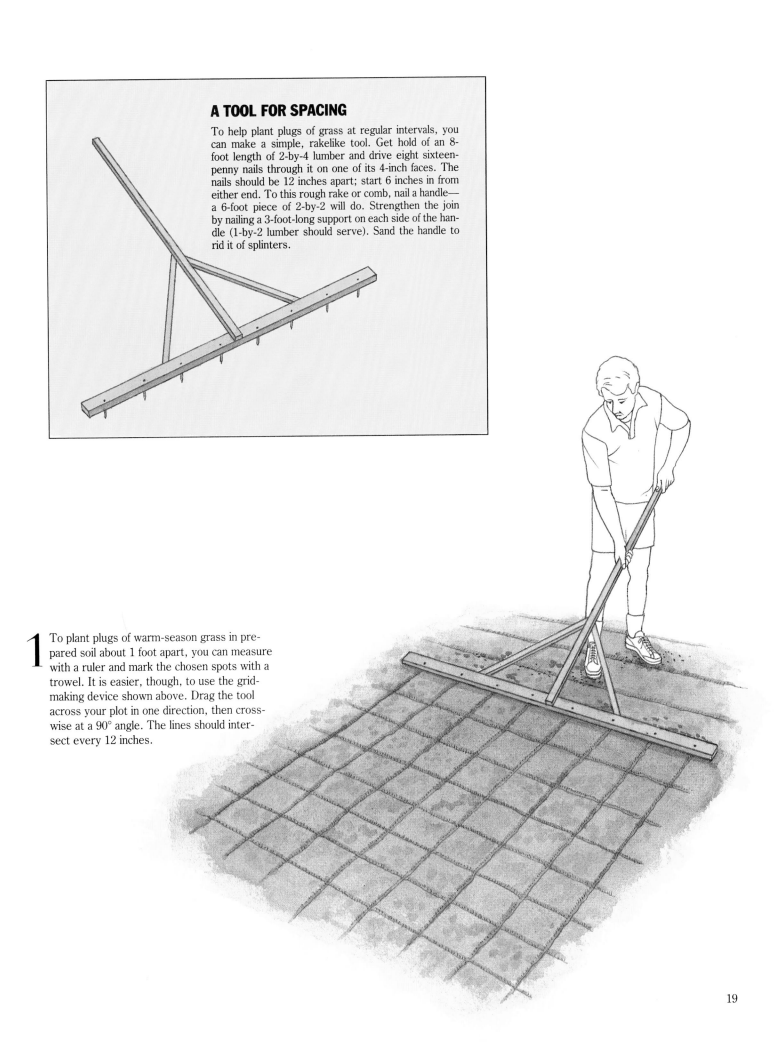

A TOOL FOR SPACING

To help plant plugs of grass at regular intervals, you can make a simple, rakelike tool. Get hold of an 8-foot length of 2-by-4 lumber and drive eight sixteen-penny nails through it on one of its 4-inch faces. The nails should be 12 inches apart; start 6 inches in from either end. To this rough rake or comb, nail a handle—a 6-foot piece of 2-by-2 will do. Strengthen the join by nailing a 3-foot-long support on each side of the handle (1-by-2 lumber should serve). Sand the handle to rid it of splinters.

1 To plant plugs of warm-season grass in prepared soil about 1 foot apart, you can measure with a ruler and mark the chosen spots with a trowel. It is easier, though, to use the grid-making device shown above. Drag the tool across your plot in one direction, then crosswise at a 90° angle. The lines should intersect every 12 inches.

19

2 Where the lines intersect, make holes with a trowel or with a special plugging tool *(below)*. You can ready all the holes and then plant, or insert the plugs as you go. Just be sure the plugs do not dry out while they wait; keep them moist with sprinklings from a hose.

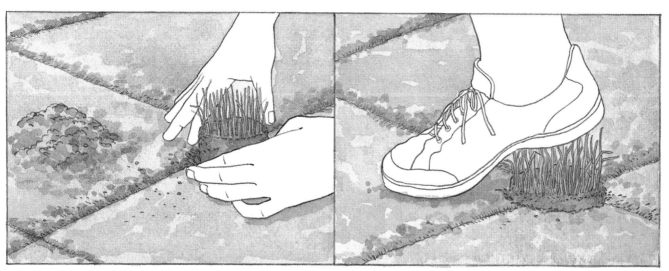

3 Put a plug in its hole *(above, left)*, making sure that the grassy top sits ⅛ to ¼ inch above the soil line. If the plugs are too deep, the grass will not spread freely and make new roots in the surrounding earth. After the plug has been planted at the right depth, tamp it down with your heel *(above, right)* to ensure good root-to-soil contact. Plant all your plugs in this fashion.

4 When all the plugs are in the ground, rake the areas between them. Smooth out any little hills and fill depressions so that the finished lawn will be smooth. Do not mound up earth around any of the plugs, however; they should remain above ground level.

5 Water the entire area thoroughly as soon as the planting is finished. An oscillating sprinkler is ideal because it spreads the water evenly without causing washouts. Continue watering liberally during the first couple of months, to be sure the plugs remain moist and become well established. □

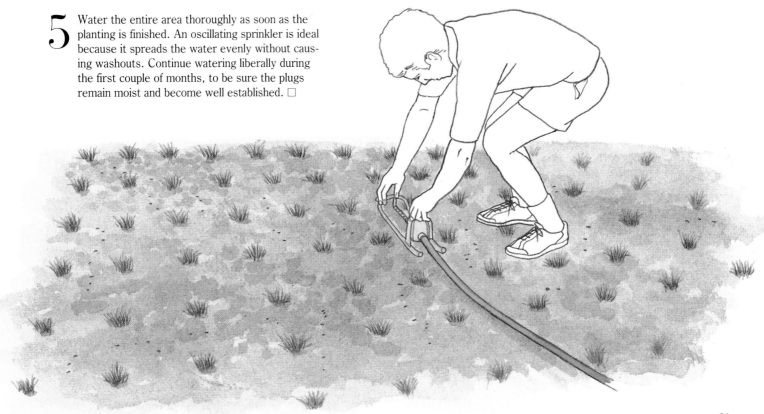

ANOTHER WAY TO START: WITH GRASS SPRIGS

Bermudagrass, zoysia and the other grasses commonly used for lawns in hot-weather regions can be planted by using sprigs—small sections of stem—instead of plugs *(pages 18-21)*. The short-term effect is less orderly, but after a year the sprigs should grow together and fill in the lawn just as well.

Sprigs generally consist of sections of shredded stem 3 to 6 inches long. Most will include roots and blades of grass. Turf farms usually sell sprigs by the bushel; one bushel should be enough to plant 200 square feet. Whether you buy the sprigs locally or by mail, ordering the right quantity is important; ordering at the right time is essential. Having no soil attached, they dry out quickly, so they should be planted soon after being shredded. The first step, then, is to decide when to do the planting. Spring and summer, when warm-season grasses do their most active growing, are best. Settle on a convenient week and begin preparing the soil *(pages 10-13)*. In ordering the sprigs, tell the turf farmer when to deliver the order. He will shred the sprigs as close to the planting date as possible and package them in airtight bags. They should, of course, be put in the ground as soon as they arrive.

One way to start a large lawn is to spread the sprigs over the entire area, till them into the ground with a rotary tiller, then press them down with a roller. This method is quick but wastes a few sprigs because some of them get buried. The drawings at right show another method—planting sprigs in furrows. This takes more time but is advisable because a higher percentage of the sprigs will take root and grow.

Bordered by spiky juniper shrubs of a contrasting hue, a large lawn of St. Augustine grass shines a bright green in strong Southern sunlight. Tough and fast-spreading, St. Augustine is easily planted from stem sections called sprigs, which will grow together to cover sizable areas in a year.

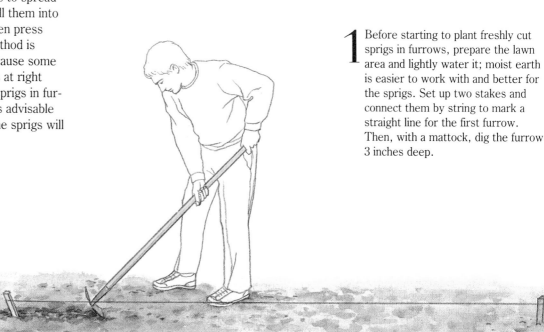

1 Before starting to plant freshly cut sprigs in furrows, prepare the lawn area and lightly water it; moist earth is easier to work with and better for the sprigs. Set up two stakes and connect them by string to mark a straight line for the first furrow. Then, with a mattock, dig the furrow 3 inches deep.

2 Place sprigs end to end the length of the furrow, firming the soil as you go *(below)*. Make sure that the grass blades stick up above the ground *(inset)*. Then move the stakes and string to mark the next furrow. With most warm-season grasses, the furrows can be 12 inches apart, but with slow-growing zoysia 6 inches is preferable.

3 After the lawn has been filled with sprigs, remove the stakes and go over the area with a roller half filled with water (for weighting); the roller will firm the soil and get rid of any air pockets around the sprigs. Next, water the area well—and keep on watering at frequent intervals for about six months, or until the sprigs have grown together. They are vulnerable to drying and will not grow and spread unless they are kept moist. □

SOWING GRASS SEED—
AN ECONOMICAL WAY TO BEGIN

S eeding is by far the most popular method of starting a new lawn. It is quick and easy; it costs much less than such methods as installing sod, plugs or sprigs; and commercially available seed offers the largest variety of both cool- and warm-season grass types.

To make sure you get the right kind of seed, think carefully about your needs before you buy. There are grasses that tolerate heavy wear (important if your lawn will double as a play area), hot dry spells (for regions with low rainfall) and shade. The dictionary at the back of this volume will help you find grasses with the specific characteristics you are looking for.

Be prepared to pay for quality. Avoid seed "bargains," which often have a low germination rate or contain a lot of "temporary" seeds that spring up fast and fade even faster. Quality grass seed contains only minimal amounts of filler material and weed seeds. The quality can to some extent be judged by the labels. A good bet is any seed package labeled "Certified." This means that the state has tested the contents and found that the seeds are accurately represented on the label. The label will also tell how many square feet the seeds in the package will cover.

Before seeding, prepare the soil as shown on pages 10-13. Never spread seed on wet soil, which can become compacted and hinder germination. Seeds can be sown by hand. But for neater, more even distribution, use a drop spreader, which deposits seeds through a long slot, or a broadcast spreader, which throws seeds in a half-circle *(opposite)*. Both kinds of spreaders can be rented at garden supply centers, as can lawn rollers, which make it easy to set the seeds firmly in place.

Bright green shoots of new grass started from seed poke through a protective layer of straw mulch, which helps keep newly broadcast seeds from blowing away and conserves moisture while they germinate.

WHAT'S IN THE BAG

Grass seeds sometimes come packaged "straight"—by the species or cultivar, such as Kentucky bluegrass—but most packages contain more than one kind of grass. The idea is to balance strengths and weaknesses. For example, some grasses are durable but slow-growing; others grow fast but are susceptible to disease or bad weather. A combination of traits should provide maximal satisfaction over the life of a lawn.

Packages labeled "mixture" contain seeds of more than one species (such as Kentucky bluegrass and fine fescue); "blends" bring together different cultivars of the same species. Both mixtures and blends combine grasses that have similar colors and textures.

1 Fill a broadcast spreader with seed and set the slot opening according to the manufacturer's instructions. Push the spreader over a prepared bed at an even, comfortable speed *(far left)*. To make sure that you leave no unseeded strips between rows, overlap the rows slightly as you go back and forth *(inset)*.

2 After you have finished broadcasting, lightly scratch the seeds into the soil with a garden rake *(right)*. Be careful not to bury or redistribute them; you just want to give each seed a thin covering of earth.

3 Roll a light lawn roller over the seeded bed. This will squeeze out air pockets and ensure that the seeds remain in close contact with soil particles and with moisture in the soil—conditions necessary for germination.

4 Mulch lightly with clean straw; you should be able to see about half the ground surface through it. The mulch will provide shade and prevent seeds from being washed away in a heavy rain. Water well; during hot weather you may have to water up to four times a day to keep the soil moist. Don't walk on the lawn until the grass is well established. □

25

INSTALLING SOD
FOR AN INSTANT LAWN

Rows of parallel lines are visible between the strips of turf on a newly sodded lawn. As the grass grows together, usually in two to four weeks, the lines will fade, creating an even surface color. Sodding is the most expensive way to start a lawn, but it yields immediate results.

The quickest way to build a new lawn is to lay down sod—turf that has been grown on a commercial farm, then harvested in uniform strips and marketed in rolls for easy installation. Sod costs up to five times more than a seeded lawn. But it has many advantages. It enables you to start enjoying the sight of green grass the moment you set down your tools; it goes anywhere, including steep slopes; and the roots of properly laid sod quickly "knit" to the soil so erosion is halted.

Careful site preparation is crucial; the soil must be turned, amended, leveled and watered ahead of time just as it would be for seeding *(pages 10-13)*. When preparing the site, leave the soil surface 1 inch lower than adjacent driveways and walkways to accommodate the thickness of the sod. Be ready to install the sod soon after it arrives; left rolled up, the strips will quickly dry out and die.

Sod strips are about 6 feet long, 2 feet wide, and between ¾ and 1 inch thick. Determine the square footage of your lawn; the sod dealer will tell you how many strips you need to cover the area. In sodding a very large lawn, mark off the site in manageable sections of 10 feet by 10 feet or so, and finish working on one section before moving on to the next.

Make sure the sod you order contains the type of grass you want. If you buy from a local dealer, examine the sod before you buy it. The grass itself should be dense, in good color, and free of disease, insects and weeds. The strips should be strong and intact. Lift one strip by an end; it should hold together like a piece of carpet. In some states you can buy "certified" sod, the composition and quality of which are guaranteed.

Both cool-season and warm-season grasses are available as sod. You can lay sod at any time, but it's best to avoid hot, dry spells. Roots establish themselves more quickly when left undisturbed; don't mow the new lawn until the grass is about 3 inches high.

1 Prepare the soil in advance as for seeding. Then, a day or two before the sod is due to arrive, lightly rake the soil surface and water it well. Align the edge of a sod roll against a straight edge such as a sidewalk (or set up stakes and string for a guideline). Unroll the strip, checking the alignment and patting the sod down at every point to make sure it lies evenly on the soil surface.

2 Lay a second strip of sod end to end with first, taking care not to overlap the ends *(left)*. Don't pull or stretch the sod in any direction; stretched sod is more likely to shrink later on, leaving unsightly gaps in your lawn.

3 Fill in the joint between the two sod strips with soil. First pull back the ends slightly, then work in fresh soil with a trowel and tamp it down *(left)*. Lay additional strips of sod end to end until you have finished the first row. Fill in and tamp down all joints.

4 Lay a second row of sod alongside the first row. Stagger the strips—in a brickwork-like pattern—so that the joints in one row never line up with the joints in adjacent rows *(right)*. This will help make an even lawn.

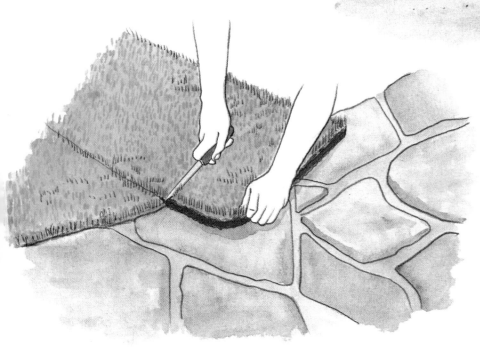

5 When you come to odd-sized or unusually shaped areas—like the ends of rows or curved corners— you will have to cut the strips of sod to fit. Use any sharp-pointed tool, such as a spade, a knife or a mason's trowel.

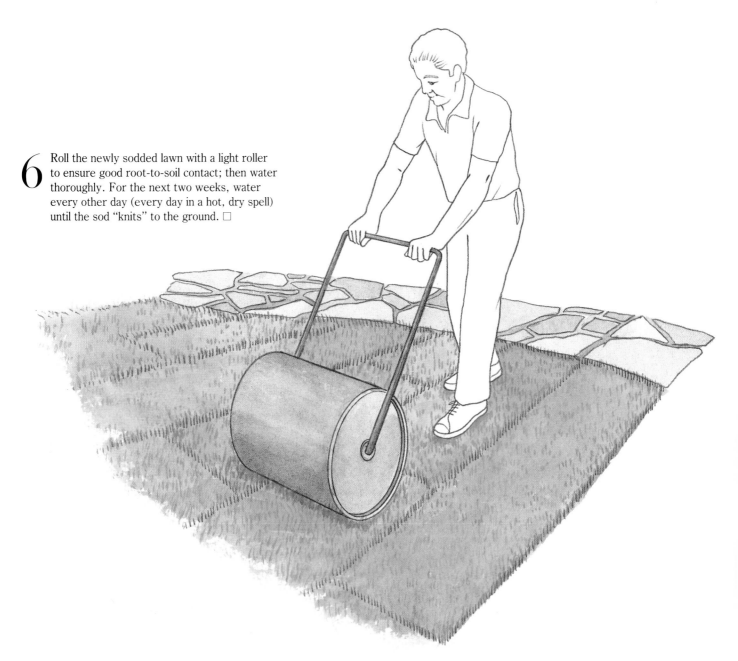

6 Roll the newly sodded lawn with a light roller to ensure good root-to-soil contact; then water thoroughly. For the next two weeks, water every other day (every day in a hot, dry spell) until the sod "knits" to the ground. □

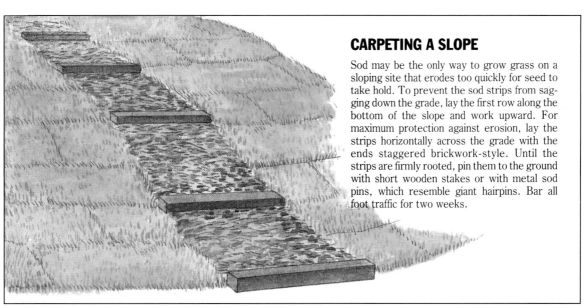

CARPETING A SLOPE

Sod may be the only way to grow grass on a sloping site that erodes too quickly for seed to take hold. To prevent the sod strips from sagging down the grade, lay the first row along the bottom of the slope and work upward. For maximum protection against erosion, lay the strips horizontally across the grade with the ends staggered brickwork-style. Until the strips are firmly rooted, pin them to the ground with short wooden stakes or with metal sod pins, which resemble giant hairpins. Bar all foot traffic for two weeks.

LOW-MAINTENANCE GROUND COVERS FROM BARE-ROOT PLANTS

The biggest and most important area you'll ever have to plant is likely to be the land directly around your house. Before settling for a traditional lawn, consider a sensible alternative: a sturdy, attractive, easy-to-maintain ground cover. A ground cover not only requires less care than a lawn, but its extensive root system does a better job of holding down soil on a slope. The principal drawback is that you can't walk on a bed of ground cover as you can on grass.

Mail-order catalogs offer ground cover plants in a wide selection of colors, shapes and growth habits. Ground covers most often come in containers, but some dealers ship them bare-root, that is, with little or no soil attached. These work just as well and cost less—a significant consideration, since it takes a substantial number of plants to serve as ground cover.

Before ordering plants, calculate the area you have to cover *(below, right)* and then figure how many plants you will need. The number will depend on the type of plant you select. As a rule, shrubs that spread should be placed no farther apart than a distance equal to their ultimate width. Perennials should be placed a distance about equal to their mature height. With vines you have a choice. If you are willing to wait a season or two for them to cover the ground completely, you can plant them 1 to 2 feet apart, and they will eventually grow together. If you are impatient and want the ground covered immediately, the vines can be planted as close together as you like—but be prepared to prune later.

To prevent erosion (especially on hills), arrange the plants in a staggered pattern so that those in one row will catch loosened soil and rain runoff from the rows above. To train plants to grow in a desired direction (toward the edge of a path, for example), secure them to the ground with pieces of bent wire or with sod pins.

Clinging to a steep slope, a dense bed of periwinkle serves as an all-season bulwark against erosion. The small purple and white flowers are an early spring bonus.

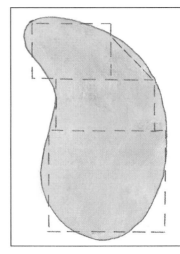

DIVIDING A WHOLE INTO PARTS

To make calculating the area of an irregularly shaped garden space easy, divide it into simple geometric figures—squares, oblongs, triangles, half circles, as appropriate. Measure the area of each separately, and then add the areas together to get a total.

1 Prepare the soil for a ground cover bed as you would for a lawn *(pages 10-13).* Then spread a 2-inch layer of organic mulch (such as pine needles) to resist erosion, reduce weed growth and conserve ground water.

2 Mark one edge of the bed with stakes and string to help you lay out a straight row. Make an opening in the mulch for insertion of the first plant. With a trowel, dig a hole wide enough for the roots to spread out comfortably and deep enough so that the topmost roots will sit about ¼ inch below the surface *(left).* Position the plant, firm the soil around it, replace the mulch and water well. Repeat for the other plants in the row. To maintain spacing, estimate visually or use a ruler.

3 When you finish planting the first row, relocate the stakes and string to guide the planting of a second row. Arrange the second row parallel to the first, but with each plant offset from its first-row neighbors to create a staggered pattern. Then move the stakes and string again, and repeat the staggered pattern with succeeding rows until the entire bed is covered. □

PLASTIC MULCH TO KEEP OUT WEEDS, LET IN WATER AND NUTRIENTS

The easiest way to keep ground covers weed-free is to deny weeds what all plants must have to live: a place in the sun. A thick layer of organic mulch (like peat moss, pine bark or straw) will hinder weed growth. But weed barriers made from plastic do an even better job since they leave fewer openings for weeds to exploit. The only breaks in the plastic are those you cut to let your own plants through.

The same property that makes plastic so effective a weed barrier—its impermeability —imposes some restrictions on its use. Ground covers that put down new roots as they sprawl, like ivy, or that multiply by spreading from their crowns, like hosta, will be frustrated by a plastic weed barrier. It should be used only with plants that grow from a central point—low-growing shrubs such as cotoneaster and dwarf varieties of yew and azalea.

It used to be that sealing off the ground with an impermeable plastic sheet also made it difficult to water and fertilize the soil around your plants. However, new materials have all but eliminated this problem. Some of the new plastics are perforated with thousands of tiny holes, and others are woven. Both kinds let air, water and fertilizer particles pass through in one direction but block weed seeds and seedlings from coming up in the other.

These new weed barriers are usually sold in sheets 3 feet wide and 50 to 100 feet long. Before installing any of them, prepare your ground cover bed for planting, as shown on pages 10-13. After planting the area with low-growing shrubs, cover the plastic weed barrier with some attractive camouflage such as shredded bark or pine bark chips.

Protected by an unseen sheet of plastic weed barrier, a juniper bed thrives. Holes have been cut in the plastic to let the juniper plants through, and a thin layer of organic mulch disguises the plastic.

1 Lay a large sheet of plastic weed barrier over a section of fully prepared bed *(below)*. Cut it to fit. Move to adjacent sections, and cut more plastic as needed to cover the entire bed. Adjacent pieces should overlap about 6 inches. Hold the plastic in place with stones.

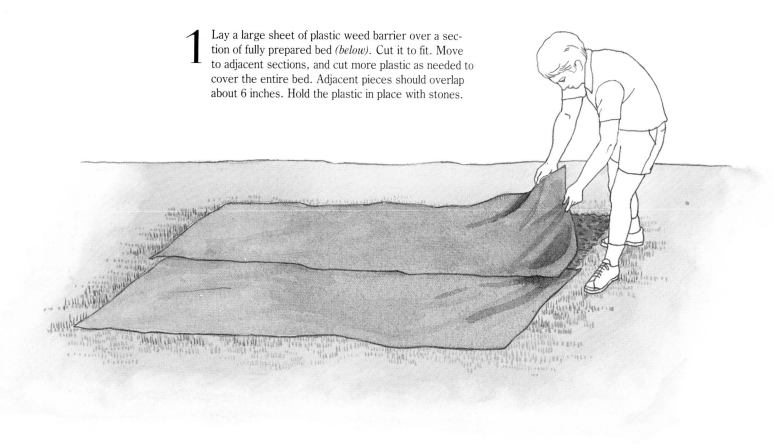

2 Arrange the plants in their containers on top of the weed barrier at recommended intervals and in staggered rows. If you are uncertain about distances, measure with stakes and string.

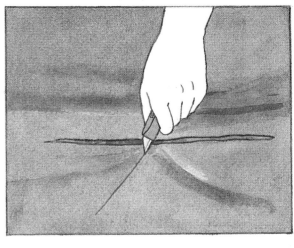

3 Lift up each plant, and use a utility knife to cut an X through the weed barrier where the plant was standing. The X-shaped slit should be large enough for the plant's root ball to pass through. Fold back the flaps of the slit and dig a hole in the exposed soil.

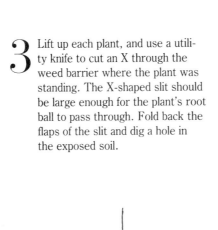

4 Carefully remove a plant from its container. With one hand on the bottom of the container and the other hand covering the soil and supporting the plant, turn the container upside down. The plant should slide out smoothly; if it doesn't, slap the side of the container several times. If the roots are thickly matted, gently untangle them with your fingers to encourage outward growth.

5 Insert the plant in its hole, making sure it sits at the same depth in the ground as it did in its container. Firm some of the dug-up soil around the plant. Set aside excess soil for use elsewhere. Water well, then fold the flaps of the slit back in place around the plant. Repeat until the entire bed is planted.

6 To hide the sheets of plastic and make the bed look natural, sprinkle a decorative mulch over the weed barrier. You can use pine bark chips, shredded bark, pine straw—or whatever is cheap and readily available in your area. □

PINE BARK

2
TAKING CARE

Mowing, watering, fertilizing, dealing with thatch and dandelions—all these are chores familiar to anyone who has a lawn. When properly done they enormously increase the beauty of the garden setting, as well as the value of the house. And the same is true of a well-groomed ground cover. Although billed as easy-care, these lawn substitutes benefit from a regular program of shearing and pruning to keep them thick and kempt.

In tackling these tasks, the operative word is "properly"; there are right and wrong ways to care for a lawn. Improperly done, mowing, watering, weeding and feeding can do more harm than good. Grass cut too short during a siege of dry weather may suffer root damage from which it may never recover. And grass cut when it is wet is apt to pick up waterborne disease spores spread by the whirling blades of the lawn mower. Similarly, too much fertilizer or too frequent watering can stimulate lush growth at the expense of stamina, and chemicals for controlling weeds can be useless if they are not geared to the particular weed. In perennial weeds, for example, it is the whole existing plant that must be targeted; in annual weeds, it is the seeds.

Guidance in handling all these tasks as well as other lawn-care procedures—dethatching, aerating, dealing with root-eating grubs—is offered on the following pages. Along with these matters are such related and critical ones as how to keep the blades of lawn mowers sharp, and how to prevent rampantly growing ground covers from getting out of hand.

WATERING:
HOW MUCH, WHEN AND WHERE

The first and most essential part of caring for lawns and ground covers, of course, is making sure they have enough water to survive and thrive. The question is, how much is enough? To be fresh and vigorous, lawns need to get the right amount of moisture—not too much, not too little—and in the right way at the right times.

Fortunately, there is a handy rule to go by: the average lawn requires 1 inch of water each week during the growing season. Much of this inch, or all of it, may be supplied by rainfall. It is a good idea, in fact, to keep track of how much rain has come down during the season and in recent weeks—a rain gauge from a hardware store will help. If nature provides the needed weekly inch, do not water the lawn any more. Excess moisture encourages weeds and makes grass more susceptible to fungi and other ailments.

But if rain has been infrequent, getting out hoses and sprinklers is very much in order. Too-dry grass exhibits several telltale signs: a wilted look, a dull gray-blue color and little resiliency when stepped on. Sprinklers should be turned on ideally once a week and allowed to run for the hour or so that it takes to supply an inch of water. One long soaking is far preferable to several short ones. It helps the water sink to a depth of 6 or 8 inches, which in turn encourages the grass roots to grow deep and strong. To check to be sure the water is getting down far enough, dig up a core of soil with a narrow trowel and examine it.

There are a few exceptions to the 1-inch rule. More water may be needed if the climate (or the summer season) is unusually hot or windy or both. And various parts of the landscape around a house may require extra moisture, as shown on the opposite page. Finally, there are ways to help save a lawn when drought and resulting water restrictions make normal watering impossible *(right)*.

A pop-up sprinkler head from an underground watering system bathes the leaves of surrounding Bermudagrass with a fine, vigorous spray. Underground systems, while not cheap to install, are efficient and convenient, and can be programmed to turn on and off automatically.

WHEN WATER IS SCARCE

Many parts of the country impose limits on lawn watering during dry seasons to save water for more vital uses. If you find that you cannot give your grass the moisture it needs, you can help it survive until wetter fall weather arrives through the following steps:

☐ Let the grass grow higher than normal by mowing less often and raising the height of the cut. This will reduce stress caused by frequent loss of plant tissue.

☐ Stop fertilizing. Fertilizers encourage grass to grow rapidly, increasing its need for water. Let growth slow down.

☐ Make a special effort to eliminate weeds, which compete with grass for moisture.

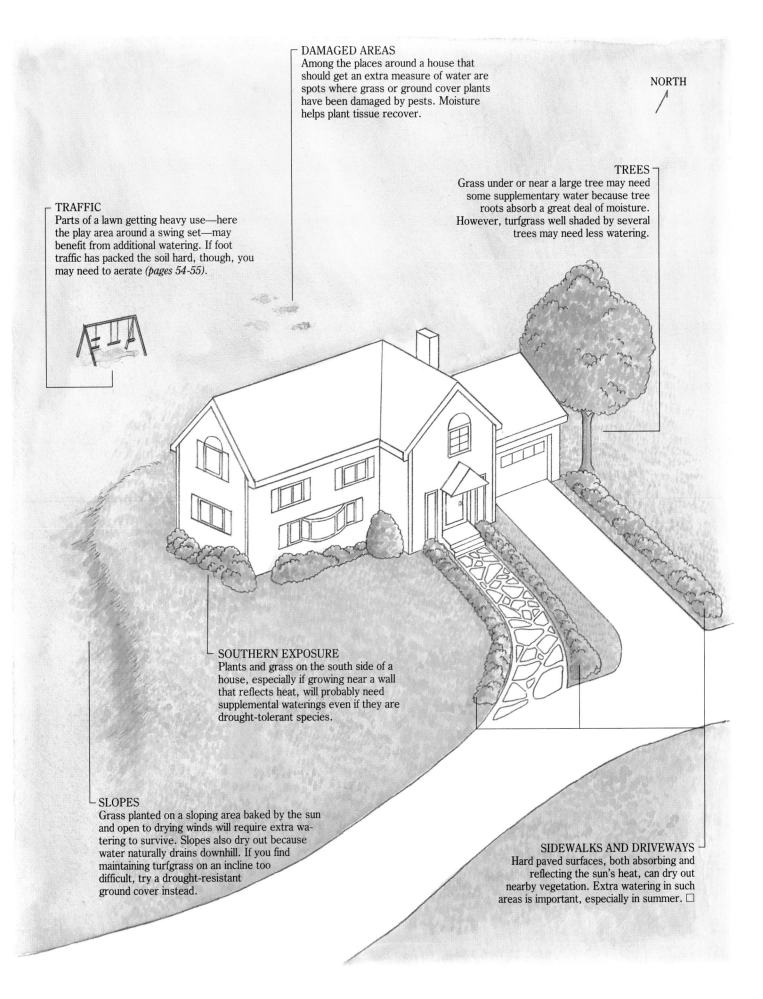

DAMAGED AREAS
Among the places around a house that should get an extra measure of water are spots where grass or ground cover plants have been damaged by pests. Moisture helps plant tissue recover.

NORTH

TREES
Grass under or near a large tree may need some supplementary water because tree roots absorb a great deal of moisture. However, turfgrass well shaded by several trees may need less watering.

TRAFFIC
Parts of a lawn getting heavy use—here the play area around a swing set—may benefit from additional watering. If foot traffic has packed the soil hard, though, you may need to aerate *(pages 54-55)*.

SOUTHERN EXPOSURE
Plants and grass on the south side of a house, especially if growing near a wall that reflects heat, will probably need supplemental waterings even if they are drought-tolerant species.

SLOPES
Grass planted on a sloping area baked by the sun and open to drying winds will require extra watering to survive. Slopes also dry out because water naturally drains downhill. If you find maintaining turfgrass on an incline too difficult, try a drought-resistant ground cover instead.

SIDEWALKS AND DRIVEWAYS
Hard paved surfaces, both absorbing and reflecting the sun's heat, can dry out nearby vegetation. Extra watering in such areas is important, especially in summer. ☐

A GUIDE
TO FERTILIZING LAWNS

A healthy, bright green lawn leads to a colorful border of flowers, shrubs and trees. Such a lawn results from a balanced diet of nutrients that produce strong roots and vigorous green grass blades.

Because they are regularly subjected to overcrowding, mowing and other indignities, turfgrasses require extra fertilizing care. An understanding of the basics of plant nutrition will help you avert problems and keep your lawn handsome and healthy.

There are 16 essential nutrients that all plants must have in order to live. They get most of what they need from the soil, air and water. The purpose of fertilizers is to supplement the few essential nutrients that the environment does not supply in adequate amounts.

Plants absorb nutrients through their roots; how efficiently they use available nutrients is determined in part by soil composition. The best way to determine which nutrients are in short supply is a soil test, which you can make with a do-it-yourself kit or have done at a state agricultural extension service.

The three nutrients that most often need to be added are nitrogen (for green leafy growth), phosphorus (for strong roots) and potassium (for general vigor). A "complete" fertilizer contains all three; the three numbers (such as 23-3-6) on the package indicate the percentages of nitrogen, phosphorus and potassium (in that order) to be found in the product.

In general, the best time to apply fertilizer is just before a period of active growth. For most of the country, this means early spring. One application of general-purpose fertilizer per year will suffice for most ground cover beds. Lawns should be fed more often, with a fertilizer that contains a higher percentage of nitrogen.

Fertilizers come in liquid form and granular form. To apply a liquid fertilizer (and any product sold as water-soluble) use a watering can or, when recommended, the nozzle of a watering hose. Granular fertilizers are applied with spreaders. Whatever you use, be sure to water thoroughly in combination with fertilizing because water is necessary to release the nutrients.

THE ESSENTIALS OF PLANT NUTRITION

Plants get all the carbon, hydrogen and oxygen they need from the air and water. Of the remaining nutrients vital to growth and health, plants need relatively large amounts of nitrogen, phosphorus, potassium, sulfur, magnesium and calcium. These are the macronutrients. The nutrients required in much smaller amounts—iron, manganese, zinc, copper, molybdenum, boron and chlorine—are known as micronutrients or trace elements. Most soils are rich enough in nutrients so that the only supplements you will have to consider are nitrogen, phosphorus and potassium (and, in certain locations, sulfur or iron). A soil test will tell you exactly what to add.

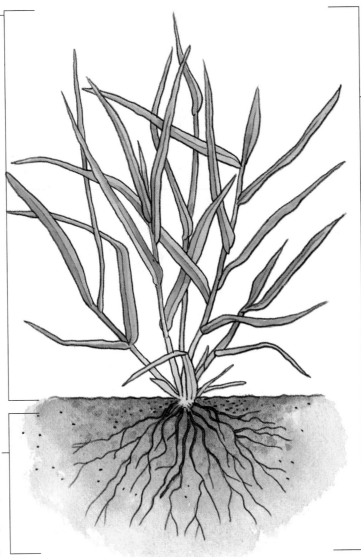

NITROGEN
Essential for leaf and shoot growth and to manufacture chlorophyll for green color. Fertilizer labels should give the source of the nitrogen. *Nitrate* nitrogen (nitrogen that does not need breaking down) is immediately available to plants and useful when you want quick greening, but it is easily washed away, so frequent supplements are necessary. *Ammoniacal* (ammonia-based) nitrogen must be converted to nitrate by microorganisms before it can be used; soil that is too cold or too wet slows microorganic activity. Decomposition by microorganisms is necessary to release *organic* nitrogen from sewage sludge and manure; but organic nitrogen remains in the soil longer than nitrates. Which type you choose depends on how fast you want results and how much time you want to spend fertilizing.

POTASSIUM
Needed for general vigor and for resistance to the stresses of drought, cold, heat and disease. Potassium has been shown to be involved in such plant metabolic processes as protein synthesis and the maintenance of salt balance. Although potassium is washed from the soil by water, most soils contain sufficient quantities to make high supplements unnecessary. It is typically supplied in fertilizers in the form of potash.

PHOSPHORUS
Promotes root growth and flower bud formation. Extra-large quantities are needed for newly seeded lawns to help initiate root development. Since phosphorus does not wash easily out of soil as nitrogen does, frequent applications are not called for; fertilizers recommended for established lawns are typically low in phosphorus. The usual source of phosphorus in fertilizers is phosphoric acid.

WHEN TO ADD FERTILIZER

Add fertilizer just before or during peak growth periods.
The two graphs below compare the peak growth periods of
warm-season and cool-season grasses. Warm-season
grasses *(upper graph)* show a steady increase in growth to a
peak in midsummer, then a steady decline through late fall.
Cool-season grasses *(lower graph)* have one peak in early
spring and another, smaller peak in the fall. Within peak
growth periods you can apply fertilizer in successive applications at your convenience, up to the total recommended
for the year. But remember: never add more than 1 pound
of nitrogen in any one month; with too much nitrogen you
risk burning the foliage and weakening growth.

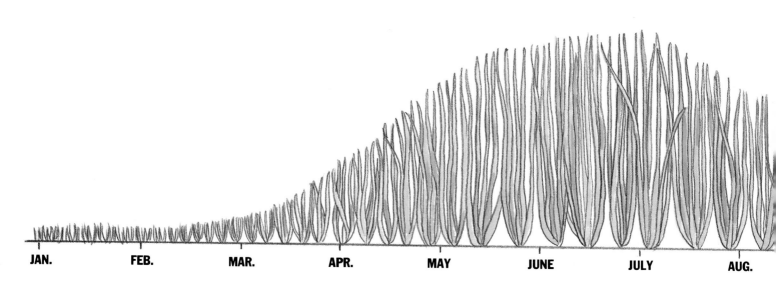

WARM-SEASON GRASSES

JAN. FEB. MAR. APR. MAY JUNE JULY AUG.

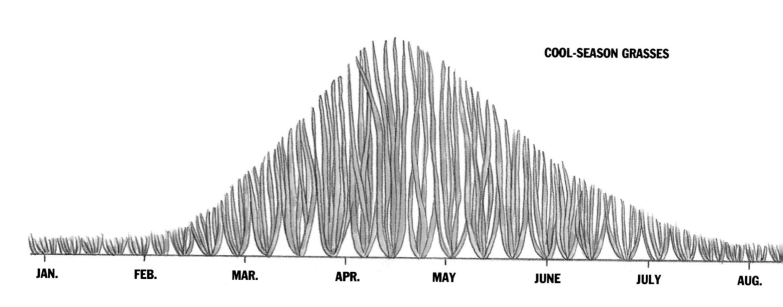

COOL-SEASON GRASSES

JAN. FEB. MAR. APR. MAY JUNE JULY AUG.

COMMON NAME	BOTANICAL NAME	TYPE	POUNDS OF NITROGEN PER 1,000 SQUARE FEET PER YEAR	
			MINIMUM	MAXIMUM
BAHIAGRASS	PASPALUM	WARM-SEASON	½ LB.	2½ LBS.
BENTGRASS	AGROSTIS	COOL-SEASON AND TRANSITIONAL	1½ LBS.	2 LBS.
BERMUDAGRASS	CYNODON	WARM-SEASON	3 LBS.	6 LBS.
BLUEGRASS	POA	COOL-SEASON	2½ LBS.	6 LBS.
BUFFALOGRASS	BUCHLOE	WARM-SEASON AND TRANSITIONAL	½ LB.	2½ LBS.
CARPETGRASS	AXONOPUS	WARM-SEASON	1 LB.	2 LBS.
CENTIPEDEGRASS	EREMOCHLOA	WARM-SEASON	½ LB.	1½ LBS.
FESCUE	FESTUCA	COOL-SEASON AND TRANSITIONAL		
CHEWINGS FESCUE	F. RUBRA COMMUTATA	COOL-SEASON AND TRANSITIONAL	1¼ LBS.	3 LBS.
CREEPING RED FESCUE	F. RUBRA RUBRA	COOL-SEASON AND TRANSITIONAL	1¼ LBS.	3 LBS.
HARD FESCUE	F. DURIUSCOLA	COOL-SEASON AND TRANSITIONAL	1¼ LBS.	3 LBS.
SHEEP FESCUE	F. OVINA	COOL-SEASON AND TRANSITIONAL	NONE	NONE
TALL FESCUE	F. ARUNDINACEA	COOL-SEASON AND TRANSITIONAL	2½ LBS.	6 LBS.
RYEGRASS	LOLIUM	COOL-SEASON	2 LBS.	6 LBS.
ST. AUGUSTINE GRASS	STENOTAPHRUM	WARM-SEASON	3 LBS.	6 LBS.
WHEATGRASS	AGROPYRON	COOL-SEASON	1 LB.	3 LBS.
ZOYSIA	ZOYSIA	WARM-SEASON	3 LBS.	6 LBS.

HOW MUCH TO USE

Almost all turfgrasses need higher doses of nitrogen than ornamental grasses or ground covers. In the dictionary at the back of this volume, you will find guidelines for fertilizing turfgrasses expressed in terms of nitrogen—specifically, pounds of nitrogen per 1,000 square feet of lawn per year. Depending on weather conditions and how much work you are willing to do, you can adjust the number of applications to achieve the total nitrogen dose recommended. The table above gives two choices: the lower figure is the minimum dose required for healthy growth, the higher figure is the maximum you can safely add for especially lush growth. (Keep in mind that extra growth means extra watering and mowing.) To determine how many square feet a bag of fertilizer will cover—at the rate of 1 pound of nitrogen per 1,000 square feet of lawn—multiply the weight of the bag by the nitrogen percentage stated on the label, then multiply by 1,000. □

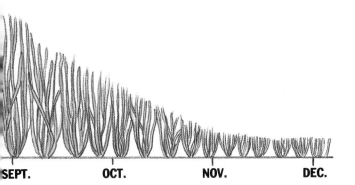

SEPT.   OCT.   NOV.   DEC.

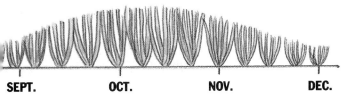

SEPT.   OCT.   NOV.   DEC.

THREE BASICS OF LAWN CARE: MOWING, EDGING AND TRIMMING

Practically all gardeners think they know how to mow a lawn. But the fact is that mowing is one of the least understood aspects of lawn care. How the grass is mowed and how often can vitally affect a lawn's health as well as its looks.

The first concern is how low to cut—and this depends on the type of grass. Some can safely be shaved down to half an inch in height, but others should be kept a good deal higher or they will sicken and burn out. Each sort of grass, in fact, has its own preferred height of cut (see the Dictionary of Lawns and Ground Covers, which begins on page 108). As a general rule, most lawns should be mowed no lower than 1½ to 2 inches. Trying for a super-smooth carpet effect will damage the grass and its roots by removing too much energy-producing top growth.

There is also a general rule for how often to mow: when the grass has grown about one-third higher than its proper cutting level. This may mean more frequent mowings during the growing season than a once-a-week trim. But letting a lawn become shaggy is a mistake. When it is finally mowed, too much of the top growth gets cut at one time, which can put the grass in shock and cause some yellowing. Also, frequent mowings produce small snippets of cut leaves that can be left to sift down through the grass and return nitrogen to the soil. Longer cuttings must be collected in a catching bag or raked up; otherwise they will smother the lawn.

It is also wise to vary the cutting pattern *(opposite, above)* and to do some edging and trimming after mowing for a finished look. Two last provisos: be sure the mower blades are sharp *(pages 46-49)*—and for that reason be especially careful of fingers and toes. Wear heavy-duty shoes and never tinker in any way with a power mower while it is running. When making the finishing touches with a power trimmer *(opposite)*, be sure to wear goggles as a precaution against flying stones.

A curving corner of a lawn, neatly mowed and crisply trimmed, shows off a colorful flower bed of red tuberous begonias and clumpy, purple sweet alyssum.

1 To mow a good-sized lawn, follow a spiral pattern *(inset),* one time going essentially clockwise, the next time counterclockwise. Mowing spirally eliminates tiring backtracking and stopping, and reversing directions from one mowing to the next keeps the grass from always being pressed down the same way. It is easiest to move from the outside inward.

2 To trim grassy areas next to walls, fences and trees that a lawn mower cannot reach, use grass shears or, to save time, a power trimmer. Some trimmers have small gasoline motors, but most run on electric current and require an outdoor extension cord *(right).* Generally trimmers cut by means of a whirling nylon filament in the head. When trimming, hold the cutting head close to the ground.

3 To make a tidy edge where your lawn meets a sidewalk or a driveway, use a single-wheeled edging machine *(left).* The wheel rides along the pavement while a rotary blade in the head shears off the straggling grass. □

KEEPING A LAWN MOWER IN CONDITION

Proper lawn care begins with proper care of your lawn mower. Fertilizing and watering will stimulate grass growth, but without regular mowing thick grass can be an eyesore. For a lush look, a well-sharpened mower is a must. If mower blades are not absolutely sharp, you risk injuring your lawn every time you mow it. Dull blades tear at grass instead of cutting it and leave ragged tips that turn brown and not only look unattractive but are susceptible to pests and diseases. After every four or five cuttings, examine the blades; if the edges are rounded or nicked, they need sharpening.

There are basically two types of lawn mowers—reel and rotary. Both have blades that require periodic sharpening. Because of their intricate shape and assembly, reel-mower blades are not suitable for sharpening at home. They should be taken to a professional blade sharpener.

You can have the blades of a rotary mower professionally sharpened, but you can do the job yourself with a coarse file or an electric grinder. The grinder will give more even results.

When grinding the blade of a rotary mower, be sure to maintain the original angle of its two cutting edges and the balance between them. Use a bevel square to establish the angle, then check after each pass through the grinder and correct any deviation on the next pass.

To keep the blade in balance, the same amount of metal must be removed from each edge. After grinding, test the blade for balance and correct it if necessary by grinding a little more metal from the heavier edge. Mowing with an unbalanced blade can impair the mower itself.

Since the heat generated by grinding softens metal, immerse the blade in a container of cold water after every second or third pass through the grinder, to preserve its hardness, or temper.

Observe all safety precautions. Wear goggles to protect your eyes against sparks and flying bits of metal shavings, and wear one work glove—not two (page 49).

A freshly mown lawn lies snugly alongside a house and a walled garden area. The even height and clean-edged tips of the cut grass are achieved by mowing with sharp, smooth blades.

ABOUT MOWERS

All lawn mowers fall into two basic types: reel and rotary. There are many variations on these types, and new refinements appear each year, but the mowers illustrated here are representative of the two basic types.

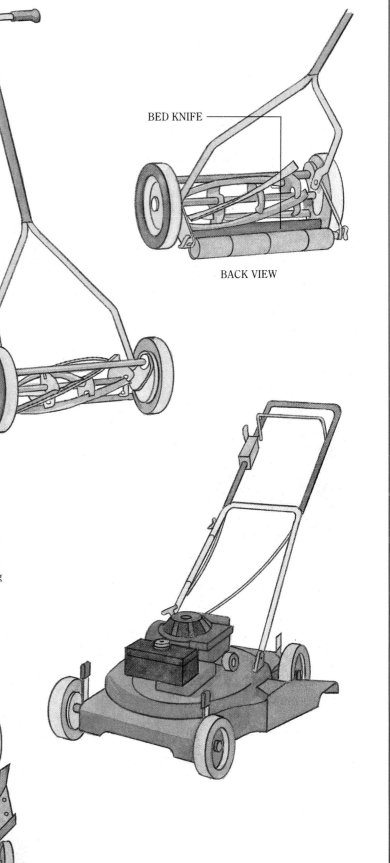

BED KNIFE

BACK VIEW

REEL MOWER

A reel mower has a set of blades that strike a fixed blade (called a bed knife) as they revolve on a reel; grass tips are caught between the two. The cutting width ranges between 12 and 18 inches. A reel mower can cut as close as ½ inch off the ground—closer than any rotary mower can manage. Reel mowers come in manual and gas-powered models. They work best on short grass and on fairly flat surfaces.

ROTARY MOWER

A rotary mower cuts with a rapidly rotating double-ended horizontal blade. It may be powered by gas or by electricity. Its rotary blade will never produce the kind of manicured look that a reel mower can achieve. But rotary mowers are fast, effective on bumpy and sloping surfaces, and make quick work of tall grass that would tangle up a reel mower. The cutting width ranges between 16 and 24 inches; the cutting height can be adjusted from 1½ to 3 inches. The most familiar model is a push-type *(right)*. There are also self-propelled models; the engine turns the wheels and all you have to do is steer the mower. For the largest lawns, there are riding mowers and lawn tractors, which have twice the cutting width of manually directed models. Some models come with grass-catching bags.

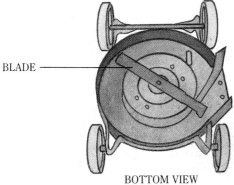

BLADE

BOTTOM VIEW

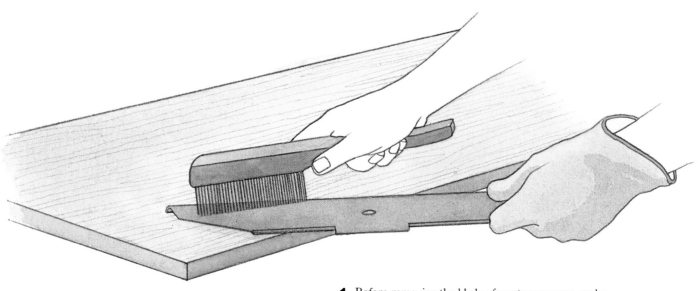

1 Before removing the blade of a rotary mower, make sure that the gas tank is empty and that the spark plug is disconnected so the engine cannot accidentally fire up. Lay the mower on its side to expose the blade assembly *(page 47)*. Since designs vary, follow the manufacturer's instructions for removing the blade, and note which way the blade is right side up. With a wire brush, clean encrusted dirt and grass from the entire blade.

2 Before grinding each cutting edge, slip the blade into a bevel square and note the cutting angle *(right)*; it is important to maintain the angle of the beveled edges as you sharpen. Keep checking the angle as you grind; if it changes even slightly, correct it on the next pass through the grinder.

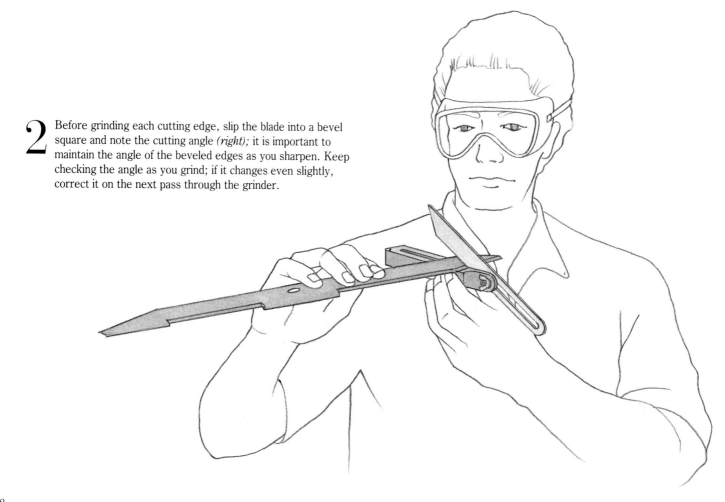

3 Turn on the grinder; lay one cutting edge of the blade on the tool rest in front of the grindstone; pull the blade evenly across the spinning stone. Always wear protective goggles and a work glove on the hand you use to steady the blade. Do not wear a glove on the hand that feeds the blade into the grinder, since the grindstone may grab the glove and pull it into the mechanism.

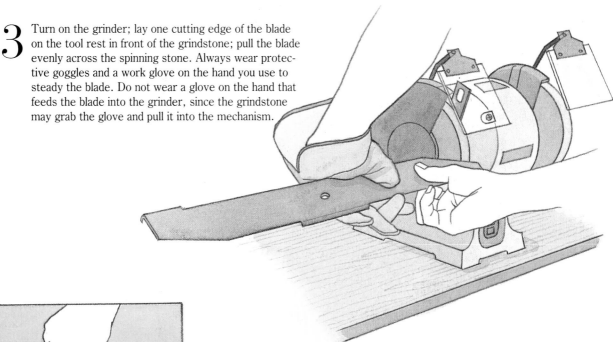

4 Alternately grind the two cutting edges. To keep the blade balanced, each edge must pass through the grinder the same number of times so that the same amount of metal is removed from each edge. To preserve the blade's hardness, plunge it into cold water after every two or three passes through the grinder *(left)*. After each pass, check the cutting angle and correct it if necessary.

5 When you think both edges are sharp enough, test on a level surface for balance; you can use a balance point of the sort sold in hardware stores, or improvise a balance by inserting a screwdriver or a pencil through the center hole and holding the blade securely upright. If one side of the blade is heavier than the other, it will dip down. In that case, gently grind the heavier side again, testing after each pass, until balance is restored. □

RIDDING A LAWN
OF UNWELCOME WEEDS

Sooner or later, all lawns are attacked by crabgrass and other invasive weeds. The weeds differ in growth habits, but the basic techniques for combating them are the same. First there is old-fashioned digging. A few isolated weeds are best removed with a trowel or a fork-tongued weeding tool. But if a lawn is large and the weed invasion spreading, the only practical answer is a chemical herbicide. Choosing the right one calls for some knowledge of weed types.

Like garden flowers, weeds are mainly of two sorts, annuals and perennials. The annuals grow from seed each year, produce seeds themselves and then die. Some set seeds that germinate in the spring; others have seeds that start up in the fall. In either case, the remedy is a preemergent herbicide —one that kills the seeds before the weeds can grow. For summer weeds, the preemergent should be applied about the time that forsythia blooms in the spring; for winter weeds, it should be spread in the fall.

Perennial weeds produce seeds, of course, but they also propagate themselves by spreading on their roots. They need a postemergent herbicide. As the name implies, postemergents kill weeds after they have emerged and begun to grow large. Most effective on most perennials are the so-called systemics, which poison a weed's entire system. For variations among weeds and specific information on fighting them, see pages 102-105.

Both preemergent and postemergent herbicides come in selective varieties, which are designed to kill only certain weeds, and in nonselective types that annihilate just about any plant they touch. For all ordinary purposes, the selective kinds are the best to use. When handling those that come in liquid form and, mixed with water, need to be sprayed as shown on these pages, always wear protective clothing: a long-sleeved shirt, trousers, rubber gloves and goggles.

A smooth and virtually weed-free expanse of healthy lawn provides a handsome setting for a ranch-style house. The most practical way to control a large invasion of weeds is with chemical herbicides.

SPRAYERS FOR HERBICIDES

For a lawn of moderate size, a backpack tank *(below, left)* or a compression tank *(middle)* is large enough. With a backpack, which holds about 3 gallons of water-diluted herbicide, you need to pump with one hand while aiming the spray tube with the other. Compression tanks are pumped beforehand to build up pressure; they range in size from quart containers to 5-gallon ones. For large lawns, battery-powered, 12-gallon sprayers—some are mounted on wheels *(right)*—make the task easier. There are also rotary spreaders *(not shown)* for dry granular herbicides.

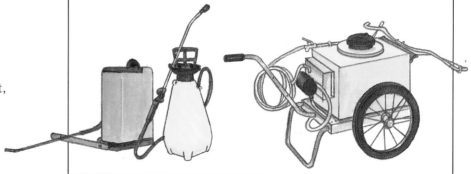

1 A few days before applying a herbicide, mow your lawn and give it a good watering. You should not mow it for several days after putting down the chemical because in mowing you will be cutting away treated foliage and thus reducing the effectiveness of the herbicide. Watering ahead of time will encourage the weeds to grow and make them more susceptible to the poison.

2 Following the directions on the herbicide container, mix the chemical with water in your spray tank—here a backpack type. It is safer to put the water in first; this reduces the chance of splashing the herbicide about. Once the tank is full, begin spraying, keeping the nozzle close to the ground and hitting the weeds directly.

3 Keep children and pets away from the treated areas for several hours, until the herbicide is thoroughly dry. Do not water your lawn for some days; watering will dilute the chemical and reduce its effect. In a week or so, when the weeds have died, rake them up and throw them away to make room for new grass to grow. □

A BIOLOGICAL REMEDY FOR BEETLE GRUBS

The most devastating pests that can afflict a lawn are Japanese beetles or, more precisely, their larvae, or grubs. Hatching from eggs laid under the grass, the grubs feed voraciously on the roots until, in severe cases, the rootless grass can be rolled up like a rug. The most common signs of infestation are brown, dead patches in the lawn. To look for grubs, cut and fold back small sections of turf and examine the soil underneath. To be sure any uncovered grubs are those of Japanese beetles, send a couple to the nearest agricultural extension office.

Far the most effective way to battle the grubs is with a substance called milky spore, the dustlike dormant form of a bacterium called *Bacillus popilliae,* which was found back in the 1930s to be the natural bacterial enemy of Japanese beetles. Today it is the active ingredient in several insecticide powders sold in garden supply centers. As far as researchers know, the bacterium has no harmful effects on humans.

The milky spore powder should be placed carefully under the grass of an infested lawn *(opposite).* It need be applied only once in a decade at most because the bacteria multiply as they attack the grubs, becoming more numerous and effective in time. In fact, milky spore products only start working really well three years after application, but then continue working for 15 years or more.

Milky spore can be put down whenever the ground is not frozen, but the best time is late spring, when new grubs are hatching, or early fall, before the grubs burrow into the soil for the winter.

Showing no signs of the brown patches caused by Japanese beetle grubs, a handsome sun-dappled lawn thrives in the partial shade of well-spaced trees. Beetle grubs, archenemies of turfgrass, are best kept in check with milky spore, a bacteria-based powder that kills the invaders.

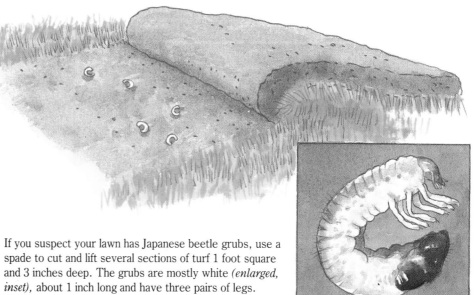

1 If you suspect your lawn has Japanese beetle grubs, use a spade to cut and lift several sections of turf 1 foot square and 3 inches deep. The grubs are mostly white *(enlarged, inset),* about 1 inch long and have three pairs of legs. Three grubs or more per square foot indicates trouble.

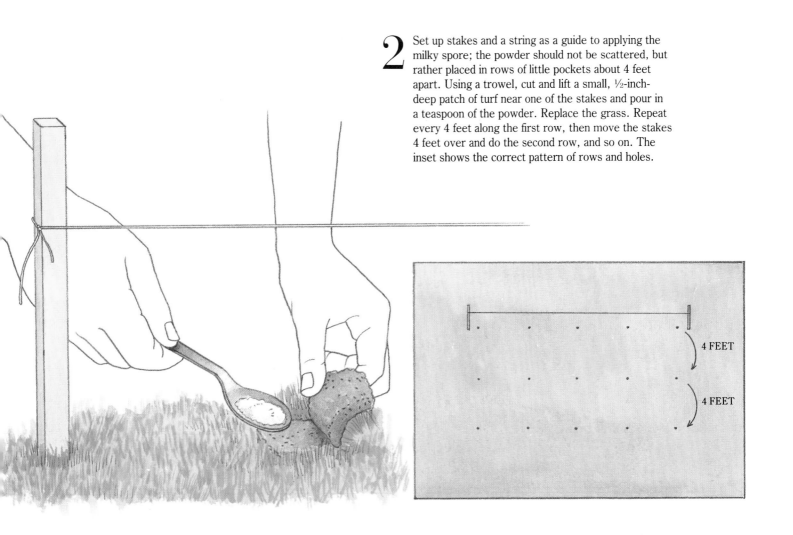

2 Set up stakes and a string as a guide to applying the milky spore; the powder should not be scattered, but rather placed in rows of little pockets about 4 feet apart. Using a trowel, cut and lift a small, ½-inch-deep patch of turf near one of the stakes and pour in a teaspoon of the powder. Replace the grass. Repeat every 4 feet along the first row, then move the stakes 4 feet over and do the second row, and so on. The inset shows the correct pattern of rows and holes.

4 FEET

4 FEET

3 After you have done enough rows to cover the infested turf, water the lawn well for at least 20 minutes. This will help wash the spores into the soil and down to root level. Water again the next day, and the next; in fact, it is a good idea to keep the lawn moist for a week or two to help the milky spore compound spread and begin affecting the grubs. □

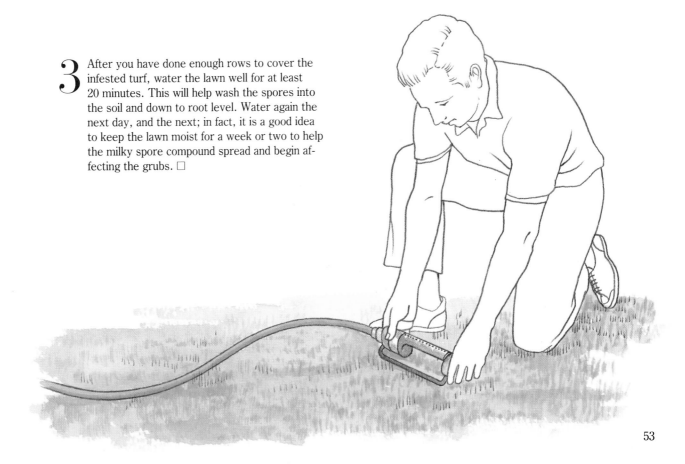

A GRASS ROOTS CAMPAIGN
TO LIVEN UP A FADED LAWN

The close-knit, thriving grass of an extensive lawn looks half-gold, half-green in the slanting rays of an early-morning sun. To be this full and vigorous, lawn grasses need occasional aerating along with other care, to avoid compaction and to get oxygen and nutrients to the roots.

Even the most carefully planted and tended stretches of lawn can, for no apparent reason, lose their velvety sheen and begin to look lackluster. The hidden cause of the malady is almost invariably compaction; the soil beneath the grass has become dense and hard, with the result that the air, water and fertilizer that grass needs cannot reach the roots. The sections of a lawn getting the most use suffer worst and soonest.

The only reliable remedy is aeration—pulling out cores, or plugs of soil, so that moisture, nutrients and above all oxygen can get directly to root level. For a small lawn or a limited problem area, there are manual aerating tools similar in appearance to garden forks, but the prongs are hollow and pull up plugs of soil. For a larger spread of grass, the sort of powered aerating machine shown opposite is a must for doing the job better, faster and with much less effort. Such machines can be rented from most garden equipment centers.

In either case, the aerator should pull up plugs of soil about ½ inch in diameter and 3 inches long, leaving good-sized holes that reach well into the root zone of the grass. The plugs can be broken up and used as topsoil or thrown away. Similarly, the holes can be left to fill in naturally, or a top dressing can be sifted into them *(opposite)*.

The best time to aerate is when the lawn is actively growing—but not when the weather is very hot. And the ground should be moist. In most parts of the country, these requirements point to spring and early fall. How often to do it depends on how fast the soil compacts—and that depends in turn on the amount of traffic the lawn gets and on how dense and clayey the soil is. Conscientious golf course superintendents religiously aerate their greens and fairways twice a year, which is why golf course grass always looks so green and flawless despite the relentless pressure of feet, golf carts and golf clubs.

1 One day after giving the lawn a good watering, run the aerating machine back and forth across your entire lawn. Examine the plugs that the aerator pulls up; if the soil is hard and dry, you may find they are crumbly and less than a full 3 inches long. If so, give the lawn another good watering, wait until the moisture has soaked in and try again.

2 If the soil under your lawn is clayey, rake up the plugs and throw them away. With lawns, the less clay the better. Plugs that seem to be good brown loam, however, can be broken up with the back of a garden rake; pulverized and sifted for stones, the cores make good topsoil.

3 Scatter a top dressing of peat moss over the aerated lawn with a shovel, then use the back of the rake to distribute it evenly and push it down into the aeration holes. Peat moss is light enough to let air into the root zone and helps retain moisture. This is also a good time to spread some fertilizer. Water the lawn thoroughly. □

PEAT MOSS

DETHATCHING
TO ADMIT AIR AND NUTRIENTS

Every lawn eventually accumulates a layer of old dead grass, unraked leaf bits and other detritus that is called thatch. It sits between the soil and the living grass, looking yellowish, matted and unattractive—and it can do a lawn real harm. If thick enough, thatch shuts off oxygen, moisture and fertilizer from the grass's roots, and it provides a cozy home for pests and plant diseases. Getting rid of it is an important part of maintaining a healthy lawn.

The best way to tell whether a lawn needs dethatching is shown below, at right. A little thatch is no problem, and can even help by conserving moisture in the ground. But a mat that is ½ inch thick or more should be removed. Warm-season grasses—the zoysias and Bermudas commonly grown in the South—build up thatch more quickly than the blues and fescues used for lawns in northern areas. As a general rule, the denser warm-weather varieties should be dethatched every year, others perhaps once in three years.

Dethatching should be done when the grass is actively growing, so it will recover quickly afterward. Spring and fall are good times in the North, late spring and summer in the South.

There are tools for dethatching by hand; they look similar to rakes but the tines are sharp-pointed and somewhat curved. They are fine for a small plot. But for most lawns a motorized dethatcher is far preferable. Motorized dethatchers work much like gas-powered lawn mowers and can be rented from most garden equipment centers. The illustrations on the facing page show how to use one.

Looking like green broadloom, a manicured lawn stretches away from a handsome border of decorative shrubs and flowers. Dethatching plays an important part in keeping turfgrass bright by improving its oxygen intake and removing the underlying mat of old, dead and discolored plant material.

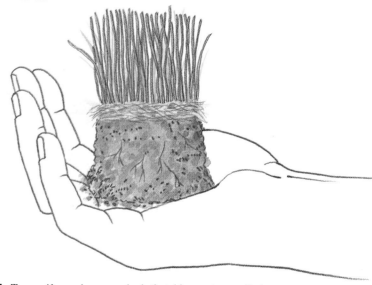

1 To see if your lawn needs dethatching, cut a small plug of turf about 2 inches deep with an old knife or a trowel. Examine its profile. You should see, from the bottom up, a layer of soil and roots, a stratum of thatch and then the green, growing grass. If the thatch is more than ½ inch thick, dethatching is in order.

2 Set the dethatching machine so that the adjustable rotating tines will dig down ½ inch. This should be deep enough to lift the top layer of thatch. Go over the entire lawn, making parallel passes; move north-south first, for example, and then south-north.

3 Rake up the thatch that has been dislodged and throw it away. (You can put it in a compost pile if the grass has not been treated with chemicals.) If your lawn is generally healthy, a properly set dethatcher should not lift up a large amount of green grass. But some grass will come up with the thatch; this is normal and unavoidable.

4 Set the tines on the dethatcher a fraction of an inch lower and go over the lawn again, this time perpendicular to your first passes. If you initially moved north and south, go east and west this time. Again, rake up the thatch and discard it. After that, fertilize *(pages 40-43)*, and then give the lawn a good watering to help the grass recover. ☐

PRUNING TO KEEP GROUND COVERS IN CHECK

Bright yellow blooms peek from a well-tended bed of the perennial ground cover called St.-John's-wort that has been neatly shaped by careful shearing. This plant, like other many-stemmed ground covers, can be sheared periodically without harm to the foliage, and flowers will soon reappear.

Some ground cover plants are decorous growers, staying within bounds and encroaching on nearby lawn areas or walkways slowly if at all. Others, though, are exuberant in their habits, spilling out of their plots and encroaching on their neighbors. These spreaders need pruning a couple of times a season to keep them in check. Even the slow growers can benefit from some judicious snipping now and then, to keep them shapely and to remove dead or aging sections.

There are essentially two ways to prune ground covers *(right)*. One is shearing—a wholesale lopping of the ends of branches or foliage. Used on creeping, low-growing shrubs and on plants that have numerous leaves— blue fescue, for example—shearing helps keep them healthy, compact and the proper size. Shearing can also prevent them from going to seed, which makes them neater as well as more vigorous. The other sort of pruning is thinning—a selective cutting of entire branches or stems. Once more, this can bring plants back to their proper size, and it also cures overcrowding. Thinning is the right way to prune shrubby ground covers such as juniper, Russian cypress and cotoneaster.

Pruning can be done any time during the growing season, but with flowering plants it is best undertaken soon after the plants have bloomed. This avoids snipping off the next year's flower buds, which will not have formed yet. And do not wait until late summer. Pruning encourages new growth and tender fresh shoots that sprout late in the season and can be killed by autumn's first hard frosts.

SHEARING PERENNIALS, GRASSES AND VINES

To prevent vertical-growing ground covers from flopping over into a messy tangle, gather the stems or the leaves in one hand and cut off the tops with garden shears *(left)*. A full one-third of the top growth can be sheared from grasses such as blue fescue and perennials such as thyme and phlox. New, fresh and more vigorous growth will come up quickly. Shearing is also the right way to cut back vines such as wintercreeper and prostrate shrubs to prevent them from crawling across your lawn or terrace. For these plants, use large grass shears or hedge shears, snipping vertically *(below)*.

THINNING WOODY SHRUBS

The main task here is to spot the individual branches or stems that need to be removed—dead and damaged ones of course, but also those that spoil the shape of the plants or cause overcrowding. Shrubby ground covers often need to have excess growth removed, to open up the bed and let in more sunlight and air. When thinning branches or stems, always cut off the ones you are removing at the base, as shown, where they meet a lateral branch or the main trunk. The best tool is a sharp pair of pruning shears. □

SPRING RENOVATION
FOR GROUND COVERS

Following an early-spring mowing and raking, this bed of gazania has rebounded with new vigor—and a cheerful display of vibrantly colored blossoms.

Winter can be hard on even winter-hardy ground covers. Although they survive the cold with their foliage largely intact, they often show ugly brown or straggly patches (the result of lack of moisture) when spring comes.

The first sign of warmer weather should be your signal to remove all dead or damaged stems and leaves. This not only improves the appearance of the bed but clears the way for the first vigorous growth of the new season.

Even ornamental grasses like pampas grass, whose weather-beaten foliage adds visual interest to a wintry landscape, will benefit from a thorough spring renovation.

You can clean up any ground cover bed with a pair of pruning shears—a time-consuming job. Fortunately, some evergreen ground covers grow low enough to the ground to be mowed. These include yarrow, snow-in-summer, Mondo grass and lily turf.

To avoid tearing up the plants, make sure the blades of your mower are absolutely sharp before you begin. If necessary, sharpen them *(pages 46-49)*. Set the mower to the highest setting (usually between 2½ and 3 inches) and run it once over the bed.

Whether you renovate a ground cover bed by hand pruning or with a mower, it is a good idea to fertilize immediately afterward. This will help nurture the emerging new growth. After fertilizing, lay down a fresh layer of mulch, such as pine straw, to slow evaporation from the soil surface and help control weeds.

1 To mow a low-growing ground cover, check the blades of your lawn mower to make sure they are at their sharpest. Sharpen them if necessary. Set the mower to the highest setting and run it over the ground cover bed *(below)*. A single pass should be sufficient.

2 Use a rake to gather all the clipped foliage together *(left);* rake gently to minimize the danger of uprooting any plants. Dispose of the clippings.

3 After mowing and clearing the bed, use your hands or a spreader to apply a general-purpose granular fertilizer. For the correct amount, follow instructions on the label. Water thoroughly to soak the fertilizer into the soil.

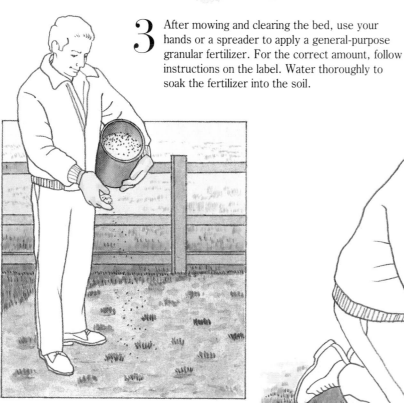

4 Cover the fertilized bed with a light mulch such as pine straw. This will improve the bed's appearance, conserve moisture and hinder weed growth. Don't hesitate to lay mulch right over the clipped plants; the summer's new growth will easily penetrate the mulch layer. □

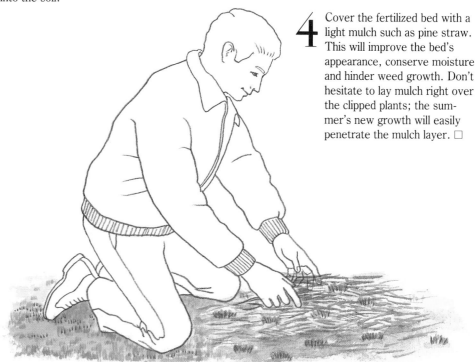

RESTRAINING UNRULY ORNAMENTAL GRASSES

Most ground covers grow and spread above ground, where they can easily be pruned back when they get too pervasive. But several of the more versatile and hardy ground cover plants, including ribbon grass, eulalia grass and bamboo, sprout from rhizomes, stems that creep underground. And rhizomes can pose a problem. Most of the bamboos that have creeping rhizomes are notorious spreaders, and the ornamental grasses can be invasive, too, burrowing sideways into lawns and flower beds, where they are unwelcome. Pruning the plants above ground only encourages further underground creeping.

There is a way, however, to grow these useful, handsome ground covers without having them take over the neighborhood, namely to plant them in good-sized containers sunk inconspicuously into the ground. Large, stiff-sided plastic tubs will do; so will galvanized metal washtubs. For drainage reasons they will need to have their bottoms taken off. A sharp knife should deal with plastic tubs, tin snips and a hacksaw with metal tubs.

An alternative, shown here, is to buy thin sheets of aluminum or galvanized steel 18 to 24 inches wide, bend them into cylinders and either weld the ends together or secure them with bolts. How long the sheets should be depends on the size of the desired containers. Rule of thumb: a 6-foot-long sheet will make a container 2 feet in diameter. In any case, the sunken tubs or metal rings will keep any wandering rhizomes within bounds and out of other parts of the garden—and the containers will be large enough for the grasses or bamboo to thrive.

The long pale blades of Japanese silver grass arch gracefully behind a low-growing dark green ground cover. The Japanese silver grass, which can be invasive, is kept in check by metal barriers sunk out of sight in the ground.

1 Using your bottomless tub or cylinder of sheet metal as a guide, draw a circle on the ground where you want to start planting. Dig a hole that is as wide across as the tub or cylinder and deep enough to hold it with about an inch of rim showing above ground level. Sink the tub or cylinder into the hole *(below);* then pour about 2 inches of gravel in the bottom to help with drainage.

2 Enrich the earth you dug up with some organic matter—peat moss, compost or rotted leaves. Partially refill the hole with the soil; when you place the plant on top, the upper surface of the root ball of the plant should be an inch or so below the rim of the container.

3 Knock your plant out of its pot and gently untangle the roots. Place the plant on the soil, then fill in around it, leaving the top inch of the container clear. Firm the soil and water it generously.

4 Backfill around the outside of the container with the remaining earth, raking the last bits flush with the rim to help hide it. You can finish off by covering the area around the plant with a light mulch. □

BORDERS FOR OTHER CREEPERS

A number of ground covers, although not as invasive as ornamental grasses, tend to spread eventually. If you have cypress spurge, strawberry, speedwell or goutweed *(above)* bordering a lawn, you may want to check the ground cover's spread with some shallow edging. Handiest are black plastic edging strips that are about 5 inches wide. Dig a shallow trench along the border of the ground cover bed and insert the edging in the trench so its upper edge is flush with the surface of the soil. It should keep shallow-rooted spreaders from encroaching.

3
MULTIPLYING AND DIVIDING

Once established, ground covers tend to be self-perpetuating, constantly renewing themselves, season after season, year after year. Most of them do so by rapidly and easily putting down new roots whenever a leaf node along a trailing stem comes in contact with the ground. A few ground covers, notably the popular hosta, arrange things otherwise. These plants, which are called clumping plants, renew themselves by sending up shoots from belowground around the base of the parent plant. These characteristic patterns of reproduction, so useful in keeping the ground cover thick and green, are also helpful in generating new plants whenever existing plants, for whatever reason, sicken and die, and need to be replaced.

When clumping plants fail, it is often because the parent plant has come to the end of its life span and has grown thin and woody. Its replacements, however—the shoots—are already at hand, and need only be cut free and repositioned to fill the gap. With other plants the replacement process takes a bit longer. Most of them can be started from stem cuttings, taken from the plant in the spring or early summer, which are rooted in a soilless medium. A trailing stem can be pinned to the soil until it has sent out new roots, at which point the stem is severed from the parent plant.

All three of these methods of obtaining new plants—from trailing stems, from stem cuttings and from shoots—are explained on the following pages. In addition, for gardeners who want to experiment, there is information on the special nurturing requirements of plants grown from seed. And finally, there are instructions for creating a propagation bed to get young stem cuttings off to the best start.

PROPAGATION AND REJUVENATION ALL IN ONE

The varied colors and leaf patterns of hosta plants lend visual excitement to the shady area underneath a tree. Ground covers like hosta are easily divided, providing additional plants and keeping established ones vigorous.

Some perennial ground covers and ornamental grasses (like hosta and miscanthus) spread by establishing new clumps along their outer edges. With most of the plant's energy directed toward the perimeter, the center eventually becomes choked with old, woody growth. But that is easily remedied, because, fortunately, clumpy perennials lend themselves to periodic division—a process that not only restores their vigor but generates plenty of material for new beds.

Depending on the appearance of your plants, you'll probably want to divide every few years. If a plant has a woody center but healthy exterior clumps, it is ready for dividing. Each clump has its own root system. If you keep these roots intact when you divide the plant, each newly separated clump will be capable of quickly establishing itself as an independent plant.

Before dividing a clumpy perennial *(opposite),* water the ground well to make digging easier and to fortify the roots against the shock of transplanting. Then lift the plant with a spade and immediately pull apart the individual sections with your hands. If the clumps are bound together by inter-meshed roots or crowns, cut them apart with a knife. Don't be afraid to exert some force if you encounter resistance; this will not harm the plant.

Once you have removed all the vigorous outer clumps, examine what is left. Any center sections that look dry and lifeless should be discarded.

If you divide an entire bed of ground cover, you will end up with enough new plants to fill an additional bed. Since roots should not be exposed to the air a moment longer than necessary, prepare the new bed ahead of time and plant the new divisions as quickly as possible.

The best time to divide is in early spring or early fall, when most plants are dormant.

1 Before dividing a ground cover plant, water the soil thoroughly, to make digging easier and reduce the shock to the plant's root system. With a sharp spade, dig straight down several inches around the plant. To spare the root system, be careful not to dig too close to the plant. Lift the entire plant on the blade of the spade.

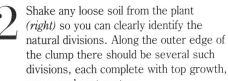

2 Shake any loose soil from the plant *(right)* so you can clearly identify the natural divisions. Along the outer edge of the clump there should be several such divisions, each complete with top growth, crown and root system.

3 With a sharp knife, cut through any roots or plant tissue binding individual sections together *(above, left);* then pull each section free with your fingers *(above, right)*. Replant the new sections without delay, and keep them well watered until they are fully established. □

GROWING NEW GROUND COVERS FROM STEM CUTTINGS

A lush collection of sedum plants spills summer blossoms over a lichen-encrusted stone wall. Plants such as sedum, with their semiwoody stems, can yield a multitude of offspring from cuttings taken in spring.

One way to expand a ground cover is to propagate your own plants from stem cuttings. Any healthy plant with woody or semiwoody stems is a good candidate for this method of reproduction. Examples include sedum, yarrow, lantana, yew, Russian cypress and English ivy.

The best time to take cuttings is in late spring or early summer, when the stems are actively growing. Sharp tools are a must; smooth, clean tissue will root more readily than tissue that is ragged and crushed. Use a sharp knife, a pair of sharp shears or a fresh razor blade.

To expose as much rooting surface as possible, cut the stem on a slant just below a leaf or a node—the point on the stem where leaves are attached. Cuttings should be between 2 and 6 inches long. To encourage rooting, dip the cut ends in rooting hormone powder just before planting. Shake a little powder onto a piece of paper, roll the cut end in powder and shake off the excess. After you have treated all the cuttings, discard any powder that is left on the paper, to guard against spreading infection.

Plant the cuttings indoors in flats or pots, or outdoors in a propagating bed *(pages 72-75)*. Plant them in a well-drained, soilless rooting medium; soil-based mixes tend to be too heavy and, unless labeled "sterile," may carry diseases.

Depending on the type of plant, cuttings may take from two weeks to four months to develop vigorous roots. They are most likely to root quickly if kept in an evenly warm environment with high humidity and good light. When they show new top growth, they are ready for transplanting to a more permanent home.

1 Fill a container with premoistened, soilless rooting medium, such as builder's sand, a mix of half sand and half peat moss, or half peat moss and half perlite. Tamp down lightly; add more medium if necessary to bring the top surface to within ½ inch of the rim.

2 Select a firm stem on a healthy plant and cut 2 to 6 inches from the tip with sharp pruning shears, a fresh razor blade or a sharp knife *(left)*. Make the cut directly below a node, the point where leaves attach to the stem.

3 Holding the stem cutting in your hands *(right)*, pull off all the leaves from the last inch or so of the cut end—the part that will be buried. Any leaves buried on the stem will decay, jeopardizing the chances for successful root formation.

4 Shake a small amount of rooting hormone powder onto a piece of paper and roll the bottom inch of the cutting in it. Shake excess powder from the stem, leaving no more than a thin coat; too much powder can actually hinder root formation.

5 With a pencil, poke a hole 1 to 2 inches deep in the rooting medium *(left)*. The hole should be wide enough so that you can insert a stem cutting without scraping off its coat of hormone powder.

6 Ease the stem cutting into the hole and tamp down the medium around it. Plant as many cuttings in the pot as will fit without touching. When you are finished, write the name of the plant and the date on a plant marker and insert it in the pot for future identification.

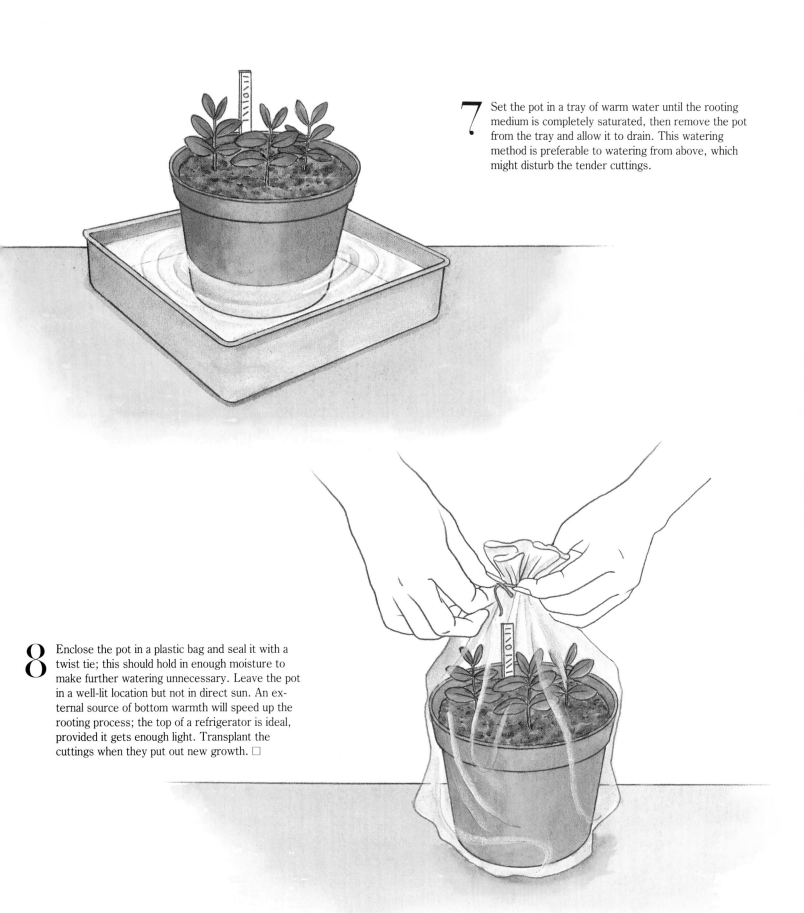

7 Set the pot in a tray of warm water until the rooting medium is completely saturated, then remove the pot from the tray and allow it to drain. This watering method is preferable to watering from above, which might disturb the tender cuttings.

8 Enclose the pot in a plastic bag and seal it with a twist tie; this should hold in enough moisture to make further watering unnecessary. Leave the pot in a well-lit location but not in direct sun. An external source of bottom warmth will speed up the rooting process; the top of a refrigerator is ideal, provided it gets enough light. Transplant the cuttings when they put out new growth. □

A SPECIAL ENVIRONMENT FOR NURTURING CUTTINGS

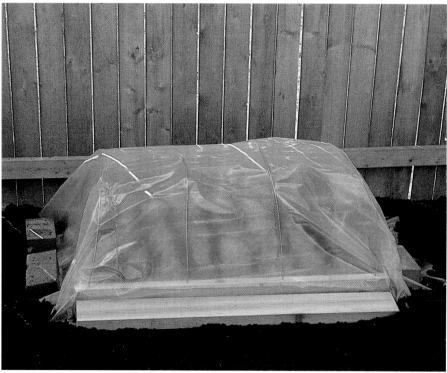

Neat, compact and out of the way, the propagation bed above has room for about 40 shore juniper cuttings inside the plastic covering. The location near a fence is ideal, protecting the bed from hot direct sunlight.

The most convenient way to nurture a number of cuttings taken from ground cover plants is to put them in an easily made propagation bed of the sort described at right and on the following two pages. Once a few supplies have been collected, the bed should not take more than half an hour to construct, and it serves the same purpose as a more elaborate cold frame. What the propagation bed will do is keep the cuttings both moist and warm—the conditions they need to develop roots and grow.

The bed stays warm in part because it is sunk in the earth. Down even a few inches, temperatures fluctuate less than at ground level. But the main reason the bed stays warm and humid is that its plastic canopy traps the heat of the sun and condenses the moisture in the ground. The plastic sheeting used should be fairly heavy, but it must be pliable. A sheet 4 feet by 6 ought to be large enough for a propagation bed measuring 3 feet long and 2 feet wide, such as the one described here. A bed this size can accommodate as many as 50 to 100 small cuttings; a larger bed can be made, of course, if more room is needed.

The only materials required besides the plastic are three 3-foot lengths of weatherproofed 2-by-4-inch lumber—two to outline the bed and one to weight the movable plastic cover—and four 3-foot-long pieces of moderately stiff wire. The wire is needed to make hoops that will support the plastic in a canopy. For tools, collect a spade for digging the bed, a drill for making small holes in a couple of the 2-by-4s and a staple gun to help fasten the plastic to the wood.

Cuttings need light to prosper, so the bed should be dug somewhere fairly bright—but not in direct sunlight, which would turn it into an oven. It should also be located away from backyard traffic. The best time to make the bed and plant it is spring or early summer, so the cuttings can be transplanted when they should be, in the fall.

1 Begin by spading out an area about 2 by 3 feet, or as long and wide as you want the propagation bed to be. The area should be neat, sharp-edged and about 1 foot deep. This will allow plenty of room for the drainage and planting materials that will go in the hole *(below),* while keeping the cuttings and their developing roots at ground level.

2 Cover the bottom of the bed with at least 3 inches of coarse gravel for good drainage. Then lay a sheet of window screening, cut to size, on top of the gravel. This will keep the rooting medium, which you will pour in next, from sifting down into the gravel layer.

3 Fill the bed to the top with new, clean, weed-free builder's sand. Sand is good rooting material for the cuttings because it is loose and drains well. Rake the sand so that it is level.

73

4 Sink two precut 2-by-4s into the long sides of the bed *(left)*. Drill small holes at 1-foot intervals in the tops of the boards to hold the ends of the wires. The holes should match up on the two boards. Bank some of the soil you spaded up against the outsides of the 2-by-4s to help hold them in place.

5 Insert a 3-foot length of wire into a hole in one of the boards, then loop the other end into the corresponding hole in the second 2-by-4. Repeat the process with the other wires. The wire itself should be heavy enough to hold its shape and support the weight of a plastic canopy.

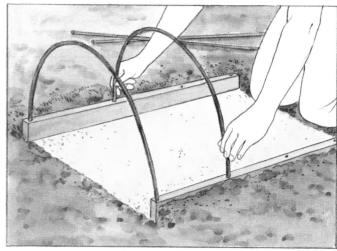

6 Cut a sheet of clear plastic so that it fits over the wires but has plenty of extra on both sides and at the ends. The excess will be needed when you tackle the next three steps, which are shown on the facing page.

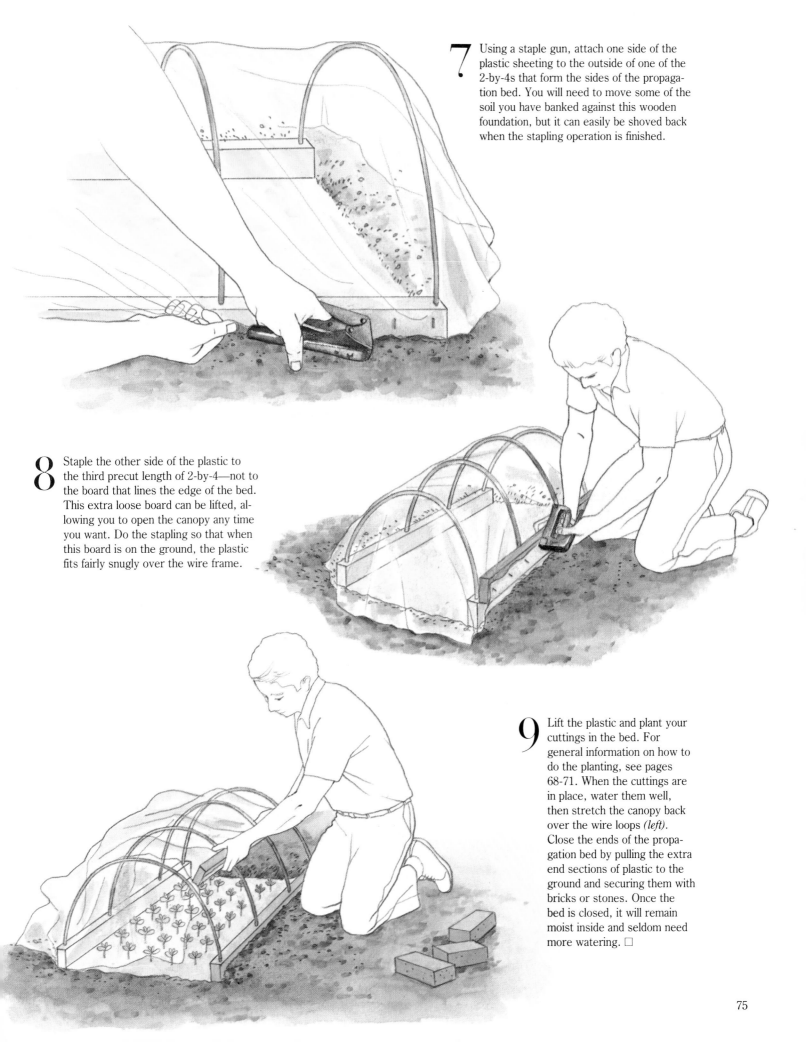

7 Using a staple gun, attach one side of the plastic sheeting to the outside of one of the 2-by-4s that form the sides of the propagation bed. You will need to move some of the soil you have banked against this wooden foundation, but it can easily be shoved back when the stapling operation is finished.

8 Staple the other side of the plastic to the third precut length of 2-by-4—not to the board that lines the edge of the bed. This extra loose board can be lifted, allowing you to open the canopy any time you want. Do the stapling so that when this board is on the ground, the plastic fits fairly snugly over the wire frame.

9 Lift the plastic and plant your cuttings in the bed. For general information on how to do the planting, see pages 68-71. When the cuttings are in place, water them well, then stretch the canopy back over the wire loops *(left)*. Close the ends of the propagation bed by pulling the extra end sections of plastic to the ground and securing them with bricks or stones. Once the bed is closed, it will remain moist inside and seldom need more watering. □

PROPAGATION
BY ROOTING LOW-LYING STEMS

Nature sometimes causes the low-lying branches of shrubs and vines to be buried beneath a layer of soil. If conditions are right, roots may form on such a buried branch, which then becomes capable of surviving as an independent plant apart from its parent. The method of propagation known as layering imitates this natural process. Good candidates for layering include shrubby plants like bearberry, cotoneaster, cypress spurge and juniper, and vining ground covers like Boston ivy and English ivy.

A great advantage of layering over stem cuttings is that the layered branch is sustained by the parent until its roots have matured. This minimizes the risk of rot and disease, especially with woody and semiwoody plants that take a long time to root.

To encourage root formation, cut away a small portion of bark and wood with a knife or a razor, then coat the cut with rooting hormone powder before burying that portion of the branch in the ground. Cover it with a light mulch to keep it moist during the six months to a year it requires to root.

The best time to layer is in spring or early summer, so that the buried branch has an entire growing season to put down its own root system. Check in the fall to see whether sturdy roots have formed. If a layered branch shows new growth at the tip and resists gentle tugging, it is ready for life on its own.

Where winters are mild, you can cut the layered branch from the parent and replant it as soon as roots develop. Where winters are extremely cold, you may prefer to leave the rooted branch in place until the following spring; this will do no harm to either the new plant or its parent.

The stems of a variegated periwinkle, a vining ground cover, spread out over the surface of a mulched bed. Ground covers that have low-lying stems and branches often root themselves naturally, but the gardener can lend a hand and help them root, and thus gain new plants.

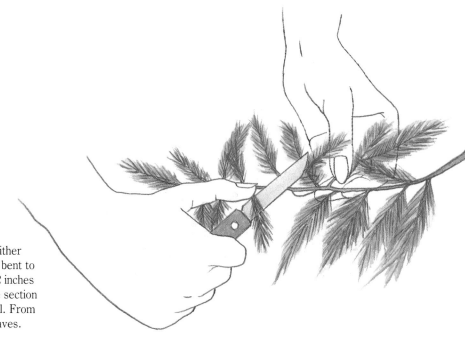

1 Find a healthy branch or stem that either grows close to the ground or can be bent to the ground without breaking; 6 to 12 inches from the tip, it should have a flexible section that can be easily tucked into the soil. From this section, strip 2 to 3 inches of leaves.

2 With a sharp knife, remove bark and wood along the underside of the section from which you have stripped the leaves *(right)*. The cut should be no deeper than half the thickness of the wood and should cover an area about twice the diameter of the branch.

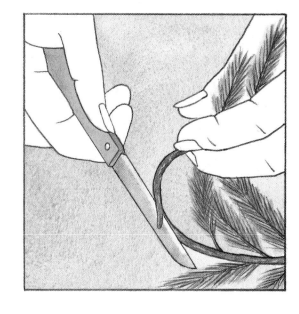

3 Sprinkle a small amount of rooting hormone powder onto a clean piece of paper. Dip a clean paint brush in the powder and brush some powder onto the cut you have just made in the branch *(left)*.

4 Dig a hole 1 to 2 inches deep. Insert the cut section of the branch and hold it down *(right)* while you refill the hole and tamp down the soil. To make sure the branch stays in the ground, secure it with a small rock or a twist of wire. Spread mulch lightly over the refilled hole.

5 In the spring, check for signs of root formation—new growth from the branch tip and resistance to tugging. If you are unsure, loosen the soil around the hole and examine the underside of the cutting directly. If the roots are well developed, cut the layered branch from the parent and replant it; if not, leave it in the ground for a few more months. □

SOWING SEEDS: MORE PLANTS FOR LESS MONEY

Considering how many plants are needed to fill out even a small bed, ground covers and ornamental grasses are expensive to buy from a nursery. A sensible alternative is to start your own plants from seed. With seed, you not only save money, you also have a wider selection of plants to choose from and you get a jump on the growing season because seedlings raised indoors can be safely moved outside the moment the weather warms up. And since all the important variables—soil, light, moisture and temperature—are under your control, the chances of successful germination are high.

To reduce the risk of damping-off—a fungus disease that attacks seedlings—seeds should be sown in a light, well-drained rooting medium. Either buy a ready-made mix or make your own by combining one part peat moss and one part builder's sand. Pour the medium into a clean nursery flat or some other shallow container that has several drainage holes.

Read the seed packet to find out when to start your seeds. Also take note of any special instructions for pretreating seeds. To germinate, most seeds should be kept in an environment that has high humidity and temperatures in the 75° to 80° F range. But certain seeds will not sprout unless first subjected to a period of "artificial winter" in a refrigerator; this chilling process is known as stratification. Other seeds must be either nicked with a knife or soaked in water overnight to soften their outer coats before germination can begin.

Once seedlings emerge, give them plenty of bright sunlight; a south-facing windowsill is ideal. If you cannot provide sufficient natural illumination, place the seedlings under a bank of fluorescent bulbs for several hours a day.

Bright sun highlights the geometric regularity of a bed filled with sandwort plants. Ornamental grasses and ground covers such as sandwort can be inexpensively started from seed and propagate readily.

1 Into a nursery flat (or some other container that has several drainage holes) pour about 2 inches of premoistened rooting medium such as a mix of half peat moss and half builder's sand. Tamp down lightly.

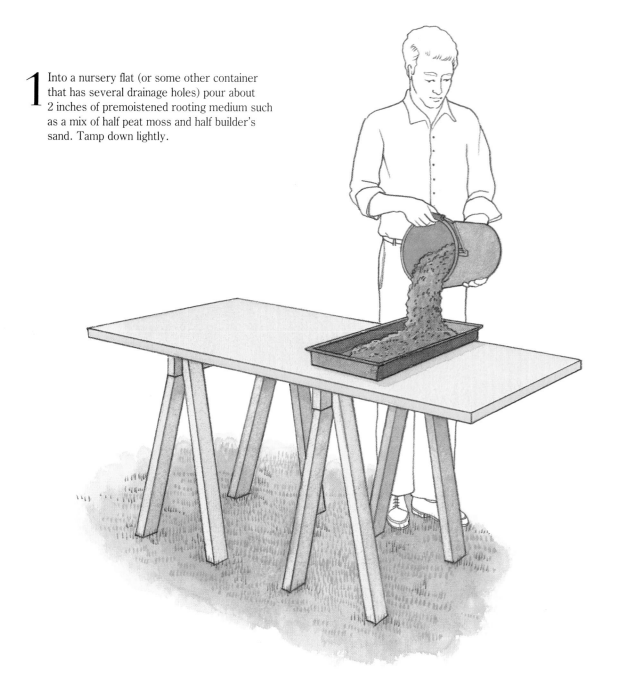

2 With a plant label or a pencil laid flat, make shallow grooves in the medium several inches apart. The recommended depth varies with the type of seed; follow the instructions on the seed packet. In general, seeds should be planted at a depth equal to twice their width.

3 Drop seeds into the grooves at a rate of one to five per inch, depending on the size of the seeds. Unless the seed packet tells you to leave the seeds exposed to light, cover them with a thin layer of rooting medium.

4 After planting, water thoroughly. If your container is small enough, let it soak in a pan of water until the medium is saturated to the top. If your container is a large one (as shown here), water gently from above; use a hose fitted with a breaker or a watering can with a rose attachment. Let excess water drain from the container.

5 To maintain the high humidity that is necessary for speedy germination, cover the container with clear plastic wrap and tape it in place or enclose the container in a plastic bag and seal it with a twist tie. Leave the container in a warm spot, such as a sunny windowsill or the top of a refrigerator.

6 When seedlings start coming up, remove the plastic covering. From this point on, adequate light is crucial to prevent the plants from growing weak and spindly. If the rows become crowded, thin out the seedlings until they are separated by a space equal to their own height. To thin, use scissors to snip off at the base each of the seedlings that is to go. Transplant the seedlings when they show two or three pairs of leaves (pages 82-85). □

PREPARING SEEDLINGS AND CUTTINGS FOR LIFE OUTDOORS

Seedlings and cuttings can become weak and spindly if they are left too long in their cramped rooting containers. Such plants will have a tough adjustment later on when they are transferred to the garden.

To build up their strength ahead of time, give seedlings and cuttings more room by moving them to larger pots at the first signs of root development. Seedlings are ready to transplant when they have sprouted a second pair of leaves; cuttings are ready when they show new leaf growth and resist gentle tugging.

The tender young roots of seedlings and cuttings can be irreparably damaged if they are exposed to the air for too long during transplanting. To minimize this danger, fill the new pots with soil before you begin.

Always match the size of the pot to the size of the plant. If a plant is too large for its pot, its roots will be constricted. If a plant is too small for its pot, water may collect in the excess soil and cause the roots to rot. In general, 2½- to 3-inch-wide pots are the right size for young transplants.

Seedlings and cuttings can be lifted more easily if you first moisten the medium in which they have been growing. Since the slightest touch can bruise their fragile stems, the plants should be handled only by their leaves.

After a few days in their new, larger quarters, the plants will have recovered from the shock of transplanting, and it will be time to start getting them accustomed to conditions outside. To begin the process, leave the plants outdoors in a shaded, protected location for no more than an hour; then gradually increase their daily exposure to sun, wind and fluctuating temperatures until the plants are "hardened off" and ready to be moved outdoors.

After being transplanted from a crowded flat, variegated ivy stem cuttings stretch toward the light in their individual plastic pots. When strong roots have developed, the plants will be ready to move one more time to their permanent home in the garden.

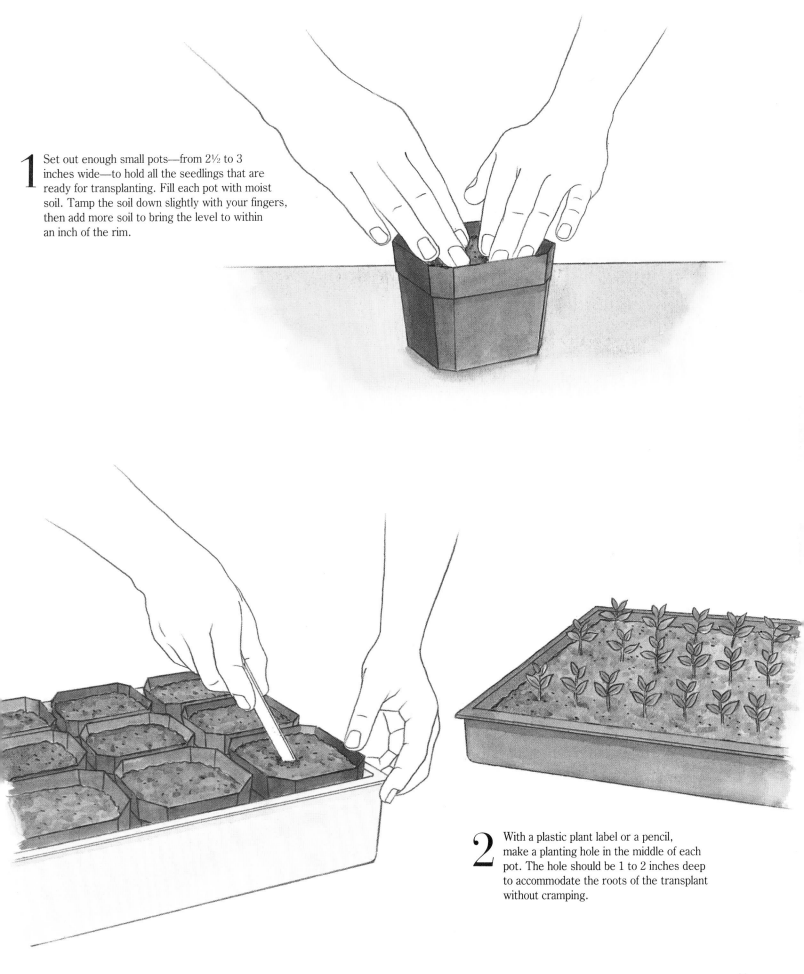

1 Set out enough small pots—from 2½ to 3 inches wide—to hold all the seedlings that are ready for transplanting. Fill each pot with moist soil. Tamp the soil down slightly with your fingers, then add more soil to bring the level to within an inch of the rim.

2 With a plastic plant label or a pencil, make a planting hole in the middle of each pot. The hole should be 1 to 2 inches deep to accommodate the roots of the transplant without cramping.

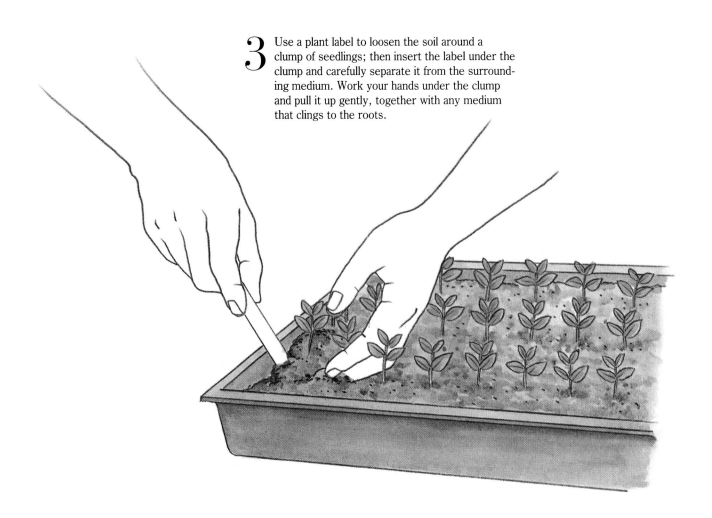

3 Use a plant label to loosen the soil around a clump of seedlings; then insert the label under the clump and carefully separate it from the surrounding medium. Work your hands under the clump and pull it up gently, together with any medium that clings to the roots.

4 Place the clump of seedlings on a clean surface and gently separate individual plants with your fingers. Carefully untangle any intertwined roots. To avoid damaging the fragile stems, handle the plants by their leaves.

5 Holding a seedling by its leaves, lower it straight down into a planting hole. If the roots begin to curl against the sides of the hole, use a finger to straighten them. Each seedling should sit at the same depth in the new pot as it sat in the rooting medium. Firm the soil around it.

6 Finish transplanting all your seedlings. Add water to each pot until water starts to drain from the bottom. Or if you prefer, set all the pots in a pan of water and let them stand until the top of the soil gets wet, then pour any remaining water from the pan. Remove the pots and let them drain. □

4
MAKING THE MOST OF NATURE

L awn grasses have been the subject of intensive study for so many years that almost nothing about them is a mystery. Their climate preferences, tolerance of sun and shade, the pests and diseases to which they are prone, and the weeds that afflict them are all known in voluminous detail. Consequently, the care of a lawn, though labor-intensive, can be reduced to a predictable routine. By consulting the map of climatic regions on page 89, together with the checklist of year-round lawn-care activities on pages 94-95 and the listing of pests and diseases on pages 98-101, it should be possible to move through the cycle of sowing, mowing and spraying without any major crisis—barring some natural disaster. And to enable you to tell one unwelcome weed from another, there is a gallery of the commonest of these lawn invaders—with pictures, descriptions and information on how to drive them out—on pages 102-105.

Ground covers have their own problems. The zone map on page 88, used in conjunction with the dictionary entries in the next chapter, can be a guide to selecting plants that will grow best in your area. Similarly, the maintenance chart and the trouble-shooting list on pages 90-93 and 96-97, respectively, can be helpful guides to when to prune, propagate, mulch and spray various kinds of ground covers.

Finally, to round out this chapter, there are about half a dozen handy tips. Among them is a method for keeping a lawn of warm-season grass green all winter, a secondary use for intrusive bamboo canes and some advice on choosing fire-retardant ground covers—which should be welcome information to gardeners living in areas where brush fires are periodic nuisances.

CLIMATE MAPS
FOR LAWNS AND GROUND COVERS

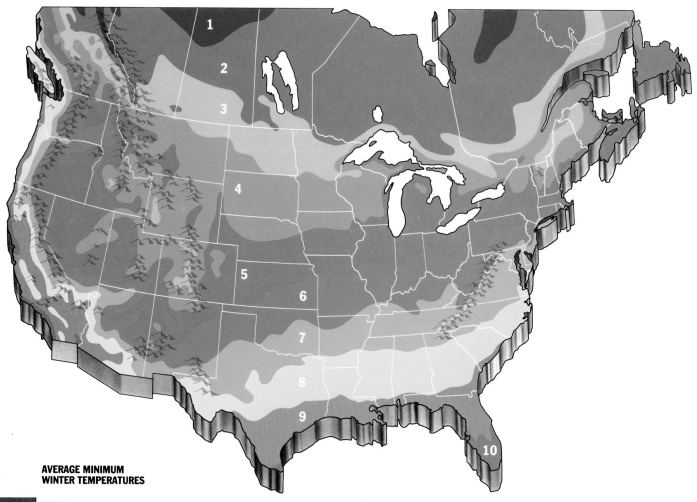

**AVERAGE MINIMUM
WINTER TEMPERATURES**

ZONE 1:
below −50°

ZONE 2:
−50° to −40°

ZONE 3:
−40° to −30°

ZONE 4:
−30° to −20°

ZONE 5:
−20° to −10°

ZONE 6:
−10° to 0°

ZONE 7:
0° to 10°

ZONE 8:
10° to 20°

ZONE 9:
20° to 30°

ZONE 10:
30° to 40°

When you select a turfgrass, a ground cover or an ornamental grass for your yard, the most critical question to ask is whether the plant will survive in your climate. With ground covers and ornamental grasses, ability to survive winter varies from plant to plant. Some ground covers and ornamental grasses cannot survive freezing temperatures; others need winter frost in order to produce flowers and foliage in spring.

To find out if a ground cover or an ornamental grass will grow where you live, first determine the range of winter temperatures in your area. The zone map *(above, left)*, compiled by the U.S. Department of Agriculture, divides North America into 10 zones based on average minimum temperatures.

Once you know which zone you live in, you can consult the Dictionary of Grasses and Ground Covers *(pages 108-150)* to find the winter climate a particular plant requires. For example, a ground cover such as heather, which can grow in Zones 4 through 7, will not survive the severe winters of Zones 1 through 3, but it needs some winter frost to produce new growth each year and thus does not thrive in the mild winters of Zones 8, 9 and 10. And the zonal range tells not only whether a plant can be grown in your area, but also how it will fare. A tropical ornamental grass such as arundo, which ranges in height from 12 to 20

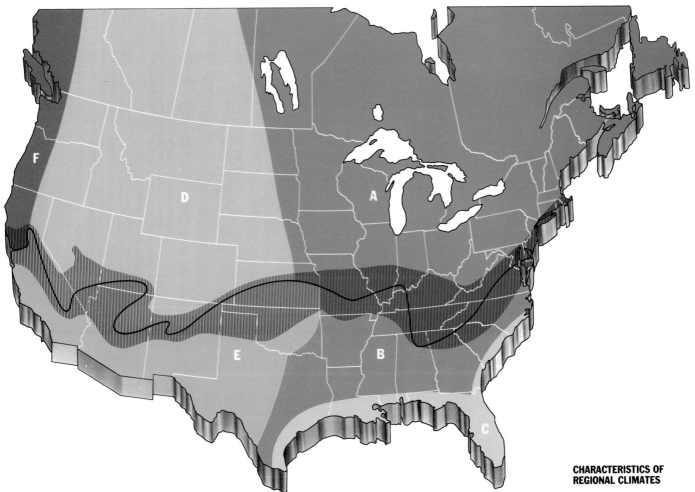

feet, can be grown in Zones 7 through 10, but it will reach its greatest height in Zones 9 and 10, because it flourishes best in the warmest climates.

The ability of turfgrasses to survive the cold is easier to discern. All are categorized as either warm-season or cool-season grasses, and they grow in the type of climate the category name suggests. Warm-season grasses, such as Bermudagrass and zoysia, do best in the mild climate of the southern United States. They respond to summer heat with rapid growth, then become dormant and turn brown during winter's cold. Cool-season grasses, such as fescue and Kentucky bluegrass, thrive in northern regions, where winters are cold. They do most of their growing in the cool weather of spring and fall; in summer, their growth slows. On the region map *(above, right)* the areas for cool- and warm-season grasses are separated by the black line that divides the country. The gray area indicates a transitional zone, where either type of grass may be used, depending on local conditions such as elevation and the amount of sun the lawn receives.

Winter temperature is but one factor that contributes to a healthy lawn; others such as humidity and rainfall also play major roles. The region map above divides North America into six regions based on year-round climates. Each turfgrass in the Dictionary has a letter that corresponds to one or more of these regions to indicate the areas in which that grass will flourish.

CHARACTERISTICS OF REGIONAL CLIMATES

REGION A:
Hot summers in the southern area
Cool summers in the northern area
Cold winters
Variable humidity
Moderate rainfall, 20 to 40 inches per year

REGION B:
Hot, humid summers
Mild winters with moderate humidity
High rainfall, 40 to 60 inches per year

REGION C:
Hot, humid summers
Mild winters with moderate humidity
High rainfall, 40 to 60 inches per year

REGION D:
Warm, dry summers
Cold, dry winters
Low rainfall, 10 to 20 inches per year

REGION E:
Hot, dry summers
Mild winters, except at high altitudes
Low rainfall, 10 to 20 inches per year

REGION F:
Cool, humid summers
Cool, humid winters
Very high rainfall, 40 to 80 inches per year

A CHECKLIST FOR GROUND COVERS AND ORNAMENTAL GRASSES

	ZONE 1	ZONE 2	ZONE 3	ZONE 4	ZONE 5
JANUARY/FEBRUARY	• Spray broad-leaved evergreen ground covers with antidesiccant • Replace mulch as needed	• Spray broad-leaved evergreen ground covers with antidesiccant • Replace mulch as needed	• Spray broad-leaved evergreen ground covers with antidesiccant • Replace mulch as needed	• Spray broad-leaved evergreen ground covers with antidesiccant • Replace mulch as needed	• Spray broad-leaved evergreen ground covers with antidesiccant • Replace mulch as needed
MARCH/APRIL	• Start seeds of ground covers and ornamental grasses indoors	• Start seeds of ground covers and ornamental grasses indoors	• Start seeds of ground covers and ornamental grasses indoors	• Start seeds of ground covers and ornamental grasses indoors	• Start seeds of ground covers and ornamental grasses indoors • Plant ground covers and perennial ornamental grasses
MAY/JUNE	• Plant ground covers • Plant annual and perennial ornamental grasses • Take ground cover stem cuttings for propagation • Layer ground cover stems for propagation • Divide ground covers and perennial ornamental grasses • Prune ground covers • Cut back ornamental grasses to encourage new growth • Remove weeds or apply an herbicide • Fertilize ground covers and ornamental grasses • Water as needed • Replace mulch as needed • Check for insects, diseases	• Plant ground covers • Plant annual and perennial ornamental grasses • Take ground cover stem cuttings for propagation • Layer ground cover stems for propagation • Divide ground covers and perennial ornamental grasses • Prune ground covers • Cut back ornamental grasses to encourage new growth • Remove weeds or apply an herbicide • Fertilize ground covers and ornamental grasses • Water as needed • Replace mulch as needed • Check for insects, diseases	• Plant ground covers • Plant annual and perennial ornamental grasses • Take ground cover stem cuttings for propagation • Layer ground cover stems for propagation • Divide ground covers and perennial ornamental grasses • Prune ground covers • Cut back ornamental grasses to encourage new growth • Remove weeds or apply an herbicide • Fertilize ground covers and ornamental grasses • Water as needed • Replace mulch as needed • Check for insects, diseases	• Plant ground covers • Plant annual and perennial ornamental grasses • Take ground cover stem cuttings for propagation • Layer ground cover stems for propagation • Divide ground covers and perennial ornamental grasses • Prune ground covers • Cut back ornamental grasses to encourage new growth • Remove weeds or apply an herbicide • Fertilize ground covers and ornamental grasses • Water as needed • Replace mulch as needed • Check for insects, diseases	• Plant ground covers • Plant annual and perennial ornamental grasses • Take ground cover stem cuttings for propagation • Layer ground cover stems for propagation • Divide ground covers and perennial ornamental grasses • Prune ground covers • Cut back ornamental grasses to encourage new growth • Remove weeds or apply an herbicide • Fertilize ground covers and ornamental grasses • Water as needed • Replace mulch as needed • Check for insects, diseases

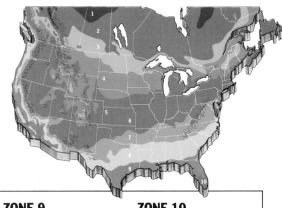

	ZONE 6	ZONE 7	ZONE 8	ZONE 9	ZONE 10	
	• Spray broad-leaved evergreen ground covers with antidesiccant • Replace mulch as needed • Start seeds of ground covers and ornamental grasses indoors	• Spray broad-leaved evergreen ground covers with antidesiccant • Replace mulch as needed • Start seeds of ground covers and ornamental grasses indoors	• Start seeds of ground covers and ornamental grasses indoors	• Start seeds of ground covers and ornamental grasses indoors • Plant ground covers • Plant annual and perennial ornamental grasses • Divide ground covers and perennial ornamental grasses • Remove weeds or apply an herbicide • Prune ground covers • Water if ground is dry • Check for insects, diseases	• Start seeds of ground covers and ornamental grasses indoors • Plant ground covers • Plant annual and perennial ornamental grasses • Divide ground covers and perennial ornamental grasses • Remove weeds or apply an herbicide • Prune ground covers • Water if ground is dry • Check for insects, diseases	**JANUARY/FEBRUARY**
	• Start seeds of ground covers and ornamental grasses indoors • Plant ground covers and perennial ornamental grasses	• Start seeds of ground covers and ornamental grasses indoors • Plant ground covers and perennial ornamental grasses • Fertilize ground covers and ornamental grasses • Divide ground covers and perennial ornamental grasses • Prune ground covers • Remove weeds or apply an herbicide	• Plant ground covers • Plant annual and perennial ornamental grasses • Take ground cover stem cuttings for propagation • Layer ground cover stems for propagation • Divide ground covers and perennial ornamental grasses • Prune ground covers • Cut back ornamental grasses to encourage new growth • Remove weeds or apply an herbicide • Fertilize ground covers and ornamental grasses • Apply mulch for summer • Water as needed • Check for insects, diseases	• Plant ground covers • Plant annual and perennial ornamental grasses • Take ground cover stem cuttings for propagation • Layer ground cover stems for propagation • Divide ground covers and perennial ornamental grasses • Prune ground covers • Cut back ornamental grasses to encourage new growth • Remove weeds or apply an herbicide • Fertilize ground covers and ornamental grasses • Apply mulch for summer • Water as needed • Check for insects, diseases	• Plant ground covers • Plant annual and perennial ornamental grasses • Take ground cover stem cuttings for propagation • Layer ground cover stems for propagation • Divide ground covers and perennial ornamental grasses • Prune ground covers • Cut back ornamental grasses to encourage new growth • Remove weeds or apply an herbicide • Fertilize ground covers and ornamental grasses • Apply mulch for summer • Water as needed • Check for insects, diseases	**MARCH/APRIL**
	• Plant ground covers • Plant annual and perennial ornamental grasses • Take ground cover stem cuttings for propagation • Layer ground cover stems for propagation • Divide ground covers and perennial ornamental grasses • Prune ground covers • Cut back ornamental grasses to encourage new growth • Remove weeds or apply an herbicide • Fertilize ground covers and ornamental grasses • Water as needed • Replace mulch as needed • Check for insects, diseases	• Plant ground covers • Plant annual and perennial ornamental grasses • Take ground cover stem cuttings for propagation • Layer ground cover stems for propagation • Divide ground covers and perennial ornamental grasses • Prune ground covers • Cut back ornamental grasses to encourage new growth • Remove weeds or apply an herbicide • Water as needed • Replace mulch as needed • Check for insects, diseases	• Plant ground covers and perennial ornamental grasses • Take ground cover stem cuttings for propagation • Layer ground cover stems for propagation • Prune ground covers • Remove weeds or apply an herbicide • Water as needed • Check for insects, diseases	• Plant ground covers and perennial ornamental grasses • Take ground cover stem cuttings for propagation • Layer ground cover stems for propagation • Prune ground covers • Remove weeds or apply an herbicide • Water as needed • Check for insects, diseases	• Plant ground covers and perennial ornamental grasses • Take ground cover stem cuttings for propagation • Layer ground cover stems for propagation • Prune ground covers • Remove weeds or apply an herbicide • Water as needed • Check for insects, diseases	**MAY/JUNE**

	ZONE 1	ZONE 2	ZONE 3	ZONE 4	ZONE 5
JULY/AUGUST	• Plant ground covers and perennial ornamental grasses • Prune ground covers • Remove weeds or apply an herbicide • Water as needed • Check for insects, diseases	• Plant ground covers and perennial ornamental grasses • Prune ground covers • Remove weeds or apply an herbicide • Water as needed • Check for insects, diseases	• Plant ground covers and perennial ornamental grasses • Prune ground covers • Remove weeds or apply an herbicide • Water as needed • Check for insects, diseases	• Plant ground covers and perennial ornamental grasses • Prune ground covers • Remove weeds or apply an herbicide • Water as needed • Check for insects, diseases	• Plant ground covers and perennial ornamental grasses • Prune ground covers • Remove weeds or apply an herbicide • Water as needed • Check for insects, diseases
SEPTEMBER/OCTOBER	• Water if the ground is dry • Prepare soil for spring planting • Apply mulch for winter	• Water if the ground is dry • Prepare soil for spring planting • Apply mulch for winter	• Water if the ground is dry • Prepare soil for spring planting • Apply mulch for winter	• Water if the ground is dry • Prepare soil for spring planting • Apply mulch for winter	• Water if the ground is dry • Prepare soil for spring planting
NOVEMBER/DECEMBER	• Spray broad-leaved evergreen ground covers with antidesiccant	• Spray broad-leaved evergreen ground covers with antidesiccant	• Spray broad-leaved evergreen ground covers with antidesiccant	• Spray broad-leaved evergreen ground covers with antidesiccant	• Spray broad-leaved evergreen ground covers with antidesiccant • Water if the ground is dry • Apply mulch for winter

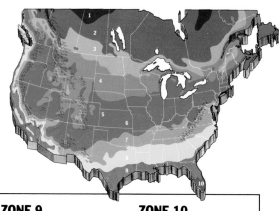

ZONE 6	ZONE 7	ZONE 8	ZONE 9	ZONE 10	
• Plant ground covers and perennial ornamental grasses • Take ground cover stem cuttings for propagation • Prune ground covers • Remove weeds or apply an herbicide • Water as needed • Check for insects, diseases	• Plant ground covers and perennial ornamental grasses • Take ground cover stem cuttings for propagation • Prune ground covers • Remove weeds or apply an herbicide • Water as needed • Check for insects, diseases	• Plant ground covers and perennial ornamental grasses • Take ground cover stem cuttings for propagation • Prune ground covers • Remove weeds or apply an herbicide • Water as needed • Check for insects, diseases	• Plant ground covers and perennial ornamental grasses • Take ground cover stem cuttings for propagation • Prune ground covers • Remove weeds or apply an herbicide • Water as needed • Check for insects, diseases	• Plant ground covers and perennial ornamental grasses • Take ground cover stem cuttings for propagation • Prune ground covers • Remove weeds or apply an herbicide • Water as needed • Check for insects, diseases	**JULY/AUGUST**
• Plant ground covers and perennial ornamental grasses • Divide ground covers and perennial ornamental grasses • Prune ground covers • Remove weeds or apply an herbicide • Water as needed • Prepare soil for spring planting	• Plant ground covers and perennial ornamental grasses • Divide ground covers and perennial ornamental grasses • Prune ground covers • Remove weeds or apply an herbicide • Water as needed	• Plant ground covers and perennial ornamental grasses • Divide ground covers and perennial ornamental grasses • Prune ground covers • Remove weeds or apply an herbicide • Water as needed • Check for insects, diseases	• Plant ground covers and perennial ornamental grasses • Take ground cover stem cuttings for propagation • Divide ground covers and perennial ornamental grasses • Prune ground covers • Remove weeds or apply an herbicide • Water as needed • Check for insects, diseases	• Plant ground covers and perennial ornamental grasses • Take ground cover stem cuttings for propagation • Divide ground covers and perennial ornamental grasses • Prune ground covers • Remove weeds or apply an herbicide • Water as needed • Check for insects, diseases	**SEPTEMBER/OCTOBER**
• Spray broad-leaved evergreen ground covers with antidesiccant • Water if the ground is dry • Prepare soil for spring planting • Apply mulch for winter	• Spray broad-leaved evergreen ground covers with antidesiccant • Water if the ground is dry • Prepare soil for spring planting • Apply mulch for winter	• Spray broad-leaved evergreen ground covers with antidesiccant • Water if the ground is dry • Prepare soil for spring planting • Apply mulch for winter	• Plant ground covers and perennial ornamental grasses • Divide ground covers and perennial ornamental grasses • Prune ground covers • Water as needed • Check for insects, diseases	• Plant ground covers and perennial ornamental grasses • Divide ground covers and perennial ornamental grasses • Prune ground covers • Water as needed • Check for insects, diseases	**NOVEMBER/DECEMBER**

A CHECKLIST FOR LAWNS

	REGION A	REGION B	REGION C
JAN./FEB.	• Sharpen mower blades	• Sharpen mower blades • Test soil pH; adjust if necessary • Weed lawn or apply an herbicide • Mow and edge as necessary • Water if ground is dry • Check for insects, diseases	• Sharpen mower blades • Sow grass seed • Test soil pH; adjust if necessary • Weed lawn or apply an herbicide • Mow and edge as necessary • Water if ground is dry • Check for insects, diseases
MAR./APR.	• Sow grass seed • Lay sod • Test soil pH; adjust if necessary • Dethatch • Aerate • Weed lawn or apply an herbicide • Mow and edge as necessary • Water if ground is dry • Check for insects, diseases	• Sow grass seed • Lay sod • Plant sprigs and plugs of warm-season grasses • Dethatch • Aerate • Weed lawn or apply an herbicide • Mow and edge regularly • Water regularly • Check for insects, diseases	• Sow grass seed • Lay sod • Plant sprigs and plugs of warm-season grasses • Dethatch • Aerate • Weed lawn or apply an herbicide • Mow and edge regularly • Water regularly • Check for insects, diseases
MAY/JUNE	• Sow grass seed • Lay sod • Dethatch • Aerate • Weed lawn or apply an herbicide • Mow and edge regularly • Water regularly • Check for insects, diseases	• Lay sod • Plant sprigs and plugs of warm-season grasses • Dethatch • Aerate • Weed lawn or apply an herbicide • Mow and edge regularly • Water regularly • Check for insects, diseases	• Lay sod • Plant sprigs and plugs of warm-season grasses • Dethatch • Aerate • Weed lawn or apply an herbicide • Mow and edge regularly • Water regularly • Check for insects, diseases
JULY/AUG.	• Lay sod • Aerate • Weed lawn or apply an herbicide • Mow and edge regularly • Water regularly • Check for insects, diseases	• Lay sod • Dethatch • Aerate • Weed lawn or apply an herbicide • Water regularly • Mow and edge regularly • Check for insects, diseases	• Lay sod • Dethatch • Aerate • Weed lawn or apply an herbicide • Mow and edge regularly • Water regularly • Check for insects, diseases
SEPT./OCT.	• Sow grass seed • Lay sod • Dethatch • Aerate • Weed lawn or apply an herbicide • Mow and edge regularly • Water regularly • Check for diseases	• Sow grass seed • Overseed dormant warm-season grasses • Lay sod • Dethatch • Aerate • Weed lawn or apply an herbicide • Mow and edge regularly • Water regularly • Check for insects, diseases	• Sow grass seed • Overseed dormant warm-season grasses • Lay sod • Dethatch • Aerate • Weed lawn or apply an herbicide • Mow and edge regularly • Water regularly • Check for insects, diseases
NOV./DEC.	• Rake leaves from the lawn	• Overseed dormant warm-season grasses • Weed lawn or apply an herbicide • Mow and edge as necessary • Water if ground is dry • Check for insects, diseases • Rake leaves from the lawn	• Overseed dormant warm-season grasses • Weed lawn or apply an herbicide • Mow and edge as necessary • Water if ground is dry • Check for insects, diseases • Rake leaves from the lawn

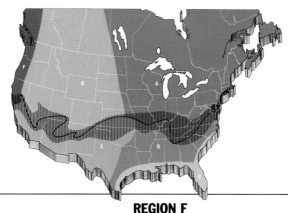

REGION D	REGION E	REGION F	
• Sharpen mower blades	• Sharpen mower blades • Sow grass seed • Test soil pH; adjust if necessary • Weed lawn or apply an herbicide • Mow and edge as necessary • Water if ground is dry • Check for insects, diseases	• Sharpen mower blades	JAN./FEB.
• Sow grass seed • Lay sod • Test soil pH; adjust if necessary • Weed lawn or apply an herbicide • Dethatch • Aerate • Mow and edge as necessary • Water if ground is dry • Check for insects, diseases	• Sow grass seed • Lay sod • Plant sprigs and plugs of warm-season grasses • Dethatch • Aerate • Weed lawn or apply an herbicide • Mow and edge regularly • Water regularly • Check for insects, diseases	• Sow grass seed • Lay sod • Test soil pH; adjust if necessary • Dethatch • Aerate • Weed lawn or apply an herbicide • Water if ground is dry • Mow and edge as necessary • Check for insects, diseases	MAR./APR.
• Sow grass seed • Lay sod • Dethatch • Aerate • Weed lawn or apply an herbicide • Mow and edge regularly • Water regularly • Check for insects, diseases	• Lay sod • Plant sprigs and plugs of warm-season grasses • Dethatch • Aerate • Weed lawn or apply an herbicide • Mow and edge regularly • Water regularly • Check for insects, diseases	• Sow grass seed • Lay sod • Dethatch • Aerate • Weed lawn or apply an herbicide • Mow and edge regularly • Water regularly • Check for insects, diseases	MAY/JUNE
• Lay sod • Aerate • Weed lawn or apply an herbicide • Mow and edge regularly • Water regularly • Check for insects, diseases	• Lay sod • Dethatch • Aerate • Weed lawn or apply an herbicide • Mow and edge regularly • Water regularly • Check for insects, diseases	• Lay sod • Aerate • Weed lawn or apply an herbicide • Mow and edge regularly • Water regularly • Check for insects, diseases	JULY/AUG.
• Sow grass seed • Lay sod • Water regularly • Mow and edge regularly • Dethatch • Aerate • Weed lawn or apply an herbicide • Check for diseases	• Sow grass seed • Overseed dormant warm-season grasses • Lay sod • Dethatch • Aerate • Weed lawn or apply an herbicide • Mow and edge regularly • Water regularly • Check for insects, diseases	• Sow grass seed • Lay sod • Dethatch • Aerate • Weed lawn or apply an herbicide • Mow and edge regularly • Water regularly • Check for diseases	SEPT./OCT.
• Rake leaves from the lawn	• Overseed dormant warm-season grasses • Weed lawn or apply an herbicide • Mow and edge as necessary • Water if ground is dry • Check for insects, diseases • Rake leaves from the lawn	• Mow and edge as necessary • Water if ground is dry • Rake leaves from the lawn	NOV./DEC.

WHAT TO DO WHEN THINGS GO WRONG WITH GROUND COVERS

PROBLEM	CAUSE	SOLUTION
Leaves are mottled with white, then lose their color and develop a dull bronze sheen. Tiny black specks are visible on the undersides of the leaves. Eventually, a fine white webbing appears on the plant.	Spider mites, nearly microscopic pests that suck the sap from plants. Mites are particularly active in hot, dry environments and they produce new generations every few days.	Adult mites can be knocked off plants with a strong stream of water every three days; repeat treatment is necessary for control. In severe cases, spray with an insecticidal soap or a miticide three times, three days apart. To help prevent infestation, keep plants well watered and spray the undersides of the leaves with water every few days.
Small, rounded or oblong holes appear in leaves and may appear in flowers. Eventually, plants may be stripped of foliage.	Beetles, including Asiatic, blister, chafer, flea and Japanese beetles. They are from ¼ to ¾ inch long and have hard shells.	Small colonies can be picked off plants by hand. The larvae of Japanese beetles can be controlled organically with milky spore *(pages 52-53)*. If the infestation is severe, apply an insecticide.
Leaf edges turn brown and die. Leaves are spotted with irregular brown patches. Broad-leaved evergreens are especially susceptible.	Too much sun or too much wind, especially in winter. Wind and sun cause rapid water evaporation. When the ground is dry or frozen, the roots cannot transfer sufficient water to the leaves.	Cut out affected leaves. Make sure ground covers are well watered in late fall. To lessen water evaporation, spray evergreens with an antidesiccant in fall.
Jagged holes appear in leaves; stems may be chewed or broken off. The problem is especially severe in spring.	Caterpillars, which are the larvae of butterflies and moths. Caterpillars emerge in spring and hide on the undersides of leaves.	Hand-pick and destroy large caterpillars. Spray affected plants with *Bacillus thuringiensis,* called Bt, a bacterium fatal to caterpillars but harmless to other organisms. Apply Bt in early spring to prevent infestation.
Upper leaf surfaces lose color and are mottled with white or yellow. The undersides of the leaves are covered with small black specks. Plants cease to grow.	Lace bugs, tiny flat bugs $\frac{1}{16}$ to ⅛ inch long with clear, lacy wings and hoodlike coverings on their heads. The bugs suck the sap from the undersides of leaves. The black specks are deposited by the bugs as they feed.	Spray with an insecticide when symptoms appear and repeat the application two or three times, seven to 10 days apart.
Foliage is covered with a white powder. New growth is distorted in shape. Leaves may curl and turn yellow. The plant may be stunted.	Powdery mildew, a fungus disease that is most severe when nights are cool and humid, and days are warm.	Mildew can be eradicated with a lime-sulfur spray, provided the temperature is not above 80° F. Mildew can be prevented with a fungicide applied every 10 days when weather conditions are favorable for the disease.

PROBLEM	CAUSE	SOLUTION
Plants cease to grow and the plant tips die back. Leaves turn yellow and fall from the plant. Thin, white bumps appear on the undersides of the leaves and the stems. Dark brown, shell-shaped masses are scattered among the white bumps. Euonymus is especially susceptible.	Euonymus scale, a tiny insect that sucks sap from plants. The male is white and the female develops a dark brown shell under which it lays eggs.	Prune out any dead or severely infested branches. Spray with an insecticide, repeating the application until all signs of scale disappear. To prevent infestation, spray plants with horticultural oil in spring, just before plant growth begins.
Leaves suddenly wilt, turn brown or black, and appear to have been scorched by fire. Twigs may also turn black, and the bark at the base of the twigs becomes dark, dry and cracked. Cotoneaster is especially susceptible.	Fire blight, a bacterial disease that spreads rapidly in warm, wet conditions. The bacteria remain in the branches through winter, and can reinfect the plant in spring.	Prune out damaged branches and destroy them. Disinfect pruning tools with alcohol after each cut. To prevent the disease, spray plants with a bactericide every five to seven days from the time new growth appears until blooming is finished.
Leaves turn pale green or yellow. The entire plant may wilt and can be pulled from the soil easily. The roots and the crown are discolored and have a sour odor.	Root rot or crown rot, fungus diseases that spread in water-logged soil and hot, humid weather. The fungi thrive in water.	Remove and destroy infected plants and the surrounding soil. Apply a fungicide to the soil before replanting. Allow the soil to dry between waterings.
Tan, brown or purple circular spots appear on either or both upper and lower leaf surfaces. Eventually, the spots merge, and the entire leaf becomes discolored and falls from the plant.	Leaf spot disease, caused by several different fungi. The fungi spread easily in wind and water.	Remove damaged leaves and spray with a fungicide to control the disease. In fall, collect and destroy plant debris, where the fungi spend the winter.
Leaves curl, wither or are distorted in shape, and the plant is stunted. A clear, shiny substance appears on leaves and stems.	Aphids, green, yellow or brown insects $\frac{1}{8}$ inch long. Aphids appear in clusters on buds, leaves and stems, where they suck sap from the plant. Aphids spread diseases.	Aphids can be knocked off plants with a strong stream of water. If the infestation is severe, apply an insecticidal soap or an insecticide.
Large, jagged holes appear in leaves. Entire leaves and young seedlings may be eaten. Shiny silver trails appear on plants and on the ground.	Snails and slugs, which are shell-less snails up to 3 inches long. They feed at night.	Saucers of beer and inverted grapefruit halves set around plants will trap snails and slugs. Snail and slug bait is also available; it should be applied at dusk, and reapplied after plants have been watered and after a rainfall.
Conifer needles turn brown, starting at the tips and progressing to the bases of the needles. Eventually, needles may drop. Evergreen leaf edges and tips turn brown or black. Leaves may drop. Symptoms usually appear on older foliage. Plants along roads and walkways are especially susceptible.	Damage from salt applied to icy roads and walkways during winter snows.	Use sand or sawdust instead of salt to melt ice. To prevent damage, spray ground covers near roads with an antidesiccant in late fall.

WHAT TO DO WHEN THINGS GO WRONG WITH LAWNS

PROBLEM	CAUSE	SOLUTION
In late spring or early summer, the lawn becomes spotted with rounded patches of yellow or brown grass. Initially, the patches are only a few inches across, but during the summer they expand to cover several feet of turf. Affected grass can be pulled out of the soil easily. Damaged areas often appear first in lawn areas adjoining pavement. Small black insects may be visible on the pavement.	Billbugs, which are black weevils up to ¾ inch long. They emerge in spring, feed on the grass and lay their eggs in the grass stems. The larvae hatch and feed on the stems. As the larvae mature, they enter the soil and feed on the roots. Adults emerge again in the fall, feed briefly, and then hibernate in areas between the lawn and adjacent pavement.	Billbugs can be controlled with insecticide applied in spring, while the young larvae are still feeding on the stems and before they move down to the roots. Mow the lawn before using an insecticide, so the chemical can easily reach the soil. If the damage is limited to small areas, the grass may recover once the larvae are controlled. Large areas may need reseeding or resodding.
In early spring and late summer, irregular patches of brown grass appear throughout the lawn. The patches may be from several inches to several feet across. Within affected areas, the grass is easily pulled up and the turf can be rolled back.	Grubs, which are white insects with curled bodies 1 to 1½ inches long. They are the larvae of beetles, including Japanese, European chafer, Asiatic garden, Oriental and June beetles. The grubs feed on grass roots, and are visible at the soil surface.	Japanese beetle grubs can be controlled organically with milky spore *(pages 52-53)*. Other grubs can be treated with insecticide applied in early spring or late summer, when the grubs are near the soil surface.
Beginning in spring and continuing through summer, small patches of the lawn turn brown and die. Within affected areas, the grass blades have jagged holes along the edges. Some blades may be severed at the soil surface.	Cutworms, gray, brown or black worms 1½ to 2 inches long. They are usually visible at the soil surface. The worms feed at night. The worms are the larvae of a night-flying moth that has striped wings.	Apply an insecticide in the evening or at night, when the worms and the moths are active. Repeat applications are necessary as long as cutworms are present.
The lawn thins out, turns light green or yellow, fails to grow, and wilts during heat or drought. The roots appear to be swollen and knotty.	Nematodes, microscopic soil-dwelling worms that feed on grass roots. Their presence can be confirmed only by soil test.	No chemical controls are available to the homeowner. Consult your local extension service for soil testing information. When nematodes are present, soil treatment by a professional fumigator is necessary.
The lawn thins out and has a bleached, dried-out appearance. Grass blades turn yellow and are covered with tiny white spots.	Leafhoppers, ⅛- to ¼-inch, wedge-shaped, yellow or light green insects that suck the juice from grass blades. They may be visible hopping from blade to blade.	Apply an insecticide as soon as symptoms appear. In the warm regions of the South and the West, leafhoppers may produce several generations a summer, and repeat applications are necessary if symptoms recur.
Large circular bare patches appear in the lawn. Jagged holes appear in grass blades. Caterpillars are visible on the grass.	Armyworms, tan, green or black, 1½-inch insects with three stripes down their backs and a V on their heads. They are the larvae of a moth that lays its eggs on the grass.	Apply an insecticide in the evening, when the moths and the worms are active. Armyworms produce several generations per year, and repeat applications are necessary if signs of the insect recur.

PROBLEM	CAUSE	SOLUTION
Circular or irregular yellow patches several feet across appear in the lawn during summer. The problem is especially severe in hot, dry areas of the lawn that receive extensive sunlight.	Chinch bugs, reddish brown or black insects ⅕ inch long that suck the juice from grass blades and stems. The insects are active in hot, dry summer weather. When conditions favor them, they can destroy a lawn in a few days.	Apply an insecticide as soon as symptoms appear, and again three weeks later to control successive generations. If symptoms recur or if hot, dry weather persists, continue treating the lawn with an insecticide throughout the summer.
Long, narrow ridges zigzag across the lawn. Mounds of soil may appear in the lawn beside holes that are the entrances to underground tunnels.	Animals such as moles, voles and gophers, which tunnel through the soil. Moles feed on insects such as grubs and ants; voles and gophers feed on roots and grass.	To get rid of moles, eliminate the grubs and ants they feed on. For other animals, several types of baits and traps are available.
Patches of grass up to 15 feet across take on an orange cast and then die. The problem appears first in shady areas of the lawn and then spreads to sunny areas.	Greenbugs, which are small, yellow or light green aphids that pierce grass blades and feed on them. The bugs then inject the blades with a toxic substance that turns them orange. Greenbugs prefer the cool, moist environment that shady areas provide.	Apply an insecticide once every seven days until symptoms disappear. Reduce the amount of fertilizer used in shady areas, because the insects feed heavily on lush new growth.
In spring, small patches of dead brown grass appear throughout the lawn. In summer, the patches enlarge to several feet across. Within affected areas, many grass blades have been cut off at the soil surface. Small whitish tunnels appear at the soil surface. At night, moths fly over the lawn in a zigzag pattern.	Sod webworms, the larvae of moths. The adult moths do not damage the lawn, but they drop their eggs onto the grass. When the larvae hatch, they construct the tunnels of soil and webbing. The worms usually feed at night, chewing off grass blades and pulling them into their tunnels.	Damaged grass may recover if the webworms are controlled as soon as symptoms appear. Apply an insecticide in the evening, when the worms and the moths are active. If symptoms persist, repeat applications may be necessary through the summer months.
Small hills of soil from 1 inch to 1 foot across appear throughout the lawn. The grass under and around the soil mounds dries out and dies.	Ants. The ants themselves do not damage an established lawn, but the anthills can smother the grass. The ants make underground tunnels among the grass roots that cause the soil to dry out and can kill the grass. Ants do eat grass seed.	Apply an insecticide to the anthills. Once the ants are controlled, reseed or resod any damaged or bare areas.
The lawn is spotted with irregular patches of brown grass. Eventually, the patches may spread to cover the entire lawn. Within the patches, the grass blades have oval or round spots with tan centers and black or purple borders.	Leaf spot disease, also called helminthosporium disease and melting out. This fungus disease occurs primarily when the weather is humid, temperatures are moderate, and the lawn receives too much water or fertilizer.	When symptoms appear, apply a fungicide four times, seven to 10 days apart. Water in the morning; moisture evaporates from the grass blades more rapidly during the day than at night.
Tufts of stunted, thick, yellow grass blades appear scattered throughout the lawn.	Yellow tuft, also called downy mildew, a fungus disease that is most active in cool, humid climates. The fungus spores spread in water.	Apply a fungicide as soon as symptoms appear. Mow only when the grass is dry; wet clippings on mowing tools can spread the disease.

PROBLEM	CAUSE	SOLUTION
Grass blades are mottled with yellow. The mottling spreads over the blade until the entire blade turns yellow and withers. The discolored blades are coated with an orange powder. The lawn may begin to thin out.	Rust, a fungus disease most active in warm, humid weather. The fungus is most likely to attack lawns that have been underfertilized, underwatered or too closely mowed. The orange powder, which consists of fungus spores, spreads easily in wind.	Apply a fungicide every seven to 10 days until symptoms disappear. Make sure the lawn receives the recommended amounts of fertilizer and water. Mow the lawn at the recommended height. Collect and destroy grass clippings.
The lawn is spotted with brown patches of wilted grass blades. The patches are from 1 to 3 inches across. They may enlarge and coalesce rapidly, often within a few days.	Pythium blight, a fungus disease that is most active in warm, humid weather and when a lawn is overwatered or overfertilized.	Apply a fungicide every five to 10 days until the symptoms disappear. Do not water or fertilize more than the recommended amount. Mow only when the grass is dry; wet clippings on mowing tools can spread the disease.
Grass is covered with a whitish gray powder. Eventually, the grass turns yellow, then brown, withers and dies. Lawns in the shade are most susceptible.	Powdery mildew, a fungus disease most active when nights are cool and damp, and days are hot and humid.	Apply a fungicide every seven to 10 days until symptoms disappear. Thin out the lower branches of large trees that shade the lawn. Water only in the morning; moisture evaporates from the grass blades more rapidly during the day than at night.
The lawn is spotted with penny-sized, copper-colored patches. The patches enlarge and coalesce to cover large areas.	Copper spot, a fungus disease most active in rainy weather when temperatures are between 50° and 75° F. The disease is most severe when a lawn is insufficiently fertilized or the soil is too acidic.	Apply a fungicide. Make sure that the lawn receives the recommended amount of fertilizer. Test the soil pH; if it is too acidic, apply lime.
A ring of lush, dark green grass appears in the lawn. The ring may be a few inches or several feet in diameter. Mushrooms may grow in the ring.	Fairy ring, caused by soil-dwelling fungi. The fungi do not attack the grass, but they feed on organic matter in the soil, thus depriving the grass roots of nutrients. The lush, dark green growth is caused by the concentrated release of nutrients as the fungi break down organic matter.	There are no effective chemical controls. Remove excess thatch, which is decomposing organic matter and attracts fungi. You can improve the appearance of the lawn by mowing more frequently and removing the mushrooms.
Large, rounded patches of grass 2 feet across turn yellow and then brown. The border of each patch may turn purple. The blades in the center of the patch may be unaffected.	Rhizoctonia blight, also called brown patch, a fungus disease most active in hot, humid weather, when the lawn has been overfertilized or overwatered.	Apply a fungicide as soon as symptoms appear, and repeat the application at least three times, seven to 10 days apart. Continue as long as hot, humid weather persists. Remove excess thatch, which attracts the fungus.
The lawn is spotted with circular or irregular reddish brown patches from 2 inches to 2 feet across. Thin, red threads intertwine with the grass blades.	Red thread, a fungus disease that produces the red, threadlike growth. It is most active in humid weather and temperatures between 30° and 60° F. The disease spreads rapidly when a lawn does not receive adequate fertilizer or the soil pH is too acidic.	Apply a fungicide four times, seven to 10 days apart. Make sure the lawn receives the recommended amount of fertilizer. Test the soil pH; if it is too acidic, apply lime. Water only in the morning; moisture evaporates from the grass blades more rapidly during the day than at night.

PROBLEM	CAUSE	SOLUTION
The lawn is spotted with silver-dollar-sized brown patches that may enlarge and coalesce to cover large areas. Within the affected areas, individual grass blades have yellow or tan spots with reddish brown borders.	Dollar spot, also called sclerotium rot, a fungus disease most active when the weather is humid and temperatures are mild, between 60° and 85° F. The disease is most likely to spread in lawns that are insufficiently watered or fertilized.	Apply a fungicide twice, seven to 10 days apart. Make sure the lawn receives the recommended amount of fertilizer and water. Water only in the morning; moisture evaporates from the grass blades more rapidly during the day than at night.
As winter snows melt, the lawn becomes spotted with patches of yellow or tan dry grass. The patches are 2 inches to 2 feet across. The grass blades within the patches are matted together, and a pink or grayish white, cottony growth may appear on them.	Snow mold, a fungus disease. There are two common types of snow mold: pink snow mold, also called fusarium patch; and gray snow mold, also called typhula blight. Both occur in winter and spring, when the ground remains wet from melting snow.	Apply a fungicide in early spring, when symptoms appear, and rake to break up the dry, matted blades. To prevent the disease, apply a fungicide in late fall or early winter. Do not fertilize in late fall; soft, lush growth is more susceptible to the disease.
Patches of yellow grass appear scattered throughout the lawn. Within the discolored areas, the grass blades are streaked with yellow and covered with stripes of black, sooty powder. Eventually, affected blades split lengthwise, wilt and die.	Stripe smut, a fungus disease most active in moderate temperatures, between 50° and 68° F. The disease usually occurs in spring and fall, especially in lawns that are overwatered or overfertilized.	Apply a fungicide when symptoms appear. If the disease occurs in spring, reduce the amount of water and fertilizer applied during the summer to help prevent its recurrence in fall.
Patches of lawn acquire a yellow cast. Within the affected areas, individual grass blades are mottled with yellow. Eventually, the entire lawn turns yellow and begins to thin out. St. Augustine grass is the only susceptible turfgrass.	St. Augustine decline (SAD), a virus disease. The virus itself does not spread, but it can be transmitted to healthy grass by greenbugs and other aphids and by diseased clippings carried on mowing tools.	There are no chemical controls for SAD. Greenbugs and other aphids should be controlled *(pages 97, 99)*. Clean mowing tools thoroughly after each use. If damaged areas do not recover, they may be reseeded with disease-resistant varieties of St. Augustine.
Round patches of light green grass develop in scattered areas of the lawn. The patches may be up to 3 feet across, and the grass at the center of the patches may remain unaffected. Eventually, the light green grass turns brown and dies.	Fusarium blight syndrome, also called summer patch and necrotic ring spot, a fungus disease that occurs in hot, humid weather. It is particularly severe when extended periods of heavy watering or rainfall are followed by drought.	When symptoms appear, apply a fungicide three times, 10 to 14 days apart. To prevent the disease from recurring the following year, apply a fungicide in late spring.
The lawn becomes spotted with rings of dead brown grass. Eventually, the rings enlarge and merge. Within the rings, the grass blades become bronze-red before turning brown. Symptoms may appear in spring, but are most severe following periods of hot, dry weather in midsummer. Bentgrass is especially susceptible.	Take-all patch, also called ophiobolus patch, a fungus disease. The fungus is active in cool, humid weather, but the symptoms of the disease may not be apparent until the lawn is stressed by summer heat. The disease is especially severe in alkaline soils.	There are no chemical cures. Applying an acid fertilizer to lower the soil pH may prevent the spread of the disease. If small areas are affected, they may be overseeded with less susceptible grasses, such as certain bluegrass and fescue species.

A GALLERY
OF WEEDS

Looked at as lone specimens, weeds can be surprisingly pleasing in form and color. But as every gardener knows, weeds are not loners; they proliferate with exasperating persistence, and if left unchecked will drive more timid plants out of a garden. In a lawn of any size, pulling them by hand and at random is impractical; therefore the gardener is best advised to distinguish one species from another, and to tackle a weed with an herbicide designed to interact with its specific growth habit, cell structure and metabolism.

In general, perennial weeds—those that put out new foliage from roots that have survived since the previous season—are broad-leaved and sprawling, and spread across the soil surface via their stems or underground by means of their roots. Annual weeds—those that sprout from seed and die in a single year—are either broad-leaved and sprawling or grassy and grow in clumps. As a rule, annual weeds can be checked with so-called preemergent herbicides, which are applied in advance to stop seeds from sprouting, and with postemergent contact herbicides, which kill whatever foliage they touch. Most perennials are best fought with postemergent systemic herbicides, which poison a plant's vascular system. For what to use, see the descriptions accompanying the pictures here and on the following pages; for how to use it, see pages 50-51.

ANNUAL BLUEGRASS *(Poa annua)* is a hardy grassy annual that grows in clumps of narrow, light green leaves and sprouts white, fluffy seed heads in spring and dies out in hot weather. To prevent seeds cast in summer from germinating in fall, use a preemergent herbicide in late summer.

BLACK MEDIC *(Medicago lupulina)* is a broad-leaved annual that forms dense mats of flat, branching stems, cloverlike foliage, small yellow spring flowers and black seeds. Use a postemergent systemic herbicide in early spring or in fall.

CHICKWEED is broad-leaved and may be either annual or perennial. Two prevalent varieties are common chickweed *(Stellaria media),* an annual that has branching stems, small, pointed, light green leaves and small white flowers, and mouse-ear chickweed *(Cerastium vulgatum, left),* a perennial that looks similar but has fuzzy, dark green leaves. Both can be controlled with a postemergent systemic herbicide applied when plants appear. Common chickweed can also be controlled with a preemergent herbicide applied in early spring or fall.

CRABGRASS is a grassy summer annual. Smooth crabgrass *(Digitaria ischaemum)* produces thick clumps of smooth, narrow, light green leaves; hairy or large crabgrass *(D. sanguinalis, left)* has shorter, hairy leaves. Use a preemergent herbicide in spring or a postemergent contact herbicide as soon as plants appear.

CURLY DOCK *(Rumex crispus, right)* is a broad-leaved perennial that grows from a long taproot in a rosette of long, oval green leaves with curled edges. The leaves may be tinged with red. Seeds are produced in a pyramidal seed head atop a slender stem. Use a postemergent systemic herbicide in spring or fall.

DANDELION *(Taraxacum officinale)* is a broad-leaved perennial with long, narrow, deeply notched green leaves that emerge in a rosette from a long taproot. It produces bright yellow flowers and fluffy white seed heads in spring. Use a postemergent systemic herbicide as soon as plants appear.

GOOSEGRASS *(Eleusine indica)*, also called silver crabgrass, is a grassy summer annual having low-growing clumps of flat, silver-green stems and narrow green leaves. It is found primarily in compacted soil and along walkways. To prevent it from taking hold, aerate compacted soil and use a preemergent herbicide in spring or a postemergent contact herbicide when the plants appear.

HENBIT *(Lamium amplexicaule)* is a broad-leaved annual that has small, scalloped leaves along stems that arch over and root where they touch the soil, and small purple spring flowers. Use a postemergent contact herbicide in spring or in fall when the plants appear.

KNOTWEED is a broad-leaved annual. Prostrate knotweed *(Polygonum aviculare)* has small, blue-green, lance-shaped leaves. The stems spread along the ground and form large, dense mats. Small white flowers blossom in late summer or early fall. Knotweed tends to grow in compacted soil. Aerate the soil and use a postemergent systemic herbicide when the plants appear.

NUTSEDGE is a grassy perennial that resembles turfgrass but has triangular instead of round stems. Yellow nutsedge *(Cyperus esculentus)* has shiny green leaves that grow upright from the base of the stem and small yellow flowers atop the stem. Purple nutsedge *(C. rotundus, above)* is similar, but its leaves are tinged with purple and its flowers are purple. Nutsedge spreads by seed and by underground tubers called nutlets. The nutlets do not respond to systemic herbicides; they require a postemergent contact herbicide.

PLANTAIN is a broad-leaved perennial. Buckhorn plantain *(Plantago lanceolata)* forms rosettes of narrow, dark green leaves up to 12 inches long and produces long, wiry stalks with bullet-shaped seed heads. Broadleaf plantain *(P. major, right)* forms rosettes of broad, oval leaves up to 6 inches long and produces short seed stalks. Both species have very long taproots. Use a postemergent systemic herbicide in fall or in early spring before the flowers appear.

PROSTRATE SPURGE *(Euphorbia supina, above)* is a broad-leaved annual that forms dense, multi-branched mats of small dark green leaves along reddish stems. The sap is milky. Apply a preemergent herbicide twice in spring at six-week intervals or use a postemergent systemic herbicide before flowers appear.

PURSLANE (*Portulaca oleracea*) is a broad-leaved annual that thrives in summer heat. It forms mats of tiny, succulent green leaves along thick reddish stems. Small yellow flowers bloom at the base of the leaves. Use a preemergent herbicide in early spring or a postemergent contact herbicide when the weeds appear.

RED SORREL (*Rumex acetosella, right*), also known as sheep sorrel, is a broad-leaved perennial that has arrow-shaped green leaves, reddish rhizomes and small reddish brown flowers atop slender stalks in spring. Use a postemergent systemic herbicide.

SPEEDWELL (*Veronica serpyllifolia, left*) is a broad-leaved perennial that has small heart-shaped leaves and tiny white flowers in late spring. It thrives in shady, moist areas. Use a postemergent systemic herbicide when the plants are in bloom.

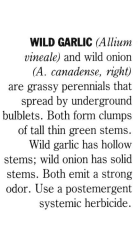

WILD GARLIC (*Allium vineale*) and wild onion (*A. canadense, right*) are grassy perennials that spread by underground bulblets. Both form clumps of tall thin green stems. Wild garlic has hollow stems; wild onion has solid stems. Both emit a strong odor. Use a postemergent systemic herbicide.

YELLOW WOOD SORREL (*Oxalis stricta, above*), also called oxalis, is a broad-leaved perennial that has cloverlike foliage, small yellow flowers and long, narrow seedpods. Flowers bloom in spring and sometimes again in fall. Use a postemergent systemic herbicide.

TIPS AND TECHNIQUES

BRINGING ORNAMENTAL GRASSES INDOORS

The graceful plumes of ornamental grasses can be cut from the plants and displayed indoors in winter. Both pampas grass and fountain grass produce tall, feathery plumes that can be dried and used in a variety of arrangements.

Cut the plumes from the plant after they are fully developed but before seeds begin to form. Make sure the stems are dry; damp stems are susceptible to mildew. Remove any undesired foliage. Short plumes can be tied together in small bunches and hung upside down. Tall plumes with arching stems should be placed upright in an open container. Both should be stored for two to three weeks in a dark, cool, dry, well-ventilated spot.

When they have dried, delicate plumes can be preserved with a light coat of hair spray. For added color, plumes may be dipped into a solution of clothing dye.

FIRE-RESISTANT GROUND COVERS

If you live in an area where fire is a perennial threat, as it is in some of the arid regions of the West, you can reduce the risk to your property by using ground covers, especially ones that have fire-retardant qualities.

All ground covers have a natural advantage over other plants: because their height is limited and they grow close to the soil, less of their surface area is exposed to air and they do not dry out as quickly as upright plants. And succulent ground covers, such as ice plant and sedum *(above),* have an added virtue; their foliage is thick and fleshy, and capable of holding water, and has a waxy coating that seals moisture in.

Some ground covers have other fire-retardant properties. Among them are English ivy, Point Reyes ceanothus, St.-John's-wort, trailing African daisy and trailing rosemary. They do not contain flammable resins and oils; they shed few leaves, and the leaves that die disintegrate rapidly; and some have sap that contains salt, which does not burn.

To get the most protection out of these plants, keep them well watered and pruned low.

WINTER COLOR FOR WARM-SEASON GRASSES

Warm-season grasses, which thrive in the heat of summer, become dormant and turn brown during the winter. Gardeners who grow these grasses in the Southern states don't have to settle for a brown lawn during the winter. They can overseed their lawns—that is, broadcast seed over the grass already growing in the soil. A lawn overseeded in the fall with a cool-season grass will sprout up as the warm-season grass goes dormant, and the cool-season grass will stay green throughout the winter. When high temperatures return the following spring, the cool-season grasses will die out as the warm-season grasses start to grow again.

To maintain such a green lawn year round, overseed in the fall as soon as the warm-season grasses begin to turn brown. Broadcast the seed as you would for a new lawn *(pages 24-25).* Use a mix of various cool-season grasses and sow them at a rate twice that recommended for a new lawn, since about half the seeds will not germinate because of competition with the existing grass and foot traffic. After sowing, cover the lawn with a thin layer of topsoil and keep the lawn moist until the cool-season grasses are established.

USES FOR GRASS CLIPPINGS

After you mow the lawn, don't discard the clippings; they make an excellent mulch for flower beds and vegetable gardens. Grass clippings contain large amounts of nitrogen and organic matter that will benefit the soil.

If you applied an herbicide to the lawn, go through at least four mowings before collecting the clippings for mulch; otherwise the herbicide will be transferred to the other plants in the garden.

Once collected, the clippings should be set aside and allowed to dry before they are used in the garden. As they dry, clippings emit a great amount of heat, which can damage plants. After they have dried, the grass clippings can be spread on the soil.

BETWEEN THE STONES

Stepping-stones are attractive and functional in any garden. To enhance their appeal, you can fill the spaces between them with a ground cover that withstands light foot traffic. Besides adding color to your walkway, a ground cover will also prevent grass and weeds from growing between the stones.

Ground covers that are both low-growing and tolerant of foot traffic include Irish moss, lippia, sandwort and yerba buena. To add a touch of fragrance, you can use Corsican mint or thyme, which emit an aroma when crushed by foot traffic.

Avoid stepping on the ground covers until they become established. Once established, they may need occasional trimming to keep them from spreading over the stones.

SPRING COLOR FOR GROUND COVERS

An area covered with herbaceous ground covers—those that die back in fall—looks barren in early spring, before the ground cover produces its warm-season growth. To enliven such an area, you can interplant groups of spring-flowering bulbs among the ground cover plants.

An herbaceous ground cover makes an ideal setting for a display of bulbs. The bulbs flower before the ground cover begins to grow, and they fade as the ground cover starts to fill in. After the bulbs bloom, their foliage turns brown, but the unattractive brown leaves are obscured by the sea of green.

For a natural-looking show of spring flowers against a ground cover, select early-blooming bulbs that are low-growing, such as snowdrop, squill, crocus and glory-of-the-snow. Plant them in the fall, between the ground cover plants, and space them according to package instructions. Left in the soil; the bulbs will continue to provide showy spring color for years to come.

BAMBOO AT STAKE

When you thin out a bed of bamboo plants, don't throw away the pruned canes; you can use them as stakes to support tall perennials, annuals and vegetables in your garden.

Bamboo canes are best cut in midsummer or later, when the canes are not actively growing. Select mature canes—those that have started to develop a hard outer bark and are turning beige in color. Young canes may be too soft and flexible to serve as stakes.

After cutting the canes to the lengths that you want, you can either strip the branches and leaves or let them remain on the cane to help hold plant ties in place.

5
DICTIONARY OF GRASSES AND GROUND COVERS

The 136 entries in this dictionary embrace three diverse groups of plants that are linked by their use in the garden or by botanical similarities. One group consists of turfgrasses, which are used in lawns, and a second category, ground covers, includes dwarf shrubs and low-growing herbaceous plants. Turfgrasses and ground covers share a common function; planted in masses, they serve as the garden's living carpet. The third group is ornamental grasses. Despite their close botanical relationship to turfgrasses, ornamental grasses are unsuited for lawns; many of them grow too tall, and most of them cannot withstand foot traffic or mowing. But they are a versatile lot; they can be used in the garden as ground covers, as borders, as specimens, as screens and as additions to flower borders.

All three groups of plants in this dictionary underscore the importance of foliage to the gardener—though flowers and fruit are bonuses with some of the ground covers and ornamental grasses, their primary esthetic value, month in and month out, is their leaves. The turfgrasses, of course, have a unique practical virtue; they are the only kind of plant that can be walked on and mowed, and they also provide a restful visual contrast to other plantings. The ground covers offer a tremendous variety of choices to the gardener. Foliage may be evergreen or deciduous; fine-textured or coarse; shiny or matte; round, oval, heart-shaped or straplike; and colors range from the pale gray of lamb's ears to the deep black-green of spreading English yew. The ornamental grasses have slender upright or arching blades and are ordinarily a soft green, but some varieties are striped or tinged with blue or red, and some have feathery seed heads.

In the entries that follow, all plants are listed by their botanical names; common names are cross-referenced. The climates in which the plants will grow are described in two ways. Ground covers and ornamental grasses are keyed to zones based on minimum winter temperatures. Turfgrasses respond to humidity, rainfall, and summer as well as winter temperatures, and are keyed to various regions accordingly. Maps of the zones and the regions appear on pages 88-89.

ACHILLEA TOMENTOSA

AEGOPODIUM PODAGRARIA 'VARIEGATUM'

AGROPYRON CRISTATUM

AGROSTIS STOLONIFERA PALUSTRIS

Achillea (ak-i-LEE-a)
Yarrow

Genus of upright and spreading perennials, some species of which are used as ground covers. Yarrow has finely divided, fernlike foliage and small flowers in flat-topped clusters. Zones 2-10.

Selected species and varieties. *A. tomentosa,* woolly yarrow, has dark green, aromatic, hairy leaves that spread to form a flat mat 2 inches high. The leaves lie at the base of the plant and are evergreen or semievergreen. Bright yellow flowers bloom in early summer to midsummer in clusters 1 inch across atop 6- to 10-inch stems. Zones 3-10.

Growing conditions. Plant yarrow in sun or part shade in any well-drained soil. It tolerates poor and dry soil. Cut the plants back after they have bloomed. Yarrow can also be mowed. It has a tendency to become weedy and may need to be thinned or divided every year. Propagate by seeds, cuttings or division.

Landscape uses. Use yarrow as a ground cover in a rock garden or as an edging. Its flowers can be cut for indoor display.

Aegopodium (ee-go-PO-dee-um)
Goutweed

Fast-growing perennial ground cover that has divided leaves with toothed margins. Small white flowers bloom in flat-topped clusters in early summer. Zones 4-10.

Selected species and varieties. *A. podagraria* has light green foliage and grows 6 inches high. Flower heads 3 inches across bloom atop 12- to 14-inch stems. The cultivar 'Variegatum' has light green leaves edged in white and is not as aggressive a grower.

Growing conditions. Goutweed grows in any moist or dry, infertile garden soil. It tolerates sun but prefers partial shade. Remove flowers after they have bloomed. Goutweed may also be mowed. It spreads by underground runners and can be kept from becoming invasive by installing metal barriers in the ground 2 feet deep. Propagate by division.

Landscape uses. Goutweed is useful where a large area needs to be covered, especially at the north side of a house, where it will receive some shade.

Agropyron (ag-ro-PY-ron)
Wheatgrass

Cool-season, cold- and drought-resistant bunching turfgrass. Region D and higher altitudes of E.

Selected species and varieties. *A. cristatum,* fairway wheatgrass, has blue-green, slightly hairy leaves with medium texture. *A. smithii,* western wheatgrass, is similar in color but coarser in appearance.

Growing conditions. Plant wheatgrass in full sun in any garden soil. Western wheatgrass is more tolerant of alkaline soil than fairway wheatgrass. Both are extremely drought-tolerant and will not grow in warm or humid climates. Wheatgrass may turn brown during hot summers. Mow to 2 inches. Fertilize with 1 to 3 pounds of nitrogen per 1,000 square feet per year. Propagate by seeds, which are slow to germinate.

Landscape uses. Wheatgrass may be grown as a lawn where foot traffic is high.

Agrostis (a-GROS-tis)
Bentgrass

A high-maintenance, cool-season and transition zone turfgrass that usually has narrow leaves and fine texture. It has a prostrate growth habit and, depending on the type, may be either bunching or stoloniferous. Region F; A where cool and humid; D with irrigation; E at high altitudes and in coastal areas.

Selected species and varieties. *A. alba,* redtop, is coarser and wider leaved than other bentgrasses and of lower quality. It is primarily used as a quick-cover grass while slower-developing grasses are being established. *A. canina,* velvet bentgrass, has soft, velvety, needlelike leaves. It is more stoloniferous than colonial bentgrass *(see below)* but not as stoloniferous as creeping bentgrass. *A. stolonifera palustris,* creeping bentgrass, is a fine-textured grass with vigorous creeping stolons. 'Arlington' is olive green, of fine texture, best adapted to dry soils, and has good tolerance to heat stress and wear. 'Emerald' is dark emerald green, of very fine texture and with good tolerance to heat stress. 'Penncross' is medium dark green, with medium-fine texture and excellent wear tolerance. 'Pennlu' is dark blue-green and of fine texture. 'Seaside' is medium light green and medium textured, and has excellent resistance to drying winter winds and seashore conditions. 'Toronto' is medium dark green and fine textured. *A. tenuis,* colonial bentgrass, is an erect, fine-textured grass. 'Exeter' is bright medium green and of fine texture. 'Highland' is dark blue-green and medium textured. 'Holfior' is medium dark green and with medium-fine texture.

Growing conditions. Bentgrass prefers full sun but will tolerate light shade. Climate must be humid. Soil should be fertile, moist, acid and well drained. Redtop is mowed to 1½ to 2 inches; velvet bentgrass, ¼ to ½ inch; creeping and colonial bentgrass, ¼ to ¾ inch. All require 1½ to 2 pounds of nitrogen per 1,000 square feet per year. Bentgrass is not wear-tolerant. Colonial and creeping bentgrasses are susceptible to most turfgrass diseases. Velvet bentgrass is susceptible to copper spot and prone to iron chlorosis. Redtop is susceptible to fusarium. Depending on the type and variety, bentgrass is propagated by either seeds or plugs. Redtop and colonial bentgrasses are propagated from seeds. Velvet bentgrass can be propagated by either method. Most creeping bentgrasses are propagated by plugs; 'Penncross' and 'Seaside' are propagated from seeds.

Landscape uses. Bentgrass should be used in showplace lawns where it will not receive foot traffic.

— — —

Ajuga (a-JOO-ga)
Bugleweed

Evergreen or semievergreen perennial ground cover with glossy, oval leaves that form mats of rosettes on the ground. Spikes of blue, violet, pink or white flowers bloom in spring. Some types spread by runners; others are clumping plants that spread more slowly by rhizomes. Zones 3-10.

Selected species and varieties. *A. genevensis* has 3-inch, coarse, toothed green leaves, hairy stems and spikes of blue flowers 5 to 14 inches high in late spring. It spreads by rhizomes. 'Pink Beauty' has pink flowers. *A. pyramidalis* has quilted green leaves up to 4 inches long and spikes of lavender-blue flowers 6 to 10 inches high in early summer. It spreads by rhizomes. Zones 4-10. *A. reptans,* carpet bugle, has dark green leaves 2 to 4 inches long and spikes of blue to purple flowers 3 to 6 inches

high in midspring. The plants send out runners that form new plants at their ends. 'Alba' has white flowers; 'Bronze Beauty' has bronze foliage and blue flowers; 'Burgundy Glow' has leaves variegated in green, white, pink and purple, and has blue flowers.

Growing conditions. Plant bugleweed in full sun or partial shade; in hot areas, it prefers partial shade. Bronze-leaved types will retain their coloring better if planted in full sun. Grow in any moist garden soil. Propagate by division.

Landscape uses. Use bugleweed as a ground cover under or in front of shrubs or in a rock garden. It is most effective planted under shrubs that flower at the same time.

— — —

Alchemilla (al-ke-MILL-a)
Lady's mantle

Perennial ground cover that has spreading and mounded clumps of round, deeply lobed, velvety foliage and small, yellow-green flowers that bloom in feathery sprays. Zones 4-9.

Selected species and varieties. *A. mollis* has silvery gray foliage and spikes of flowers 12 to 15 inches tall in late spring or early summer. Leaves may be evergreen.

Growing conditions. Plant lady's mantle in full sun or light shade in any garden soil. Keep well watered during periods of excessive heat. To prevent invasive growth from reseeding, remove flowers as they start to fade. Propagate from seeds or by division.

Landscape uses. Use as a ground cover either with shrubs or with other perennials.

— — —

Alopecurus (al-o-pe-KEW-rus)
Meadow foxtail grass

Upright perennial ornamental grass with an open habit. In spring it has cylindrical, fluffy seed heads that are cream to tan, ½ inch in diameter and 3 inches long. Zones 4-10.

Selected species and varieties. *A. pratensis* has flat leaf blades 6 inches long and ¼ to ½ inch wide. Seed heads form on 24- to 28-inch stems. 'Aureo-variegatus' has green foliage with wide gold margins. 'Aureus' has gold leaves with a green vein.

AJUGA REPTANS

ALCHEMILLA MOLLIS

ALOPECURUS PRATENSIS 'AUREO-VARIEGATUS'

ANTENNARIA DIOICA ROSEA

ARABIS CAUCASICA

ARCTOSTAPHYLOS UVA-URSI

ARENARIA MONTANA

Growing conditions. Plant meadow foxtail grass in full sun or light shade in fertile, moist, well-drained soil. Propagate by division.

Landscape uses. Plant meadow foxtail as a ground cover in informal or meadow gardens.

American barrenwort
see *Vancouveria*

Antennaria (an-te-NAR-ee-a)
Pussy-toes

Perennial ground cover that has rosettes of leaves at the base of the plant and small, tubular, funnel-shaped flowers that bloom in loose clusters. Zones 3-8.

Selected species and varieties. *A. dioica* has hairy, 1- to 1½-inch leaves that are dark green on the upper surfaces, and white and woolly on the undersides. Flowers are ¼ inch across, white tipped with pink and bloom in early summer on top of 4- to 12-inch stems. *A. dioicia rosea* has pink flowers.

Growing conditions. Plant pussy-toes in full sun and dry, sandy, acid soil. It will tolerate poor soil. Pussy-toes can become weedy from dropped seeds. Propagate from seeds or by division.

Landscape uses. Pussy-toes is useful where growing conditions are less than ideal and other ground covers will not grow well.

Arabis (AR-a-bis)
Rock cress

Perennial ground cover that has hairy leaves and masses of small, single, four-petaled flowers of white, pink or purple that bloom in midspring. Rock cress may be semievergreen or evergreen. Zones 4-8.

Selected species and varieties. *A. caucasica,* sometimes designated *A. albida,* wall rock cress, has mats of gray-green leaves that are borne in rosettes 4 to 6 inches high. Flowers are fragrant, white, ½ inch across and bloom in loose clusters 12 inches above the ground. The cultivar 'Flore Pleno' has double flowers; 'Rosabella' has pink flowers; 'Variegata' has green leaves that are edged in creamy white. *A. procurrens* has bright green leaves and ¼-inch white flowers on 12-inch stems. Zones 5-8.

Growing conditions. Plant rock cresses in full sun or light shade in sandy soil with excellent drainage. Soil for wall rock cress should be rich and may be dry or moist; for *A. procurrens* soil may be poor but should be dry. As a rule rock cresses do not grow well where summers are hot or humid. Propagate by cuttings or division or from seeds.

Landscape uses. Plant rock cress as a ground cover on a slope or on top of a wall where it can gracefully spill down over the side.

Arctostaphylos
(ark-toh-STAF-i-los)

Wide-spreading, shrubby, evergreen ground cover that has glossy, smooth, oblong leaves. Flowers are small, bell-shaped, and pink or white. Red to brown branches grow in a crooked manner and root as they grow along the ground. Long-lasting red berries are ¼ inch wide. Zones 2-10.

Selected species and varieties. *A. edmundsii,* Little Sur manzanita, has 1- to 1¼-inch light green leaves. The plant grows 6 to 24 inches tall and spreads to 12 feet across. Pink flowers bloom in winter. Zones 8-10. *A. uva-ursi,* bearberry, kinnikinick, grows 12 inches tall and has trailing branches that spread to 12 feet. Leaves are dark green, 1 inch long and turn bronze in winter. Pink flowers bloom in spring. Zones 2-7.

Growing conditions. Plant Little Sur manzanita and bearberry in full sun or partial shade in dry, sandy, acid soil with excellent drainage. Little Sur manzanita tolerates heat, drought and poor soil. Propagate by cuttings, by layering or from seeds.

Landscape uses. Bearberry is useful where a large area needs to be covered and is most attractive growing over and around rocks where the outline of its branches can be seen.

Arenaria (ar-e-NAR-ee-a)
Sandwort

Evergreen perennial ground cover that forms mats of grassy or mosslike foliage. Small white flowers have five rounded petals and bloom in late spring or early summer. Zones 3-10.

Selected species and varieties. *A. montana,* mountain sandwort, has soft, glossy, gray-green leaves 1 inch long. The plant grows 2 to 4 inches high and has 1-inch flowers. Zones 4-10. *A. verna,* Irish moss, grows 2 inches tall in mossy clumps. Smooth leaves are ¾ inch long; flowers are ½ inch across.

Growing conditions. Plant sandwort in full sun or partial shade in average, slightly acid, moist, well-drained soil. In hot climates, it prefers partial shade. Propagate by cuttings or division or from seeds.

Landscape uses. Sandwort is used as a lawn substitute and is especially useful between stepping-stones and in a rock garden.

—

Armeria (ar-MEER-ee-a)
Sea thrift

Spreading evergreen perennial that has tufts of dark green, grassy foliage and tiny flowers in 1-inch globe-shaped heads atop 6- to 12-inch leafless stems. Zones 3-9.

Selected species and varieties. *A. maritima* grows 3 to 6 inches tall and spreads to 1 foot across. White or pink flowers bloom in late spring and early summer. The cultivar 'Vindictive' has deep pink flowers.

Growing conditions. Grow sea thrift in full sun in light, sandy, dry soil with excellent drainage. Propagate by division, cuttings or seeds.

Landscape uses. Plant sea thrift as a ground cover in a rock garden or as an edging to a shrub border. It is a good choice for a seashore garden.

—

Arrhenatherum
(ar-e-na-THEER-um)
Oat grass

Perennial ornamental grass that forms erect clumps of rough-edged, flat, narrow green leaves. Zones 5-8.

Selected species and varieties. *A. elatius bulbosum,* bulbous oat grass, grows 12 to 18 inches tall. Stems 3½ to 4 feet tall produce narrow, purplish green seed heads 1 foot long in late spring. 'Variegatum' has green and white striped foliage.

Growing conditions. Plant bulbous oat grass in full sun or light shade in well-drained, fertile soil. Propagate by division.

Landscape uses. Because oat grass tolerates drought, it does well on dry slopes. Its tall seed heads make it useful as an accent planting.

Arrow bamboo see *Pseudosasa*

—

Artemisia (ar-te-MEE-zee-a)
Wormwood

Bushy perennial with some species used as ground covers. It is grown for its white or silver, deeply divided or lobed foliage. Small, inconspicuous flower heads of white or yellow are produced in late summer or fall. Zones 3-9.

Selected species and varieties. *A. schmidtiana* grows 2 feet tall and has silky, finely cut leaves that have white hairs. The foliage is aromatic. 'Silver Mound' is 8 to 12 inches tall and has 1¾-inch silver leaves. *A. stellerana,* dusty miller, has white, felty, deeply lobed leaves. The plant grows 2 feet tall.

Growing conditions. Plant wormwood in full sun or light shade in poor, dry, sandy, well-drained soil. It is essential that the plants have dry soil to survive the winter. Shear in midsummer to encourage dense growth and prevent flowering. Propagate by division and cuttings.

Landscape uses. Use wormwood as a ground cover on sunny slopes. Dusty miller is used to hold dunes in place at the seashore.

—

Arundinaria (ar-un-di-NAR-ee-a)
Bamboo

Perennial ornamental grass with woody, often hollow, stems that have obvious joints called nodes. Branches grow from the upper nodes; leaves that are rough and lance-shaped grow from these branches. Bamboo spreads rapidly by underground runners and may be invasive. It seldom if ever blooms. Zones 8-10.

Selected species and varieties. *A. pygmaea,* pygmy bamboo, grows 8 to 12 inches high and has 5-inch-long, ¾-inch-wide bright green leaves. Stems are greenish purple; nodes are purple. *A. viridistriata* grows 30 to 36 inches tall and has 8-inch-long, 1¼-inch-wide green leaves that have a yellow stripe and a velvety texture when young.

Growing conditions. Grow pygmy bamboo in full sun; *A. viridistriata* prefers partial shade; the leaves will curl in full sun. To restrict the invasive growth of bamboo, water lightly, do not fertilize, cut off new stems as they appear in spring and install an underground barrier 2 feet deep in

ARMERIA MARITIMA 'VINDICTIVE'

ARRHENATHERUM ELATIUS BULBOSUM 'VARIEGATUM'

ARTEMISIA SCHMIDTIANA 'SILVER MOUND'

ARUNDINARIA VIRIDISTRIATA

ARUNDO DONAX 'VARIEGATA'

ASARUM EUROPAEUM

AXONOPUS AFFINIS

BAMBUSA PHYLLOSTACHYS AUREA

the ground. Propagate by division or by root cuttings.

Landscape uses. Use bamboo as a ground cover in a large area or where soil erosion control is needed.

Arundo (a-RUN-doh)

Perennial ornamental grass with an open, upright, arching habit, tall and woody stems, coarse and stiff leaves, and large silky plumes that last from summer into winter. Zones 7-10.

Selected species and varieties. *A. donax,* giant reed, grows 12 to 20 feet tall and has leaves 1 to 2 feet long and 2½ inches wide. Foliage is light green to blue-green. The variety 'Variegata', striped giant reed, grows 3 to 8 feet tall and has foliage striped with white. Zones 8-10.

Growing conditions. Plant giant reed in full sun and moist, well-drained soil. Cut branches to the ground before new growth starts in spring. Propagate by division or from seeds.

Landscape uses. Giant reed does well by the side of a stream or a pool, and where soil erosion control is needed. Because of its large size, it is useful as a tall accent plant.

Asarum (AS-a-rum)
Wild ginger

Fast-growing, spreading, evergreen or deciduous perennial ground cover that has shiny, leathery, heart-shaped aromatic leaves on long leafstalks. Flowers are small, ½ to 1 inch across, purplish to brown, bell-shaped, and usually hidden by the foliage in late spring and summer. Zones 3-9.

Selected species and varieties. *A. canadense,* Canadian wild ginger, is deciduous, 6 to 8 inches high and has 3- to 6-inch leaves. *A. caudatum,* British Columbia wild ginger, has evergreen, 3- to 6-inch leaves and grows 6 to 7 inches tall. Zones 6-9. *A. europaeum,* European wild ginger, has evergreen, 2- to 3-inch leaves and grows 7 inches tall. Zones 5-9. *A. shuttleworthii,* mottled wild ginger, has evergreen, mottled, 1- to 3-inch leaves. It grows 8 inches tall. Zones 6-9.

Growing conditions. Plant wild ginger in shade in slightly acid, moist, well-drained soil. Propagate by division, by root cuttings or from seeds.

Landscape uses. Wild ginger is a good choice to cover the ground under trees.

Avena grass see *Helictotrichon*

Axonopus (ak-so-NO-pus)
Carpetgrass

Warm-season turfgrass that has a very coarse texture and a light green color. Region C.

Selected species and varieties. *A. affinis,* common carpetgrass, is low-growing and spreads by stolons that root along the ground, forming a dense sod. Tall, unsightly seed heads may appear in summer.

Growing conditions. Grow carpetgrass in full sun. Soil should be sandy, moist, acidic and of low fertility. Mow to a height of 1 to 2 inches. Fertilize in spring with 1 to 2 pounds of nitrogen per 1,000 square feet per year. Brown patch is the most common problem of carpetgrass. Propagate from seeds or by plugs.

Landscape uses. Carpetgrass does not tolerate wear and therefore should be used on lawns that will not receive heavy foot traffic. Because it is slow-growing, it requires less frequent mowing than other grasses and is useful on slopes where mowing is difficult.

Azalea see *Rhododendron*
Bahiagrass see *Paspalum*
Bamboo see *Arundinaria; Bambusa; Pseudosasa; Sasa; Shibataea*

Bambusa (bam-BOO-sa)
Bamboo

Ornamental grass that forms dense clumps of hollow, shiny stems with prominent joints. Lance-shaped leaves grow from the joints. Zones 8-10.

Selected species and varieties. *B. glaucescens,* hedge bamboo, has stems 3 to 20 feet tall and 1½ inches across. Narrow leaves are 6 inches long. 'Silverstripe' grows 10 feet tall and has striped foliage. *B. phyllostachys aurea* grows up to 30 feet tall.

Growing conditions. Grow hedge bamboo in full sun or light shade in rich, moist, well-drained neutral soil. It is a clump-forming bamboo and is therefore not as aggressive as other bamboos. Propagate by division or by layering.

Landscape uses. Hedge bamboo may be grown as an accent plant or as a hedge or in a container.

—

Barrenwort see *Epimedium; Vancouveria*

Bearberry see *Arctostaphylos*

Bellflower see *Campanula*

Bentgrass see *Agrostis*

—

Bergenia (ber-JEN-ee-a)

Evergreen or deciduous perennial ground cover that forms dense clumps of large, thick, fleshy, shiny basal leaves. The foliage is textured, has crinkled or scalloped edges, and turns purple or red in autumn. Small, single flowers bloom in nodding heads atop long stems in spring and summer. Zones 3-9.

Selected species and varieties. *B. ciliata* has dark green, round, hairy leaves. Flowers of white, rose or purple bloom in late spring on stems that are 9 to 12 inches long. Zones 6-9. *B. cordifolia,* heartleaf bergenia, has dark green, heart-shaped, wavy leaves. Pink flowers blossom on 12- to 18-inch red stems in late spring. *B. crassifolia,* Siberian tea, has dark green, heart-shaped leaves with edges that curve backward. Flowers of rose, pink or lilac bloom on 18-inch stems in summer.

Growing conditions. Grow bergenia in partial shade; it will tolerate full sun in cool areas or in areas with high humidity or rainfall. Rich soil is preferred, but poor and dry soils are well tolerated. Protect from wind that can tear the leaves. Propagate by division or from seeds.

Landscape uses. Plant bergenia as an accent plant or a ground cover under trees.

—

Bermudagrass see *Cynodon*

Bethlehem sage see *Pulmonaria*

Blood grass see *Imperata*

Blue-eyed Mary see *Omphalodes*

Bluegrass see *Poa*

Blue oat grass see *Helictotrichon*

Boston ivy see *Parthenocissus*

Bowles golden grass see *Milium*

—

Briza (BREE-za)
Quaking grass

Annual or perennial ornamental grass that has graceful, drooping seed heads at the ends of very thin stems. The plant appears to be constantly in motion. Perennial in Zones 5-10.

Selected species and varieties. *B. maxima,* large quaking grass, is an annual and grows 12 to 24 inches tall. Leaves are narrow, 4 to 6 inches long and coarse. Seed heads are pale yellow to shiny gold in color. *B. media* is a perennial and grows 10 to 18 inches high with narrow, tufted foliage. Seed heads are purple, aging to gray.

Growing conditions. Quaking grass should be grown in full sun in dry and poor soil. Propagate from seeds; the perennial can also be propagated by division.

Landscape uses. Plant quaking grass as an accent where it will be in a breeze so its movement can be enjoyed.

—

Broom see *Genista*

—

Buchloe (boo-KLO-ee)
Buffalograss

Warm-season and transitional zone turfgrass that is low-growing, fine textured and grayish green. Region E and warm areas of D.

Selected species and varieties. *B. dactyloides* spreads by means of stolons that branch heavily and form a tight sod. Leaf blades are curled.

Growing conditions. Plant buffalograss in full sun. It will tolerate alkaline soil. It is extremely drought-tolerant. Mow to a height of ½ inch to 1¼ inches. Fertilize buffalograss in spring with ½ to 2½ pounds of nitrogen per 1,000 square feet; fertilize again in summer if necessary. Buffalograss is fairly wear-tolerant. Propagate from seeds or by plugs.

Landscape uses. Buffalograss is suitable for use on unirrigated lawns that do not have high maintenance requirements, because it is very slow-growing.

BERGENIA CILIATA

BRIZA MEDIA

BUCHLOE DACTYLOIDES

CALAMAGROSTIS ACUTIFLORA STRICTA

CALLUNA VULGARIS 'MULLION'

CAMPANULA ELATINES GARGANICA

CAREX CONICA 'VARIEGATA'

Buffalograss see *Buchloe*

Bugleweed see *Ajuga*

Bunchberry see *Cornus*

Calamagrostis

(kal-a-ma-GROS-tis)
Feather reed grass

Vigorous perennial ornamental grass with erect clumps of rough leaves and lance-shaped seed heads on slender stems in summer. Zones 5-10.

Selected species and varieties. *C. acutiflora stricta* has dull green, 2-foot, slightly arching leaves. The seed head is 12 inches long, narrow, purplish in spring and wheat-colored in fall, and sits atop a 5-foot stem. *C. arundinacea brachytricha* has a wider, looser, pointed seed head that is white or pink changing to brown atop a 3-foot stem.

Growing conditions. Plant feather reed grass in full sun and moist, fertile soil. Sandy soil promotes the spread of the plant. Propagate by division.

Landscape uses. Plant feather reed grass as a screen or an accent plant, or alongside a pool or a stream.

Calluna (ka-LOO-na)
Heather

Evergreen shrubby ground cover that forms a spreading mound. Branches are covered with fine bright to dark green leaves and 10-inch spikes of tiny, single or double, nodding, bell-shaped flowers of white, pink or lavender. Zones 4-7.

Selected species and varieties. *C. vulgaris,* Scotch heather, grows 18 to 24 inches tall and spreads from 2 to 4 feet wide. Blooms appear in late summer and fall at the ends of ascending branches that are covered with scalelike leaves. 'Blazeway' is 18 inches tall with orange-yellow foliage. 'County Wicklow' grows 18 inches tall and has double, pale pink flowers. 'Kinlochruel' has double white flowers and bright green foliage. 'Mullion' is 18 inches high and has soft purplish pink to deep pink flowers.

Growing conditions. Grow Scotch heather in full sun or light shade in poor, moist, acid, well-drained soil. Roots are shallow and should be mulched. Protect from winter winds. Prune in early spring. Propagate by cuttings.

Landscape uses. Use Scotch heather as a ground cover on a sandy bank or in a seashore garden.

Campanula (kam-PAN-u-la)
Bellflower

Genus of perennials of which some species are used as ground covers. Blue or white bell- or star-shaped flowers bloom in summer. Leaves at the base of the plant are broad and oval; near the top of the plant they become smaller. Zones 3-9.

Selected species and varieties. *C. carpatica,* Carpathian harebell, grows 6 to 12 inches tall and has round, serrated leaves. Flowers are bell-shaped, 2 inches across and upturned, and may be blue or white. *C. elatines garganica* is a sprawling, 6- to 10-inch plant with hairy foliage and ½-inch, blue, star-shaped flowers. Zones 5-9. *C. portenschlagiana,* Dalmatian bellflower, is a spreading, 6- to 8-inch plant with heart-shaped to oval, serrated dark green leaves. Flowers are lavender-blue, 1 inch across and star-shaped, and bloom in clusters. Zones 5-9. *C. poscharskyana,* Serbian bellflower, is 4 to 6 inches tall and spreads by very long shoots that have heart-shaped or oval serrated leaves. Flowers are lilac, 1 inch across and star-shaped.

Growing conditions. Plant bellflower in full sun or partial shade in any well-drained garden soil. Carpathian bellflower prefers moist soil; Dalmatian and Serbian bellflowers like poor, sandy soil. Propagate by division, by cuttings or from seeds.

Landscape uses. Plant bellflower where summer color is needed. It is especially effective planted on top of a rock wall.

Candytuft see *Iberis*

Carex (KA-reks)
Sedge

Ornamental grass that has solid, triangular stems and tufted, arching leaves. Zones 3-8.

Selected species and varieties. *C. buchananii,* leatherleaf sedge, grows 12 to 24 inches tall. Leaves are narrow but heavy in texture. They are coppery brown in color and have curled tips. Zones 6-8. *C. conica*

'Variegata', variegated miniature sedge, grows 6 inches tall and has dark green leaves with silver edges. Zones 5-8. *C. grayii,* Gray's sedge, grows 2 feet tall and has narrow, 18-inch, bright green leaves. The seedpod that develops in the fall is pyramidal to round with numerous pointed protrusions. *C. morrowii,* Japanese sedge, forms a 12-inch mound. 'Aureo-variegata' is green with a central yellow stripe. 'Variegata' is dark green with white margins. Zones 6-8. *C. pendula,* pendulous wood sedge, is 2 feet tall with bright green foliage and drooping gray-green seed heads that rustle in the breeze. Zones 5-8.

Growing conditions. Plant sedge in full sun or light shade in moist, fertile soil. Propagate by division.

Landscape uses. Grow sedge as an accent plant by the side of a pool, swamp or marsh. It will also do well in a container.

—

Carmel creeper see *Ceanothus*
Carpet bugle see *Ajuga*
Carpetgrass see *Axonopus*
Catmint see *Nepeta*

—

Ceanothus (see-a-NO-thus)
Wild lilac

Genus of fast-growing, deciduous and evergreen shrubs. Species used as ground cover have upright, spreading branches and small white to lilac flowers in cone-shaped clusters. Zones 7-10.

Selected species and varieties. *C. gloriosus,* Point Reyes ceanothus, grows densely 4 to 18 inches tall and spreads from 5 to 10 feet across. Toothed leaves are 1½ inches long, dark green and leathery. Flowers are light blue to lavender and bloom in spring. *C. griseus horizontalis,* Carmel creeper, grows 18 to 30 inches tall and has 2-inch, oval, dark green, glossy, leathery leaves. It can spread from 5 to 15 feet across. Flowers of deep blue appear in spring.

Growing conditions. Plant wild lilac in full sun in light, well-drained acid or neutral soil. It does not like excessive summer heat. Propagate by cuttings, by layering or from seeds.

Landscape uses. Plant wild lilac in a massed planting on a slope, at the seashore or along the roadside.

—

Centipedegrass see *Eremochloa*

—

Cerastium (se-RAS-tee-um)

Annual or perennial ground cover that has gray or gray-green hairy leaves and small, five-petaled flowers. Zones 2-10.

Selected species and varieties. *C. tomentosum,* snow-in-summer, is a fast-growing perennial that forms a mat of white, woolly, 1-inch, pointed leaves. The plant grows 6 inches high and has ½- to 1-inch flowers with notched petals that bloom in late spring and summer.

Growing conditions. Plant snow-in-summer in full sun in poor, dry, well-drained soil. Snow-in-summer can become invasive; to prevent re-seeding, cut off flowers as they fade. Mowing promotes new growth. Propagate by division, by cuttings or from seeds.

Landscape uses. Snow-in-summer is best used in a large area, on a hot, rocky slope or on top of a wall.

—

Chasmanthium
(chas-MAN-thee-um)

Perennial ornamental grass that has an upright growth habit and thin stems. Flat, serrated leaf blades appear along the entire length of the stem. Zones 5-10.

Selected species and varieties. *C. latifolium,* northern sea oats, grows 3 to 5 feet tall. Flat leaves are 9 inches long and 1 inch wide. Seed heads are 8 to 12 inches long and appear on slender, drooping stalks. The foliage and the seed heads turn bronze after frost.

Growing conditions. Plant northern sea oats in full sun to partial shade in rich, fertile, moist soil. Propagate by division or from seeds.

Landscape uses. Plant northern sea oats as an accent plant or in a woodland garden.

—

Cheddar pink see *Dianthus*
Chewings fescue see *Festuca*

CEANOTHUS GRISEUS HORIZONTALIS

CERASTIUM TOMENTOSUM

CHASMANTHIUM LATIFOLIUM

CHRYSOGONUM VIRGINIANUM

COIX LACRYMA-JOBI

COMPTONIA PEREGRINA

CONVALLARIA MAJALIS

Chrysogonum (kri-SOG-o-num)

Perennial ground cover that has oval, toothed leaves and five-petaled yellow flowers. Zones 5-9.

Selected species and varieties. *C. virginianum* grows 4 to 12 inches tall. Hairy leaves are often tinged with purple. Yellow, 1½-inch flowers bloom in spring and summer.

Growing conditions. Plant chrysogonum in partial shade in rich, well-drained soil. It flowers best during cool summers. Propagate by division, by cuttings or from seeds.

Landscape uses. Chrysogonum may be planted as a ground cover under trees or shrubs.

Cinquefoil see *Potentilla*
Clover see *Trifolium*

Coix (KO-iks)

Annual ornamental grass that has an upright habit and flat, coarse leaves appearing along the stems.

Selected species and varieties. *C. lacryma-jobi*, Job's tears, grows 3 feet tall. Leaves are light green, sword-shaped, 1 to 2 feet long, 1½ to 2 inches wide and have prominent midribs. Hard, shiny, ¾-inch, bead-like fruits form in fall at the ends of the stems; they are green at first and fade to white or gray.

Growing conditions. Grow Job's tears in full sun to light shade in moist, rich, well-drained soil. It needs a long, hot summer for the beads to develop. Propagate from seeds.

Landscape uses. Use Job's tears as an accent plant or near water.

Comfrey see *Symphytum*

Comptonia (komp-TOH-nee-a)

Deciduous shrubby ground cover that grows into a dense mass, spreading by underground runners. Zones 3-10.

Selected species and varieties. *C. peregrina*, sweet fern, grows 3 to 5 feet tall. Leaves are fragrant, 4½ inches long and ½ inch wide, hairy and notched along their entire length.

Growing conditions. Plant sweet fern in full sun to partial shade in sandy, well-drained soil. It will grow in rich soil but tolerates poor and dry soil as well. Propagate by layering, by division or from seeds.

Landscape uses. Plant sweet fern on a sandy or rocky bank, especially where soil erosion control is needed.

Convallaria (kon-va-LAR-ee-a)
Lily-of-the-valley

Deciduous perennial ground cover that has upright, pointed leaves that grow from buds called pips that sprout on the rhizomes. Drooping, bell-shaped, fragrant flowers bloom along one side of the flower stalk. Zones 4-8.

Selected species and varieties. *C. majalis* has leaves 6 to 8 inches high and 2 to 3 inches wide. Waxy, white or pink flowers are ¼ to ½ inch long and bloom in late spring.

Growing conditions. Plant lily-of-the-valley in partial to full shade and moist, rich, fertile, well-drained soil. Propagate from rhizomes, making sure that each division bears at least one pip.

Landscape uses. Grow lily-of-the-valley in the shade of a house or trees, or by the side of water.

Cord grass see *Spartina*

Cornus (KOR-nus)
Dogwood

Genus of deciduous and evergreen trees and shrubs of which one species is used as ground cover. It has dull green leaves, single flowers with four to six petals or bracts, and showy berries. Zones 2-8.

Selected species and varieties. *C. canadensis*, bunchberry, is an evergreen or semievergreen shrub that grows 2 to 6 inches high and spreads to 12 feet across. Leaves are textured, 2 inches long and pointed, and appear in whorled clusters at the top of short, upright stems. Flowers are white and 1 to 1½ inches across and bloom in late spring. Clusters of edible red berries form in the fall.

Growing conditions. Plant bunchberry in full sun to partial shade in rich, moist, acid, well-drained soil. It grows best where summers are cool. Propagate by division, by cuttings or from seeds.

Landscape uses. Grow bunchberry under trees or in a woodland garden.

—

Coronilla (kor-o-NIL-a)
Crown vetch

Fast-growing, deciduous, creeping perennial ground cover that has soft green feathery leaves and pealike flowers. Zones 4-8.

Selected species and varieties. *C. varia* grows into a mat 18 to 24 inches high and 4 feet wide. Dense clusters of ½-inch pink flowers bloom in summer. 'Penngift' has good drought tolerance and grows 12 to 18 inches high.

Growing conditions. Plant crown vetch in full sun or partial shade in dry, well-drained soil. Do not fertilize. It can be mowed in early spring to encourage new growth. Propagate by root divisions or from seeds. Seeds are often sown in combination with annual ryegrass, which will die out as the crown vetch becomes established.

Landscape uses. Plant crown vetch on a bank or a slope that cannot be easily mowed. It is a good plant to use where erosion control is needed.

—

Cortaderia (kor-ta-DEER-ee-a)
Pampas grass

Perennial ornamental grass that has upright clumps of long, narrow, sharp-edged leaves and large, showy, plumed panicles in late summer and fall. Zones 8-10.

Selected species and varieties. *C. selloana* grows 8 to 12 feet tall. Its white, silver or pink plumes are 3 feet long and 6 inches wide. Plumes are more showy on female plants. 'Rosea' has pink plumes; 'Sonningdale Silver' has silver plumes.

Growing conditions. Grow pampas grass in full sun or light shade in fertile, well-drained, acid or alkaline soil. It will tolerate drought as well as moist soil. Propagate by division.

Landscape uses. Plant pampas grass as a windbreak, as an accent plant or in a large bank planting.

—

Cotoneaster (ko-toh-nee-AST-er)

Deciduous or evergreen shrubby ground cover that has stiff, spreading branches. Small white or pink flowers bloom in spring, scattered among small, shiny, thick green leaves. Red or black berries ¼ inch across appear through autumn and winter. Zones 3-9.

Selected species and varieties. *C. adpressus,* creeping cotoneaster, is deciduous and grows 12 inches high. Its stems, which grow in a fish-bone pattern, root as it grows along the ground. Leaves are ½ inch long. Flowers are pink; berries are red. Zones 5-9. *C. dammeri,* bearberry cotoneaster, is an evergreen growing 12 inches tall with trailing branches that spread to 6 feet across. Leaves are 1 inch long and shiny dark green, turning reddish purple in winter. Flowers are white; berries are red. Zones 6-9. *C. horizontalis,* rockspray cotoneaster, is a deciduous shrub that grows 2 to 3 feet high and has fan-shaped branches. Foliage turns orange-red in fall and may be evergreen in Zones 8-10. Flowers are white or pink; berries are red. Zones 5-9. *C. salicifolius,* willowleaf cotoneaster, is an evergreen that has narrow, 1½- to 3-inch leaves that turn purple in winter. White flowers bloom in 2-inch clusters; berries are red. The plant can reach 15 feet in height and width, with an arching habit. 'Repens' is a dwarf variety growing 12 inches tall. Zones 5-9.

Growing conditions. Grow cotoneaster in full sun or partial shade in well-drained, neutral to slightly alkaline soil. Mature plants will tolerate drought and wind. Propagate by cuttings or by layering.

Landscape uses. Plant cotoneaster as a ground cover in a rocky area where the outline of its branches can be enjoyed, or where it can spill over the top of a wall.

—

Cowberry see *Vaccinium*

Cranesbill see *Geranium*

Creeping Charlie see *Lysimachia*

Creeping Jennie see *Lysimachia*

Crown vetch see *Coronilla*

—

Cynodon (SIN-o-don)
Bermudagrass

Warm-season, medium- to high-maintenance turfgrass that is low-growing, vigorous and dense. It spreads by stolons and rhizomes and forms a tight sod. Regions B, C, E; it browns in the winter when temperatures drop below 50° F.

CORNUS CANADENSIS

CORONILLA VARIA

CORTADERIA SELLOANA

COTONEASTER HORIZONTALIS

CYNODON DACTYLON

CYPERUS ALTERNIFOLIUS

DACTYLIS GLOMERATA

DIANTHUS DELTOIDES

Selected species and varieties. *C. dactylon,* common Bermudagrass, is of fine to medium texture and ranges in color from light green to dark green. 'Midiron' is dark green, of medium texture and very cold-hardy. 'Midway' is blue-green, of medium texture, with good cold tolerance and minimum thatching. 'Ormond' is dark blue-green, medium textured and somewhat tolerant of wear. 'Santa Ana' is dark blue-green, has a medium texture, and tolerates wear and fluctuations of climate. 'Tifdwarf' is dark green, turning purple in cold winters, and fine textured. 'Tifgreen' is dark green, fine textured, and has excellent wear and drought tolerance. 'Tufcote' is medium dark green, of medium texture and has good wear tolerance.

Growing conditions. Bermudagrass will do well in full sun. Soil should be fine textured, fertile, well drained and have a pH that ranges between 5.5 and 7.5. The recommended mowing height is ½ to 1 inch. Fertilize Bermudagrass in early spring with 1 pound of nitrogen per 1,000 square feet and repeat in late spring and again in summer; or fertilize with ¾ pound of nitrogen per 1,000 square feet once a month for the eight-month season of active growth. Bermudagrass has good to excellent wear tolerance. It is susceptible to most turfgrass diseases and insects. The species can be propagated from seed, but named varieties must be grown from plugs or sprigs.

Landscape uses. Bermudagrass may be used in lawns that are subject to large volumes of foot traffic, as long as the high maintenance it requires is provided.

Cyperus (sy-PEER-us)

Semiaquatic ornamental grass that has long stems on top of which are sprays of foliage. Zone 10.

Selected species and varieties. *C. alternifolius,* umbrella plant, has slender stems 2 to 4 feet long. At the tops of the stems are 4- to 12-inch, lance-shaped leaves that hang down like the ribs of an umbrella. *C. papyrus,* paper plant, grows 6 to 8 feet tall and has 18-inch-long, drooping, threadlike leaves at the tops of the stems.

Growing conditions. Cyperus will flourish in full sun or light shade in rich, very moist soil. It may also be grown in pots submerged in water. Propagate cyperus by division or by cuttings.

Landscape uses. Plant cyperus by the side of a pool or a stream, or in pots in an ornamental pool.

Dactylis (DAK-ti-lis)

Perennial ornamental grass that has flat, rough and narrow leaf blades. Zones 5-10.

Selected species and varieties. *D. glomerata* 'Variegata', orchard grass, grows 1½ to 2 feet tall in dense, arching clumps. Leaves are striped in green and white. In summer seed heads form on one side of the stem only.

Growing conditions. Plant orchard grass in full sun or partial shade in light, well-drained soil. Propagate by division.

Landscape uses. Plant orchard grass as a ground cover, in a rock garden or as a specimen.

Daylily see *Hemerocallis*
Dead nettle see *Lamium*

Dianthus (dy-AN-thus)
Pinks

A broad group of annual, biennial and perennial plants, some of which are useful as ground covers. Leaves are narrow and grassy and have swollen joints. Small, five-petaled flowers blossom in dense clusters in spring or summer. Petals are often fringed, looking as if they had been cut with pinking shears. Zones 3-10.

Selected species and varieties. *D. deltoides,* maiden pink, is an evergreen perennial that forms a clump of blue-green leaves 3 to 9 inches tall. Flowers of white, pink or red blossom in summer. *D. gratianopolitanus,* cheddar pink, is an evergreen perennial that grows to a height of 6 to 8 inches and has gray-green leaves. Flowers of pink, white or red bloom singly in summer. Zones 5-10.

Growing conditions. Plant pinks in full sun or light shade in cool, neutral to alkaline, well-drained soil. Remove flowers after they have faded. Propagate by cuttings, division or layering, or from seeds.

Landscape uses. Plant pinks as a carpet plant in a rock garden or in any small area.

—

Dichondra (dy-KON-dra)

Perennial ground cover used as a lawn substitute in warm-season turfgrass areas. It has round to kidney-shaped, light green leaves that are ½ to 1 inch across. It spreads by underground runners. Zones 9 and 10.

Selected species and varieties. *D. micrantha* forms a low-growing, dense lawn. It has pale green flowers that are very small, sometimes inconspicuous, sometimes detracting noticeably from the appearance of the lawn.

Growing conditions. Grow dichondra in full sun to full shade in a fine-textured, rich, slightly acid, moist soil. Mow to a height of ½ to 1 inch whenever the cover looks uneven, which could be as infrequently as once per month. Fertilize with 1 pound of nitrogen per 1,000 square feet in early spring, late spring, summer and fall. Dichondra has limited wear tolerance and requires frequent watering. Leaf spot is the most serious disease problem. Propagate from seeds or with plugs.

Landscape uses. Choose dichondra as a substitute for turfgrass where foot traffic is limited. It grows well between stepping-stones.

—

Dogwood see *Cornus*
Dusty miller see *Artemisia*
English ivy see *Hedera*
English yew see *Taxus*

—

Epimedium (ep-i-MEE-dee-um)
Barrenwort

Evergreen or deciduous woody perennial ground cover with clumps of finely toothed, heart-shaped leaves. Foliage is light green and often tinged with red in spring and fall. On evergreen species, the old leaves fall when new leaves are produced in spring. Flowers bloom in clusters in spring and very often are hidden under the foliage. Both leaves and flowers have wiry stems. Zones 4-10.

Selected species and varieties. *E. alpinum,* Alpine epimedium, grows 10 inches high and is mostly evergreen. Flowers are red and yellow. *E. grandiflorum,* long-spurred epimedium, grows 12 inches tall and is semievergreen. Flowers are 1 to 2 inches across, larger than other epimediums, and may be white, yellow, pink or violet. New foliage is red in spring, and leaves turn bronze in fall. 'Rose Queen' has large fuchsia-colored flowers with white-tipped spurs. Zones 5-10. *E. × rubrum,* red epimedium, is deciduous and grows 12 to 15 inches tall. Flowers are bright pink to red and have white spurs. Foliage turns purple in fall. Zones 5-10. *E. × versicolor* is a 12-inch deciduous plant with green and purple foliage in spring, when the small yellow and red flowers are in bloom. 'Sulphureum' has yellow flowers. Zones 5-10.

Growing conditions. Plant barrenwort in partial shade. It will tolerate full sun in a cool climate; where the climate is hot, the foliage will burn in the sun. Soil should be rich and slightly acid. Moist soil is best, but barrenwort will tolerate dry conditions. Propagate by division.

Landscape uses. Plant barrenwort under trees and shrubs or as a ground cover in the front of a border.

Eragrostis (er-a-GROS-tis)
Love grass

Annual or perennial ornamental grass with fine-textured, narrow leaves and an erect or arching habit. Zones 5-10.

Selected species and varieties. *E. curvula,* weeping love grass, has tufted leaves at the base of the plant and light green foliage. Arching seed heads 10 to 15 inches long appear on 3- to 5-foot stems. They are dark gray-green when they form, and turn to brown as they age. *E. trichodes,* sand love grass, is a slightly spreading tufted plant that has a narrow seed head that opens into a spray 12 inches across. The head starts as purple and darkens to light brown on a 3- to 5-foot stem.

Growing conditions. Plant love grass in full sun and light, sandy, fertile soil. Propagate by division or from seeds.

Landscape uses. Plant love grass as a specimen, in a perennial border or in a naturalized area.

DICHONDRA MICRANTHA

EPIMEDIUM GRANDIFLORUM 'ROSE QUEEN'

ERAGROSTIS CURVULA

121

EREMOCHLOA OPHIUROIDES

ERIANTHUS RAVENNAE

ERICA CARNEA 'STARTLER'

EUONYMUS FORTUNEI 'SILVER QUEEN'

Eremochloa (er-e-MOK-lo-a)
Centipedegrass

Warm-season turfgrass that is slow-growing and of medium-coarse texture and spreads by thick, leafy stolons. Region C and warmest areas of B and E.

Selected species and varieties. *E. ophiuroides* is a low-growing, light green grass that may turn brown during cold winters.

Growing conditions. Plant centipedegrass in full sun or light shade. Soil should be of fine to medium texture, of low fertility and have a pH of 4.5 to 5.5. Mow to a height of 1 to 2 inches. Fertilize in spring with ½ to 1½ pounds of nitrogen per 1,000 square feet per year. Centipedegrass does not have good wear tolerance. It is relatively free of insect and disease problems. It may be propagated by seeds or plugs, but plugs are preferable because centipedegrass requires two seasons to become established from seed.

Landscape uses. Use centipedegrass in a low-maintenance lawn that receives minimum foot traffic.

Erianthus (er-ee-AN-thus)

Perennial, reedlike ornamental grass that has long, flat leaves and dense, silky, long seed heads in late summer. Zones 5-10.

Selected species and varieties. *E. ravennae,* ravenna grass, plume grass, is an upright grass with coarse, stiff, narrow leaves 3 feet long. Foliage is light green and turns brown after frost. Showy, 2-foot, silvery plumes appear on top of 7- to 14-foot stems and turn beige in fall.

Growing conditions. Plant plume grass in full sun in fertile, moist, well-drained soil. Propagate by division or from seeds.

Landscape uses. Grow plume grass as a tall accent plant or as a screen.

Erica (ER-i-ka)
Heath

Shrubby evergreen ground cover that has small, needlelike foliage that is held closely to the branches. Clusters of bell-shaped flowers of white, pink, rose, red or purple bloom in nodding spikes. Zones 3-9.

Selected species and varieties. *E. carnea,* spring heath, grows 6 to 18 inches tall and spreads from 1 to 6 feet across. Flowers bloom from winter into spring and may last from three to five months. Foliage is dark green and shiny. 'Startler' blooms in midseason with soft pink flowers. Zones 6-9. *E. cinerea,* twisted heath, grows 8 to 24 inches tall and spreads from 2 to 4 feet across. It has an open habit and dark green, shiny leaves that turn bronze in winter. Flowers bloom in summer. Zones 6-9. *E. tetralix,* cross-leaved heath, is an upright grower 12 inches high. Foliage is dark green with silvery undersides and is yellow, orange or red when immature. White or pink flowers bloom in summer and fall.

Growing conditions. Plant heath in full sun or, where summers are hot, in partial shade. Soil should be sandy, rich and well drained, and may be acid or alkaline. Do not let soil remain dry in summer. The roots are shallow and should be mulched. Heath does best where humidity is high and where there are no drying winds. Shear the plant after it flowers. Propagate by cuttings, by division or by layering.

Landscape uses. Grow heath as a low border or as a ground cover, especially among rocks or on a bank.

Eulalia grass see *Miscanthus*

Euonymus (yew-ON-i-mus)

Genus of deciduous and evergreen shrubs and vines, some of which make excellent ground covers. They are easy-care plants with smooth, waxy, leathery oval leaves. Flowers are green, yellow or white and are inconspicuous. Some species and varieties have berries. Zones 3-10.

Selected species and varieties. *E. fortunei,* wintercreeper, is an evergreen vine that roots as it grows along the ground. It grows to 12 to 24 inches tall and can spread to 20 feet. Foliage is ¾ to 2 inches across. Berries are round and pale pink. 'Colorata', purple wintercreeper, is 12 to 18 inches tall. Its leaves turn purple in fall and winter. Cream-colored berries open to reveal orange seeds. 'Minima' grows 2 inches high and has ¼-inch leaves with white veins. It rarely sets berries. 'Silver Queen' grows 2 feet high and 6 feet wide and has green and off-white foliage. It does not produce berries. Zones 5-9.

Growing conditions. Plant euonymus in full sun to full shade. Varieties with white on the foliage do best in the shade and will turn pink in the sun. Euonymus can be grown in any well-drained garden soil but does best in acid soil. Propagate by cuttings, by layering or by division.

Landscape uses. Plant euonymus in large areas under trees and shrubs or on rocks. It is useful where soil erosion control is needed.

—

Euphorbia (yew-FOR-bee-a)
Spurge

Large genus of succulent shrubs, perennials and annuals, some species of which are used as ground cover. All have thick leaves containing a juice that can be irritating to the skin. Flowers are tiny but are surrounded by colorful bracts. Zones 3-10.

Selected species and varieties. *E. cyparissias,* cypress spurge, running spurge, grows 12 inches high and spreads to 12 feet or more. Leaves are narrow, 1½ inches long and pale green, and have curled stems. Flowers are yellow and bloom in clusters.

Growing conditions. Plant spurge in full sun and dry, sandy, well-drained soil. It spreads quickly and can become quite invasive unless confined by an underground barrier or a low wall. Propagate by cuttings, by layering or from seeds.

Landscape uses. Grow cypress spurge in a large area, on a sunny bank or on a slope.

—

Feather grass see *Stipa*
Feather reed grass
see *Calamagrostis*
Feathertop see *Pennisetum*
Fescue see *Festuca*

—

Festuca (fes-TOO-ka)
Fescue

Perennial cool-season and transitional zone turfgrass; also an ornamental grass. Regions A and F; northern parts of B and E; D with irrigation.

Selected species and varieties. *F. amethystina,* large blue fescue, is an ornamental grass with upright tufts of fine blue foliage growing 18 inches high. Seed heads are small, fine textured and white. *F. arundinacea,* tall fescue, is a coarse, bunching, medi-

um to dark green turfgrass with wide blades. 'Arid' is medium to dark green, medium textured and has excellent heat and drought tolerance. 'Falcon' is low-growing, medium textured and medium green. 'Finelawn' is similar to 'Falcon' but has better shade tolerance. 'Houndog' is medium green and medium textured, and is the most heat- and drought-tolerant tall fescue. 'Jaguar' is medium textured and has good heat, drought and shade tolerance. 'Kentucky 31' shows better tolerance of climatic extremes than other tall fescues. It is coarse in texture and has been largely replaced by varieties with finer texture. 'Marathon' is similar to 'Jaguar' but has little shade tolerance. 'Mustang' is a low-growing variety that has fine to medium texture and very good shade tolerance. It is darker green than most other tall fescues. 'Olympic' is dark green, medium textured and has good heat tolerance. 'Rebel' is medium green, fine textured and has good shoot density.

F. duriuscola, hard fescue, is coarse textured, blue-green and grows in a tufted form. 'Aurora' is medium to dark green and very fine textured. 'Biljart' is dark green and fine textured. 'Reliant' is medium to dark green, fine textured and has excellent disease resistance. 'Waldina' is dark green and fine textured.

F. ovina, sheep fescue, is a relatively low-quality, tufted turfgrass with a fine texture and blue-green leaves. *F. ovina glauca,* blue fescue, is an ornamental grass with tufts of fine blue leaves. It grows 8 to 12 inches high.

F. rubra commutata, Chewings fescue, is a fine-textured, medium to dark green grass that has a bunching habit. 'Agram' is dark green and low-growing. 'Atlanta' is medium green and has good heat tolerance. 'Banner' is dark green and especially suited for coastal climates because it tolerates humidity. 'Checker' is medium green and of extremely fine texture. 'Jamestown' is medium dark green, with a low growth habit. 'Shadow' is dark green and has good disease resistance.

F. rubra rubra, creeping red fescue, is a fine-textured, medium to dark green grass that has a creeping habit. 'Ensylva' is medium dark green and has excellent drought tolerance. 'Flyer' is medium dark green and heat-tolerant. 'Illahee' is dense, slow-growing and medium green, and cannot survive low temperatures. 'Pennlawn' is dense, fast-growing, uniform and medium dark green. 'Rainier' is dark green and fast-growing.

EUPHORBIA CYPARISSIAS

FESTUCA ARUNDINACEA 'REBEL'

FESTUCA OVINA GLAUCA

123

FRAGARIA VESCA

GALIUM ODORATUM

GAULTHERIA PROCUMBENS

Creeping red, Chewings and hard fescue are all called "fine fescue" for their fine-textured leaves.

Growing conditions. Plant fescue in sun or partial shade. Creeping red fescue is the most shade-tolerant of the fescues, followed by hard fescue. Soil for tall fescue should be fertile, moist, rich and fine textured, with a pH of 5.5 to 6.5, although a pH as high as 8.5 will be tolerated. Tall fescue will tolerate wet soil. Soil for sheep fescue should be sandy or gravelly, acidic and of low fertility. Soil for creeping red fescue, Chewings fescue, blue fescue and hard fescue should be dry and sandy and should have a pH of 5.5 to 6.5. Creeping red fescue will not tolerate wet soil.

Mow tall fescue from 1½ to 2¼ inches high; sheep fescue, hard fescue and creeping red fescue from 1 to 2½ inches high; Chewings fescue from 1½ to 2 inches high, although it will tolerate lower heights.

Fertilize tall fescue with 2½ to 6 pounds of nitrogen per 1,000 square feet per year. Sheep fescue should not be fertilized. Fertilize hard fescue, creeping red fescue and Chewings fescue with 1¼ to 3 pounds of nitrogen per 1,000 square feet per year. Tall fescue is one of the most drought- and wear-tolerant turfgrasses and is more heat-tolerant than most cool-season grasses. Sheep fescue is drought-tolerant but not heat-tolerant and has good wear tolerance. Most creeping red fescues are not heat-tolerant but are drought-tolerant, and have medium wear tolerance. Hard fescue is heat-, drought- and wear-tolerant. Chewings fescue does not tolerate extremes in temperature but has quite good wear tolerance and drought tolerance. Propagate all fescues from seeds; blue fescue may also be propagated by division.

Landscape uses. Tall fescue should be used in lawns that are subject to heavy traffic, and only the finer varieties blend well with other turfgrasses. Sheep fescue is used in low-quality lawns that will not be maintained. Creeping red fescue is used in seed mixtures with other turfgrasses and is best suited to dry lawns that are located in the shade and have moderate foot traffic. Chewings and hard fescue lawns will tolerate more foot traffic than red fescue but not as much as tall fescue. Blue fescue is used as an accent plant and in borders.

Fleeceflower see *Polygonum*

Foamflower see *Tiarella*
Forget-me-not see *Myosotis*
Fountain grass see *Pennisetum*
Foxtail see *Alopecurus*

Fragaria (fra-GAR-ee-a)
Strawberry

Fast-growing perennial ground cover with three-part, dark green, oval leaves. White, six-petaled flowers are followed by edible, bumpy red fruit. Plants spread by runners at the ends of which new plantlets grow. Zones 5-10.

Selected species and varieties. *F. chiloensis,* beach strawberry, sand strawberry, forms a compact and bushy mat 6 to 8 inches high. Flowers 1 inch across have prominent yellow stamens. Fruits are ¾ inch long. Leaves 1 to 2 inches long have blue undersides. *F. vesca* grows 8 to 12 inches tall. Flowers are ½ to ¾ inch across; fruits are ⅜ to ¾ inch in diameter. Both flowers and fruits are borne throughout the season. Zones 5 and 6.

Growing conditions. Plant strawberries in full sun in slightly acid, well-drained soil. Remove runners and plantlets to keep plants from becoming invasive. Propagate from seeds or from rooted plantlets.

Landscape uses. Grow strawberries in large, sunny areas. They are especially effective at the seashore and in informal gardens.

Funkia see *Hosta*

Galium (GAY-lee-um)

Perennial ground cover that spreads by creeping stems that are encircled with whorls of lance-shaped, 1-inch, shiny green leaves. Zones 5-10.

Selected species and varieties. *G. odoratum,* sweet woodruff, grows 6 to 12 inches tall and spreads to 24 inches across. White, star-shaped, four-part flowers bloom in clusters in spring.

Growing conditions. Plant sweet woodruff in partial to full shade in moist, well-drained, slightly acid soil. Prune back each spring to prevent the plant from becoming leggy. Propagate from seeds or by division.

Landscape uses. Grow sweet woodruff under trees or shrubs in a woodland garden. Its leaves and stems are aromatic when dried, and are used in flavoring May wine.

—

Gaultheria (gaul-THEER-ee-a)

Low-growing, evergreen shrubby ground cover that has small, drooping, bell-shaped white flowers in spring or early summer followed by attractive berries in fall. Zones 3-10.

Selected species and varieties. *G. procumbens,* wintergreen, grows 3 to 5 inches high and spreads 12 to 18 inches across. Foliage is oval, 2 inches long and glossy green, turning red or purple in cold winters. Berries are red and edible; they have a wintergreen aroma and flavor.

Growing conditions. Plant wintergreen in partial shade in rich, moist, acid, well-drained soil. Propagate from seeds or by cuttings, division or layering.

Landscape uses. Plant wintergreen as a ground cover under trees or shrubs or where it will cascade over a wall or rocks.

—

Gazania (ga-ZAY-nee-a)

Perennial ground cover grown as an annual in areas where it is not hardy. Oblong leaves grow from the base of the plant. Daisylike flowers of yellow, gold, white, pink or orange bloom atop leafless stems that are 6 to 16 inches high. Blooms often have a black or white spot at the base of the petals and close at night and during cloudy weather. Zones 9 and 10.

Selected species and varieties. *G. rigens,* treasure flower, is a clumping plant with dark green leaves that have gray-green undersides. Flowers are 3 to 4 inches across. *G. rigens leucolaena* spreads by means of long, trailing stems. Foliage is silvery gray; flowers are 1½ to 2½ inches across.

Growing conditions. Grow gazania in full sun in dry, sandy, well-drained soil. Where grown as a perennial, it may be mowed every spring. Propagate by cuttings or division or from seeds.

Landscape uses. Clumping gazania is used as a filler between shrubs or as a ground cover along walkways. Trailing gazania is used in large areas and along slopes.

Genista (je-NIS-ta)
Broom

Low-growing, evergreen or deciduous shrub with divided leaves and pealike yellow or white flowers at the ends of the branches in spring or summer. It looks evergreen even when deciduous, as the thin branches remain green all winter. Zones 5-9.

Selected species and varieties. *G. pilosa* is a deciduous, fast-growing shrub whose stems root as they spread along the ground. Ascending, arching branches grow 4 to 15 inches high and spread 3 to 6 feet across. Leaves are gray-green, ¼ to ½ inch long and round to oval. 'Vancouver Gold' is 4 to 6 inches tall and has abundant gold flowers. *G. sagittalis* grows rapidly to 12 inches and produces yellow flowers in late spring and early summer.

Growing conditions. Grow broom in full sun and dry, slightly acid, well-drained soil. Do not fertilize. Broom does not transplant well. Propagate by layering or cuttings or from seeds.

Landscape uses. Plant broom on a slope, on top of a wall or as an edging to a shrub border.

—

Geranium (je-RAY-nee-um)
Cranesbill

Mounded or trailing perennial, some species of which are used as ground covers. Leaves are round and lobed or dissected. Flowers have five rounded petals and bloom from late spring through summer. Cranesbill should not be confused with the garden geranium, which belongs to the genus *Pelargonium.* Zones 4-10.

Selected species and varieties. *G. sanguineum* is 9 to 18 inches tall and has stems that spread to 24 inches across. Hairy, medium to dark green leaves turn red in fall. Flowers are 1 inch across and pink, red, purple or white. *G. sanguineum prostratum,* sometimes designated *G. lancastrense,* is 10 inches tall and has light pink flowers with red veins.

Growing conditions. Cranesbill grows best in full sun or light shade in rich, moist, well-drained soil, but it will tolerate dry soil. Propagate by division or cuttings or from seeds.

Landscape uses. Cranesbill may be planted on banks, on top of walls or as a border.

GAZANIA RIGENS

GENISTA SAGITTALIS

GERANIUM SANGUINEUM

GLYCERIA MAXIMA 'VARIEGATA'

HAKONECHLOA MACRA 'AUREOLA'

HEDERA HELIX

HELIANTHEMUM NUMMULARIUM 'WISLEY PINK'

Germander see *Teucrium*

Giant reed see *Arundo*

Ginger see *Asarum*

—

Glyceria (gli-SEER-ee-a)

Perennial ornamental grass that spreads to form upright clumps of rough leaves. Seed heads are airy and heavily branched. Zones 5-10.

Selected species and varieties. *G. maxima* 'Variegata', sweet grass, manna grass, is 2½ to 3 feet tall, with erect leaves at the center of the plant and arching leaves at the edges. Leaves are 18 to 24 inches long, 2 inches wide, and striped with white or pale yellow.

Growing conditions. Grow sweet grass in full sun in rich, fertile, moist soil. It may become invasive. Propagate by division.

Landscape uses. Sweet grass is suited for use as an accent plant at the edge of water or in a few inches of water. It may also be grown as a container plant.

—

Goutweed see *Aegopodium*

Ground pink see *Phlox*

—

Hakonechloa (hak-o-ne-KLO-a)

Perennial ornamental grass that spreads slowly by means of stolons and has soft, smooth leaves and delicate, open seed heads in late summer. Zones 5-10.

Selected species and varieties. *H. macra* grows 18 inches tall, with arching, dense, 9-inch, dark green leaves that grow with the appearance of being windswept. The cultivar 'Aureola' has bright yellow leaves with fine, warm green stripes. The blades are sometimes tinged with pink or bronze.

Growing conditions. Grow hakonechloa in light shade; it tolerates full sun but will lose its color. Soil should be fertile and well drained. Propagate by division or from seeds.

Landscape uses. Plant hakonechloa in front of shrubs, as a specimen, as a ground cover or in a container.

—

Harebell see *Campanula*

Heath see *Erica*

Heather see *Calluna*

—

Hedera (HED-e-ra)
Ivy

Woody evergreen vine that may be trained to grow either upright or as a ground cover. Ivies grown as ground covers generally have lobed leaves and seldom flower or set fruit. Stems root as they grow along the ground. Zones 5-10.

Selected species and varieties. *H. canariensis,* Algerian ivy, is a fast-growing vine that is 12 inches high when grown as a ground cover. Leaves are rounded to heart-shaped, shiny, rich green, have three to seven lobes and are 5 to 8 inches long. Zones 8-10. *H. helix,* English ivy, grows 6 inches high when grown as a ground cover. Leaves are dark green and dull on the upper surfaces, lighter on the undersides, 2 to 5 inches across and have three to five lobes. Zones 6-10. 'Baltica', Baltic ivy, has 2-inch lobed leaves with white veins that turn purple in winter. '238th Street' has lobeless leaves and withstands adverse environmental conditions. There are also many varieties with green leaves variegated in silver or white.

Growing conditions. Grow ivy in sun or shade; variegated varieties are better grown in partial shade or their leaves will burn. Rich, moist, well-drained soil is preferred, although ivy will tolerate poor, dry soil. Prune ivy once or twice each year to control its growth, especially near low-growing shrubs. Ivy may also be mowed. Ivy may become a habitat for rodents and pests when thick. Propagate by cuttings. Cuttings rooted from stems with immature, lobed leaves will produce plants with lobed foliage only, unless allowed to climb.

Landscape uses. Plant ivy under and around trees and shrubs, on banks and level ground, or where soil erosion control is needed. Algerian ivy should be used only in a large area since it grows so quickly.

—

Helianthemum
(he-lee-AN-the-mum)
Rock rose, sun rose

Woody shrub or perennial ground cover with spreading branches that root as they grow along the ground. Leaves are narrow, 1 inch long, and may be gray-green, silver or dark shiny green. Single or double rose-like flowers blossom in clusters in late spring and early summer. Zones 5-10.

Selected species and varieties. *H. nummularium* grows 6 to 8 inches high and spreads to 3 feet across. Flowers have five petals and are 1 to 2 inches across with a soft texture. Although each flower lasts only one day, the plant will bloom for several months. 'Aureum' has dark yellow flowers; 'Roseum' has pale pink ones. 'Wisley Pink' has rose-pink flowers. There are also varieties with white or red flowers. Foliage is hairy, oval and pointed.

Growing conditions. Grow rock rose in full sun and a dry or moist, sandy, neutral to alkaline soil that has excellent drainage. Prune after flowering to encourage a second bloom. Protect from winter wind. Rock rose does not like to be transplanted. Propagate by cuttings or from seeds.

Landscape uses. Plant rock rose on slopes, where it can spill over a rock or a wall, or where a fire-resistant plant is needed.

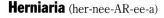

Helictotrichon
(hel-ik-toh-TRY-kon)

Perennial ornamental grass that forms a clump of stiff, fine-textured, arching blades. Narrow seed heads form on one side of a tall, erect stem. Zones 5-10.

Selected species and varieties. *H. sempervirens,* sometimes designated *Avena sempervirens,* blue oat grass, avena grass, has narrow, blue leaves 12 to 24 inches tall and seed heads that form on 3- to 4-foot stems.

Growing conditions. Grow blue oat grass in full sun or light shade in well-drained, neutral soil. It is drought-resistant once established. Propagate by division or from seeds.

Landscape uses. Blue oat grass may be used as a specimen or in a massed planting.

Hemerocallis (hem-er-o-KAL-is)
Daylily

Perennial ground cover that has arching, narrow, grasslike leaves and funnel-shaped flowers in clusters at the ends of tall, erect stems. Al-

though each flower lasts only one day, the plant will bloom for a period of three weeks or more during the summer, depending on the variety. Zones 3-10; some varieties are evergreen in Zones 6-10.

Selected species and varieties. Most of the daylilies available for gardeners are complex hybrids. By selecting varieties that are early-, mid-season- and late-blooming, you can have garden color throughout the season. Plants grow from 1 to 6 feet high and have single, semidouble or double, 3- to 8-inch flowers of white, yellow, gold, orange, red, pink, lavender or purple. 'Hyperion' grows 48 inches tall and has fragrant, soft yellow flowers in middle to late summer. 'Stella d'Oro' is 24 inches tall and has the longest blooming period of any daylily, from early to late summer. Flowers are rich gold. 'Tree Swallow' is 24 inches tall and has ruffled flowers of orchid pink with darker veining in late summer.

Growing conditions. Grow daylilies in full sun to partial shade in any garden soil. Daylilies are very easy to grow and will tolerate a wide range of growing conditions. When they become overcrowded, divide—in spring or fall. Propagate by division or from seeds, although seeds may not come true to variety.

Landscape uses. Plant daylilies on banks, in wide borders and where soil erosion control is needed.

Hen-and-chickens
see *Sempervivum*

Herniaria (her-nee-AR-ee-a)

Perennial ground cover that spreads by rooting stems densely covered with small, bright green foliage. Zones 6-10; evergreen Zones 8-10.

Selected species and varieties. *H. glabra,* rupturewort, grows into a mat 3 inches high and has ¼-inch, smooth, oblong leaves that turn bronze to red in the fall. Flowers are inconspicuous.

Growing conditions. Plant rupturewort in full sun or light shade in any garden soil that is well drained. Propagate by division or from seeds.

Landscape uses. Plant rupturewort between rocks or stepping-stones.

HELICTOTRICHON SEMPERVIRENS

HEMEROCALLIS 'HYPERION'

HERNIARIA GLABRA

127

HOSTA FORTUNEI 'AUREO-MARGINATA'

HOSTA LANCIFOLIA

HOSTA SIEBOLDIANA 'ELEGANS'

HOUTTUYNIA CORDATA 'VARIEGATA'

Honeysuckle see *Lonicera*

Hosta (HOS-ta)
Plantain lily, funkia

Perennial ground cover that has mounds of foliage at the base of the plant. Leaves vary in size from several inches to more than a foot in length; vary in shape from long and narrow to round; and are known for their colors of green, blue, yellow and gold, which may be solid or variegated. Many leaves are also deeply textured. Spikes of white, blue or lavender tubular flowers appear during the summer. Zones 4-9.

Selected species and varieties. *H. fortunei* grows 2 feet tall and has 5-inch, oval, ribbed leaves. Flowers are lavender, and appear in early summer in 3-foot spikes. 'Albo-marginata' has green leaves edged in white and flowers in late summer. 'Albo-picta' leaves turn from bright yellow in spring to light green in summer. The plant blooms in midsummer. 'Aureo-marginata' has green leaves with yellow edges. *H. lancifolia,* narrow plantain lily, grows 12 inches high and has glossy, dark green, pointed, 6-inch leaves. Spikes of lavender flowers bloom on 2-foot stems in late summer. *H. plantaginea,* fragrant plantain lily, grows 18 inches tall and has bright green, rounded, 10-inch leaves. Flowers are fragrant, 5 inches long, pale lavender to white and bloom on 2-foot stems in late summer. 'Grandiflora' has bright, medium green leaves. 'Royal Standard' has pale green leaves.

H. sieboldiana, blue-leaved plantain lily, grows 15 inches high and has 15-inch, heart-shaped, blue leaves that are deeply quilted. Lavender flowers bloom in early summer and are often hidden by the leaves. 'Elegans' grows 18 inches high and has hairy, blue-green leaves. 'Frances Williams' grows 4 feet tall and has large, round leaves that are blue-green with golden yellow margins. *H. undulata,* wavy-leaf plantain lily, is 12 inches tall and has 6- to 8-inch leaves with wavy margins. Lavender flowers bloom on 3-foot stems in midsummer. 'Albo-marginata' has green leaves that have white margins. Flower stems are 48 inches tall. 'Medio-picta' has 12-inch, wavy green leaves with white and gold centers. Flowering stems are 18 inches high. *H. ventricosa,* blue plantain lily, has rich green, round to heart-shaped, ribbed foliage and 3-foot spikes of blue flowers in late summer.

'Aureo-marginata' is similar but its leaves have yellow edges.

There are also a number of hosta hybrids. 'Antioch' grows 18 to 24 inches high and has leaves with green centers and gold or cream on the outer half. 'Francee' grows 18 inches tall and has heavily textured, dark green leaves with white margins. Lavender flowers bloom in late summer. 'Gold Standard' grows 18 inches high. Foliage is ribbed and light green with blue-green edges. Lavender flowers bloom in midsummer on 36-inch stems. 'Krossa Regal' has solid green, leathery, heavily veined leaves on a 3-foot plant. Spikes of lavender flowers are 5 feet high and bloom in midsummer.

Growing conditions. Plant most hostas in partial to full shade; wavy-leaf plantain lily will grow in full sun and shade. Soil should be moist, rich and well drained, but hostas will tolerate drought. Hostas are easy to grow but they are a favorite of slugs. Propagate by division. Hosta can be grown from seeds, but may not come true to variety.

Landscape uses. Plant hosta under trees, along a shady walkway, in a massed planting, as an edging or as a specimen.

Houseleek see *Sempervivum*

Houttuynia (hoo-TIN-ee-a)

Perennial ground cover that spreads by underground stems. Heart-shaped foliage is 2 to 3 inches long. Summer-blooming white flowers have a cone-shaped center that stands ½ inch above a rim of bracts. Zones 3-8.

Selected species and varieties. *H. cordata* grows 12 inches high and spreads to 18 inches across. Leaves are dark green tinged with metallic crimson, turn purple in fall and have a citrus fragrance. 'Chameleon' grows 6 to 9 inches high and has foliage of yellow, green, bronze and red. 'Flore Pleno' has double flowers. 'Variegata' has leaves splashed with green, cream and crimson.

Growing conditions. Plant houttuynia in partial to full shade in rich, moist soil. 'Chameleon' will tolerate full sun, and when grown in full sun, its leaves turn redder than when grown in the shade. Propagate by division or from seeds.

Landscape uses. Plant houttuynia under trees or by streams or ponds.

Hypericum (hy-PER-i-kum)
St.-John's-wort

Perennial or evergreen shrub that can be grown as a ground cover. It has shiny, light to medium green leaves and cup-shaped, golden yellow flowers that have prominent stamens. Zones 2-9.

Selected species and varieties. *H. calycinum* grows 12 inches high and spreads to 24 inches across. Foliage is light to medium green and has silvery undersides. Flowers are 2 to 3 inches across and appear throughout the summer.

Growing conditions. Plant St.-John's-wort in full sun or partial shade in any garden soil. It prefers moisture but will tolerate drought. Do not overfertilize. Shear back in early spring before growth starts to keep the plant compact. Propagate by cuttings, division or layering, or from seeds.

Landscape uses. Plant St.-John's-wort on banks, under trees, where soil erosion control is needed or in a large rock garden.

Iberis (i-BER-is)
Candytuft

Annual or perennial ground cover that has clusters of small, four-petaled flowers. Zones 4-10.

Selected species and varieties. *I. sempervirens* is an evergreen perennial that grows 9 to 12 inches tall and spreads into a mound 1½ to 3 feet across. Leaves are dark green, narrow, 1½ inches long and smothered by 1½-inch clusters of white flowers in midspring. 'Autumn Snow' grows 9 inches high, spreads to 3 feet wide and reblooms in the fall. 'Snowflake' grows 10 inches tall, 2 feet wide and has the largest flower of the perennial candytufts.

Growing conditions. Plant candytuft in full sun or partial shade in any well-drained garden soil. It tolerates drought but grows better in moist soil. Shear the plant after it flowers to keep it compact. Do not plant it where it will be subjected to winter winds. Propagate by cuttings or layering or from seeds.

Landscape uses. Plant candytuft in a rock garden, atop a wall or as an edging.

Ice plant see *Lampranthus*

Imperata (im-per-AH-ta)

Perennial ornamental grass that has tufts of rigid, erect, flat leaf blades. Zones 5-10.

Selected species and varieties. *I. cylindrica rubra,* Japanese blood grass, is a tufted, upright plant with leaf blades that are green on the bottom and bright red on the top. 'Red Baron' grows 18 to 24 inches tall and has extremely bright red leaves.

Growing conditions. Plant blood grass in full sun or light shade in moist, fertile, well-drained soil. Propagate by division.

Landscape uses. Plant blood grass as a specimen, as an accent or in a border.

Iris (I-ris)

Perennial or bulbous plants that have narrow, grassy or swordlike leaves. One species is grown as a ground cover. Flowers consist of erect parts known as standards and drooping parts known as falls. Zones 3-9.

Selected species and varieties. *I. cristata,* crested iris, grows to a height of 4 to 6 inches, forming a dense, spreading mat. Leaves are light green in color and ½ inch wide. Flowers of lavender or light blue have hairy white and yellow protrusions known as crests and bloom in midspring.

Growing conditions. Plant crested iris in partial shade; it will tolerate full sun only if the climate is cool and moist. Soil should be rich, acid and kept well watered. Propagate by division.

Landscape uses. Crested iris may be planted by the side of water, along steps, on slopes, between rocks or in front of shrubs.

Irish moss see *Arenaria; Sagina*
Ivy see *Hedera*
Japanese lawngrass see *Zoysia*

HYPERICUM CALYCINUM

IBERIS SEMPERVIRENS

IMPERATA CYLINDRICA RUBRA

IRIS CRISTATA

JUNCUS EFFUSUS 'SPIRALIS'

JUNIPERUS CONFERTA 'BLUE PACIFIC'

LAMIASTRUM GALEOBDOLON 'VARIEGATUM'

Juncus (JUNK-us)
Rush

Perennial ornamental grass that has round or three-sided stems, and clusters of brown or green flowers and seed heads halfway up the stem. Zones 3-10.

Selected species and varieties. *J. effusus,* soft rush, grows 2 to 3 feet tall and has upright and slightly arching light green leaves that may turn orange-red in the fall. 'Spiralis' grows 18 inches tall and has twisted stems that grow upright as well as along the ground. 'Zebrinus' has leaves banded horizontally in white or light green.

Growing conditions. Plant rush in sun or shade in very moist or even boggy soil. Propagate by division or from seeds.

Landscape uses. Plant rush next to or in water. It may also be planted in a container that is submerged in water.

Juniper see *Juniperus*

Juniperus (joo-NIP-er-us)
Juniper

Large genus of coniferous evergreen trees and shrubs, some of which are used for ground covers. Juvenile foliage is sharp and needlelike; mature foliage is softer and scalelike. Some plants have only one type of foliage or the other; some plants have both. Foliage may be light to dark green, blue-green, blue, silver or touched with gold, and often turns purple in winter. Female plants produce small, round, blue berries that are used to flavor gin. Zones 2-10.

Selected species and varieties. *J. chinensis,* Chinese juniper, has either scalelike or needlelike foliage. 'Gold Coast' has fine-textured foliage that is golden yellow when new. It grows 12 to 18 inches high and 4 to 5 feet wide. 'San Jose' grows 6 to 12 inches high and 6 to 8 feet wide, and has both scalelike and needlelike blue-green foliage. *J. chinensis procumbens,* Japanese garden juniper, grows 1 to 2 feet tall and 10 to 15 feet wide with ascending branches. It has blue-green, needlelike foliage. 'Nana' is similar in appearance but grows only half the size.

J. chinensis sargentii grows 18 inches high with scalelike leaves and stiff branches that spread to 10 feet across. Zones 4-9. *J. conferta,* shore juniper, has soft, blue-green, needlelike leaves and grows 1 foot high and 6 to 8 feet across. 'Blue Pacific' has blue foliage and grows 9 inches tall. Zones 6-9. *J. horizontalis,* creeping juniper, has blue-green, mostly scalelike foliage that turns purple in winter. The cultivar 'Bar Harbor' grows 8 to 12 inches tall and spreads to 8 feet wide. It has thin, horizontal branches and blue foliage. 'Plumosa', Andorra juniper, grows 18 to 36 inches tall and 10 feet wide, with gray-green foliage. Branches turn upward at a 45° angle. Zones 3-9.

Growing conditions. Plant juniper in full sun in acid to neutral, dry, well-drained soil. Do not overwater. Propagate by cuttings, by layering or from seeds.

Landscape uses. Junipers make good ground covers on slopes where soil erosion control is needed.

Lamiastrum (lay-mee-AS-trum)

Perennial ground cover that has square, hairy stems and coarsely toothed dark green leaves that give off a sharp odor when they are rubbed. Yellow flowers bloom in whorls in late spring and early summer. They sometimes have brown spots and are lipped like snapdragon flowers. Zones 4-10; evergreen Zones 7-10.

Selected species and varieties. *L. galeobdolon,* sometimes designated *Lamium galeobdolon,* yellow archangel, grows 8 to 12 inches high and spreads rapidly to 2 feet or more across, rooting as it spreads. Leaves are heart-shaped and 1½ to 3 inches in length; flowers are ¾ inch long. 'Variegatum' has silvery markings on its foliage.

Growing conditions. Plant yellow archangel in partial to full shade. Any garden soil will do, but rich, moist soil is best. Yellow archangel is drought-tolerant once established. It is sometimes invasive but can be controlled with an underground barrier. Propagate by division or by cuttings.

Landscape uses. Plant yellow archangel under trees and shrubs or in woodland gardens.

Lamium (LAY-mee-um)
Dead nettle

Perennial ground cover that is very similar in appearance to *Lamiastrum* except for the flower color, and is not as invasive. It has square, hairy stems and coarsely toothed leaves. Flowers are lipped and resemble snapdragons. They bloom in late spring and early summer. Zones 4-9.

Selected species and varieties. *L. maculatum,* spotted dead nettle, grows 8 to 12 inches high and spreads to 2 feet across, rooting as it spreads. Leaves are heart-shaped to oval, 1½ to 2 inches long and dark green with white markings along the central vein. They may turn pink or purple in the fall. Flowers are purple and 1 inch long. 'Album' has white flowers; 'Beacon Silver', grows 6 to 8 inches high, has pink flowers and has foliage with silvery markings; 'Variegatum' has leaves that are silver with green margins; 'White Nancy' has white flowers.

Growing conditions. Plant spotted dead nettle in partial to full shade. Any garden soil will do, but rich, moist soil is best. Spotted dead nettle is drought-tolerant once established. Propagate by division, by cuttings or from seeds.

Landscape uses. Plant spotted dead nettle under trees and shrubs, in woodland and rock gardens.

Lampranthus (lam-PRAN-thus)
Ice plant

Upright or trailing, perennial or shrubby ground cover that has succulent, curved, solid, three-sided, gray-green foliage. Yellow, orange, white, pink, purple or red daisylike flowers bloom during late winter and spring. Zones 9 and 10.

Selected species and varieties. *L. aureus* grows 18 inches tall and has transparent dots on 2-inch, spiny

leaves. Flowers are glossy, orange and 2½ inches across. *L. spectabilis,* trailing ice plant, grows 3 inches high and spreads to 12 inches across. Leaves are 3 inches long; flowers are 3 inches across and have purple, red, pink or rose petals.

Growing conditions. Plant ice plant in full sun in dry, well-drained soil. Ice plant is drought-tolerant and should not be overwatered. Propagate by cuttings or from seeds.

Landscape uses. Plant ice plant in a rock garden, on a dry slope or in a flat area.

Lantana (lan-TAN-a)

Perennial or shrubby ground cover that is often grown as an annual where it is not hardy. Small, tubular flowers bloom in dense, round clusters or spikes and change color as they age. Zones 9 and 10.

Selected species and varieties. *L. montevidensis,* trailing lantana, rapidly grows 12 to 18 inches tall and spreads from 3 to 6 feet wide. Leaves are rough textured, oval, 1 inch long and coarsely toothed. They are usually dark green but often turn purple in the winter. They have a sharp odor when crushed. Yellow, white, orange, pink, red or lilac flowers bloom on and off all year in round clusters at the ends of the branches.

Growing conditions. Plant lantana in full sun; it will mildew in shade. It will grow in any well-drained garden soil, but poor, dry soil is best. Fertilization will result in lush growth but few flowers. Prune back in early spring. Lantana will tolerate windy sites. Propagate by cuttings or from seeds.

Landscape uses. Plant lantana where it will cascade over walls and rocks or on dry banks, especially where soil erosion control is needed.

Leiophyllum (ly-o-FIL-um)
Sand myrtle

Compact, evergreen shrub with upright branches and shiny, leathery, oval, ½-inch leaves. Waxy, ¼-inch pink or white starlike flowers open from pink buds in 1-inch clusters in late spring. Zones 6-10.

Selected species and varieties. *L. buxifolium* grows 18 to 36 inches high and spreads to 36 inches across

LAMIUM MACULATUM 'BEACON SILVER'

LAMPRANTHUS SPECTABILIS

LEIOPHYLLUM BUXIFOLIUM PROSTRATUM

LANTANA MONTEVIDENSIS

LIRIOPE MUSCARI 'VARIEGATA'

LOLIUM PERENNE 'PALMER'

in a mounded form. Foliage turns bronze in autumn. *L. buxifolium prostratum* grows 10 inches tall and has low-spreading branches.

Growing conditions. Grow sand myrtle in partial shade in acid, moist, rich, well-drained soil. Propagate by cuttings or by layering.

Landscape uses. Plant sand myrtle in a rock garden, as a low edging, or on top of a wall or a ledge. It tolerates seashore conditions.

Lily-of-the-valley
see *Convallaria*

Lily turf see *Liriope; Ophiopogon*

Lippia see *Phyla*

Liriope (li-RY-o-pee)
Lily turf

Perennial ground cover that forms tufts of grassy, dark green foliage. Some varieties are variegated. Flowers bloom in late summer or fall on 4- to 8-inch spikes. Zones 5-10.

Selected species and varieties. *L. muscari,* blue lily turf, grows 12 to 18 inches tall and has ½-inch-wide leaves that grow in non-spreading, upright, arching clumps. Flowers are lilac, purple or white. Zones 6-10. *L. spicata,* creeping lily turf, grows 8 to 10 inches tall and spreads to 18 inches across. Leaves are ¼ inch wide and often hide the flowers, which are lilac, blue or white.

Growing conditions. Lily turf grows in full sun to full shade and does best in rich, moist, well-drained soil; it tolerates dry, poor soil. It may be mowed. Propagate by division.

Landscape uses. Plant lily turf under trees and shrubs, as an edging, or on hot slopes or flat areas. It tolerates seashore conditions.

Little Sur manzanita
see *Arctostaphylos*

Live forever see *Sempervivum*

Lolium (LO-lee-um)
Ryegrass

Annual or perennial cool-season turfgrass that may be upright or bunching. Regions A and F where winters are not colder than −20°; D with irrigation; B, C and E to over-seed warm-season grasses that turn brown in winter.

Selected species and varieties. *L. multiflorum,* annual ryegrass, Italian ryegrass, is light green and has a coarse texture. It is an annual grass, is neither cold- nor heat-tolerant, and is used primarily for temporary, quick cover while other grasses are becoming established or for overseeding warm-season grasses for winter color. *L. perenne,* perennial ryegrass, is medium to dark green with light green undersides and medium texture. Improved varieties known as turf-type perennial rye-grasses have a darker green color, finer texture, increased weather tolerance and blend well with other grasses in mixtures. 'All*Star' is medium dark green, fine textured, very drought-resistant and insect-resistant. 'Citation II' is dark green with medium-fine texture. It has good heat tolerance, is easier to mow than most ryegrasses and is insect-resistant. 'Diplomat' is medium dark green, fine textured and mows well. It has poor heat tolerance. 'Manhattan' is medium green, fine textured, mows well and has good cold tolerance. 'NK-200' is dark green, medium textured and has good cold tolerance. 'Omega II' is dark green, fine textured and mows well. 'Palmer' is very dark green, of medium-fine texture and very wear-tolerant. 'Pennfine' is bright, medium dark green and medium-fine textured, and retains its green color in winter better than most ryegrasses. 'Repell' is dark green, of medium-fine texture, mows very well and has insect resistance. 'Yorktown II' is dark green, fine textured and one of the ryegrasses most tolerant of cold temperatures. Zones 5-7.

Growing conditions. Ryegrass should be grown in full sun to light shade. Soil should be fertile, moist and have a pH of 6.0 to 7.0. Mow ryegrass to a height of 1½ to 2 inches. It is difficult to mow because the leaf blades are tough, and the leaf tips often turn brown after mowing. Fertilize with 2 to 6 pounds of nitrogen per 1,000 square feet per year. Perennial ryegrass has greater wear tolerance than annual ryegrass. Ryegrass establishes very quickly from seed. Pythium blight is the most serious disease problem of ryegrass.

Landscape uses. Perennial rye-grasses are used in mixtures with other turfgrasses in lawns that receive average wear. Both annual and perennial ryegrasses are used to overseed dormant warm-season grasses during the winter.

London pride see *Saxifraga*

Lonicera (lo-NIS-er-a)
Honeysuckle

Genus of fast-growing shrubs and vines, some of which are used as ground cover. Flowers are slender and tubular with prominent stamens, and are followed by non-showy black or red berries. Zones 5-10.

Selected species and varieties. *L. henryi* is an evergreen vine that has narrow, dark green, shiny, 3-inch leaves, and purplish red or yellow flowers that bloom in pairs in early summer. Berries are blue to black. Zones 6-10. *L. japonica* is a faster-growing vine that reaches 2 to 3 feet in height and spreads to 10 feet across. Leaves are oval, 1 to 3 inches long, dark green and evergreen in warm climates. Fragrant flowers of white with a purple tint bloom in pairs all summer, fade to yellow as they age and are followed by black berries. 'Halliana', Hall's honeysuckle, is the most rapid growing, reaching 3 feet in height and spreading to 30 feet across. Flowers are similar in appearance to the species but lack the purple tint. Zones 7-10.

Growing conditions. Grow honeysuckle in sun or shade in any fertile, moist, well-drained soil. It likes heat and is drought-resistant when established. Honeysuckle can be hard to manage and needs to be pruned every year. Propagate by cuttings, layering or division, or from seeds.

Landscape uses. Plant honeysuckle on banks. Hall's honeysuckle must be planted in large areas and is used where soil erosion control is needed.

Loosestrife see *Lysimachia*
Love grass see *Eragrostis*
Lungwort see *Pulmonaria*

Luzula (LOOZ-u-la)
Wood rush

Densely tufted, perennial ornamental grass that has a fine to medium texture. Leaves are soft and flat, and both leaves and stems are covered with soft, fine hairs. Single flowers bloom in spikes or clusters in spring. Zones 4-9.

Selected species and varieties. *L. nivea,* snowy wood rush, is an upright, arching plant growing 18 to 24 inches tall. Flowers are white and bloom in round clusters. *L. sylvatica,* great wood rush, grows 12 inches tall and has narrow, pointed leaves. Flowers are orange to brown in color and bloom in nodding clusters at the ends of the stems. *L. sylvatica marginata* has cream-colored margins on its foliage.

Growing conditions. Grow wood rush in partial to full shade in rich, moist, acid soil. Propagate by division or from seeds.

Landscape uses. Plant wood rush as a ground cover, in a rock garden or in a woodland garden. It is especially useful where soil erosion control is needed.

Lysimachia (lis-i-MAH-kee-a)
Loosestrife

Genus of upright and trailing perennials, some of which are effective as ground covers. Stems are leafy. Single flowers of yellow, white, pink, purple or blue bloom in the leaf axils or in clusters at the ends of the stems. Zones 4-9.

Selected species and varieties. *L. nummularia,* moneywort, creeping Charlie, creeping Jennie, grows 1 to 2 inches tall and spreads rapidly to 2 to 3 feet across. Shiny, round, ¾-inch leaves that look like coins are found along creeping stems that root as they grow. One-inch, yellow, cup-shaped flowers bloom in the leaf axils during spring and summer.

Growing conditions. Moneywort may be grown in full sun to full shade, but the climate should be cool to grow it in full sun. Soil should be rich and moist. Moneywort can become quite invasive. Propagate by division or by cuttings.

Landscape uses. Plant moneywort in large areas, where it can grow over walls or rocks, or near water.

Maiden grass see *Miscanthus*
Maiden pink see *Dianthus*
Manilagrass see *Zoysia*
Manna grass see *Glyceria*
Manzanita see *Arctostaphylos*
Mascarenegrass see *Zoysia*

LONICERA JAPONICA 'HALLIANA'

LUZULA NIVEA

LYSIMACHIA NUMMULARIA

MAZUS REPTANS

MENTHA REQUIENII

MICROBIOTA DECUSSATA

MILIUM EFFUSUM 'AUREUM'

Mazus (MAY-zus)

Low-growing, mat-forming perennial ground cover that has toothed leaves and purple, blue or white flowers in clusters at the ends of the branches. Zones 6-9; evergreen in Zone 9.

Selected species and varieties. *M. reptans* grows 2 inches high and spreads to 18 inches across, rooting as it grows. Bright green, lance-shaped leaves are 1 inch long. Flowers are ¾ inch long; they are purple and white, spotted with orange, and bloom in spring and summer in one-sided clusters.

Growing conditions. Grow mazus in full sun or partial shade in moist, well-drained soil. It can become invasive where soil is rich. Propagate by division or from seeds.

Landscape uses. As mazus withstands light foot traffic, it can be planted between stepping-stones. It can also be used between rocks or at the water's edge.

Meadow foxtail grass

see *Alopecurus*

Mentha (MEN-tha)
Mint

Upright or low-growing perennial that has square stems, aromatic foliage, and lavender or white tubular flowers in spikes or clusters at the ends of the stems. Zones 3-10.

Selected species and varieties. *M. requienii,* Corsican mint, creeping mint, grows ½ to 1 inch tall and spreads 6 to 12 inches across. Foliage is bright green, flat, round, ⅛ inch in diameter and has a mossy appearance. Very tiny, light purple flowers bloom in early summer. Zones 5-10.

Growing conditions. Grow Corsican mint in sun or partial shade in moist soil. All mints can become very invasive. Propagate by division or from seeds.

Landscape uses. Plant Corsican mint as a mat under shrubs or between stepping-stones.

Metake see *Pseudosasa*

Microbiota (my-kro-by-O-ta)

Evergreen coniferous shrub with bright green, feathery, scalelike foliage that covers branches that arch in a fanlike manner. The foliage turns copper-colored in fall. Zones 2-10.

Selected species and varieties. *M. decussata,* Russian cypress, Siberian carpet cypress, grows 18 to 24 inches tall and spreads to 4 to 6 feet across with a flat top.

Growing conditions. Grow Russian cypress in sun or shade in dry, well-drained soil. Propagate by cuttings or layering.

Landscape uses. Use Russian cypress under trees or in open spaces.

Milium (MIL-ee-um)
Wood millet

Loosely tufted annual or perennial ornamental grass with flat leaf blades and loose seed heads. Zones 5-10.

Selected species and varieties. *M. effusum* 'Aureum', Bowles golden grass, has soft, narrow, arching, bright yellow or yellow-green leaf blades that are 8 to 12 inches long. Yellow flowers and seed heads form on 18-inch stems.

Growing conditions. Bowles golden grass may be grown in partial to full shade in moist, rich, fertile soil. It can become invasive from dropped seeds. Propagate by division or from seeds.

Landscape uses. Plant Bowles golden grass as a ground cover or in a woodland garden.

Mint see *Mentha*

Miscanthus (mis-KAN-thus)

Perennial ornamental grass that forms clumps of upright, stiff leaves and has showy, feathery seed heads in fall. Zones 5-10.

Selected species and varieties. *M. floridulis,* giant miscanthus, is a coarse-textured plant growing 10 feet tall. Leaves are pale green and 3 feet long; seed heads are white. *M. saccariflorus,* eulalia grass, forms a narrow clump 6 to 10 feet high. Leaves are 3 feet long and 1 inch wide and turn rusty brown in fall. Plumes are silvery white. *M. sinensis,* Japanese silver grass, Chinese silver grass, grows to 8 feet or more. Leaves 2 to 3 feet long and 1 inch wide grow in narrow clumps and turn beige or orange-brown in fall. Seed heads are pink. 'Gracillimus', maiden grass, is fine textured and grows 5 feet high in a graceful, arching habit. Leaves are narrow and curl at the ends. 'Purpurascens', red-leaved miscanthus, grows 3 to 5 feet tall. Its leaves turn red in late summer. 'Strictus' grows 6 to 8 feet tall in a very narrow, upright form. Foliage is striped horizontally in yellow. 'Variegatus', striped eulalia grass, grows 5 feet tall and has narrow green foliage striped in white and yellow. 'Zebrinus', zebra grass, grows 6 to 8 feet tall in a narrow form. Foliage has yellow horizontal stripes.

Growing conditions. Plant miscanthus in full sun or light shade in a moist, moderately fertile soil. Tall varieties may need staking if the soil is too fertile or if light is too low. Eulalia grass is invasive and may need to be restricted with underground barriers. Propagate by division or from seeds.

Landscape uses. Plant miscanthus as a barrier plant or specimen, or along the waterside.

Mitchella (mi-CHEL-a)

Woody or perennial evergreen ground cover that has small, round, dark green foliage with white veins. Flowers are funnel-shaped, ½ inch long and appear in pairs at the ends of short stems growing from the leaf axils. Zones 4-8.

Selected species and varieties. *M. repens*, partridge berry, grows 1 to 2 inches high and spreads 12 to 24 inches across. Stems are slender and root as they creep along the ground. Flowers are fragrant, pink or white, and bloom in summer. Scarlet berries ¼ inch across either follow the flowers or may appear at the same time.

Growing conditions. Grow partridge berry in partial to full shade in rich, moist, acid soil. It may be slow to establish but will grow quickly after several years. Propagate by cuttings, division or rooted runners.

Landscape uses. Plant partridge berry in woodland gardens, under trees and shrubs, or where it will cascade over rocks.

Molinia (mo-LIN-ee-a)

Perennial ornamental grass that forms tufted clumps of upright and arching leaves. Leaf blades are soft, narrow and flat. Flowers and seed heads appear in panicles on stiff stems. Zones 5-8.

Selected species and varieties. *M. caerulea,* moor grass, has erect leaves 6 to 12 inches long and green or purple spikes of flowers and seeds on 3-foot stems. 'Variegata', variegated purple moor grass, has mounds of soft, fine-textured leaves striped in creamy yellow. Seed heads are purplish green on 1- to 2-foot stems.

Growing conditions. Moor grass will flourish in full sun or light shade in rich, moist, acid soil. Propagate by division.

Landscape uses. Plant moor grass as an accent or as a specimen plant. Tall plants may be used in background plantings; low ones as edgings.

Mondo grass see *Ophiopogon*

Moneywort see *Lysimachia*

Moor grass see *Molinia*

Moss pink see *Phlox*

Mother of thousands see *Saxifraga*

Mother of thyme see *Thymus*

Mountain cranberry see *Vaccinium*

Mountain pink see *Phlox*

Myosotis (mu-o-SO-tis)
Forget-me-not

Annual, biennial or perennial ground cover that has narrow oblong leaves and clusters of small, tubular, five-lobed flowers. Zones 4-10.

Selected species and varieties. *M. scorpioides* is a perennial that grows 18 inches tall and wide, spreading by creeping roots. Flowers are blue with a pink, yellow or white eye and bloom in delicate, airy clusters at the ends of the stems in spring and summer. *M. scorpioides semperflorens* grows 8 inches high.

Growing conditions. Grow forget-me-not in partial to full shade in rich, moist soil. It may be short-lived but it self-sows readily. Forget-me-not is prone to spider mite and mildew. Propagate by division or from seeds.

Landscape uses. Plant forget-me-not as a filler plant under bulbs or other perennials or alongside water.

Myrtle see *Vinca*

MISCANTHUS SINENSIS 'ZEBRINUS'

MITCHELLA REPENS

MOLINIA CAERULEA 'VARIEGATA'

MYOSOTIS SCORPIOIDES

135

NEPETA MUSSINII

OMPHALODES VERNA

OPHIOPOGON JAPONICUS

OPUNTIA HUMIFUSA

Nepeta (ne-PEE-ta)

Genus of erect and trailing annuals and perennials, some of which are used as ground covers. Stems are square and covered with heart-shaped, hairy leaves. Small, tubular, ½-inch flowers of blue or white are clustered around the stems, often in whorls. Zones 4-10.

Selected species and varieties. *N. mussinii,* catmint, is an evergreen perennial that has soft, gray, aromatic 1-inch leaves. It grows 12 to 24 inches tall and spreads into a mound-shaped plant 24 inches across. Flowers of blue or lavender-blue bloom in 6-inch spikes in late spring and early summer.

Growing conditions. Catmint may be grown in full sun or partial shade and in any well-drained soil, but poor, dry soil is best. Cut back after flowering for a second bloom. Catmint becomes invasive. Propagate by division or from seeds.

Landscape uses. Use catmint as an edging plant or in a large rock garden.

Northern sea oats
see *Chasmanthium*

Oat grass see *Arrhenatherum; Helictotrichon*

Omphalodes (om-fa-LO-deez)

Erect or trailing annual or perennial, with some species used as ground covers. It has lance-shaped to heart-shaped leaves at the base of the plant and smaller leaves along the flowering stems. Tubular, five-lobed flowers are pink or blue and bloom in loose, one-sided racemes. Zones 5-9.

Selected species and varieties. *O. verna,* blue-eyed Mary, creeping forget-me-not, grows 8 inches tall and spreads to 24 inches across. Fast-growing stems root as they creep along the ground. Flowers are blue, have a white center, are ½ inch across and bloom among the leaves in loose clusters in spring.

Growing conditions. Blue-eyed Mary may be grown in full sun to partial shade in cool, neutral, dry or moist soil. Propagate by division or from seeds.

Landscape uses. Plant blue-eyed Mary on slopes or flat areas or under trees and shrubs.

Ophiopogon (o-fi-o-PO-gon)
Mondo grass, lily turf

Evergreen perennial that has tufts of basal, grasslike leaves and loose, erect clusters of ¼-inch, nodding flowers that are often hidden by the foliage. Zones 7-10.

Selected species and varieties. *O. japonicus* grows 6 to 12 inches high and has dark green, soft, curved foliage that is 8 to 16 inches long and ⅛ inch wide. It spreads quickly by underground stolons. Flowers are white or pale lavender and bloom in summer. *O. planiscapus* 'Arabicus', black mondo grass, grows 8 to 10 inches high and 12 inches wide. Leaves are arching; they are green when new but purplish black when mature. Flowers are white, pink or purple and bloom in summer.

Growing conditions. Mondo grass may be grown in full sun to full shade, but partial shade is preferred where summers are hot. Any garden soil is acceptable; mondo grass will tolerate heat and drought. Propagate by division.

Landscape uses. Plant mondo grass under trees, on slopes or flat areas, or as an edging. It tolerates seashore conditions.

Opuntia (o-PUN-cha)

A large group of perennial cacti that grow either upright or prostrate, some of which are used for ground cover. Spiny segments are flat or cylindrical. Zones 5-10.

Selected species and varieties. *O. humifusa,* sometimes designated *O. compressa,* prickly pear, has flat, oblong to oval segments 2 to 6 inches long. It spreads horizontally along the ground. Yellow flowers are 2 to 3 inches across and bloom on short, conical stems in early summer. Green to purple, 2-inch oval fruits appear in fall. This is the hardiest of the cacti.

Growing conditions. Grow prickly pear in full sun and sandy, dry, well-drained soil. It is very drought-tolerant. Propagate by breaking off the pads and rooting them in sand, or from seeds.

Landscape uses. Plant prickly pear on dry or rocky slopes or flat areas or in rock gardens. Because of the sharp spines, keep from areas where there is foot traffic.

Orchard grass see *Dactylis*
Oregon boxwood see *Paxistima*

Osteospermum
(os-tee-o-SPER-mum)

Spreading annuals, perennials and shrubs that have oval leaves and daisylike flowers that bloom on long stems and close at night and on cloudy days. Zones 9 and 10.

Selected species and varieties. *O. fruticosum,* trailing African daisy, grows 12 inches high and spreads rapidly to 4 feet across, rooting as it spreads. Thick leaves are 1 to 3 inches long. Flowers are 2 inches across and bloom on 4-inch stems. The center of the flower is purple to violet; the petals are lilac fading to white on the upper sides and deeper lilac or rose on the undersides.

Growing conditions. Grow trailing African daisy in full sun in light, well-drained soil. Water during the summer months; the plant will tolerate drought the rest of the year. Propagate by cuttings or layering, or from seeds.

Landscape uses. Trailing African daisy may be planted on a slope, where it can cascade over a wall or as a border plant.

Pachysandra (pak-i-SAN-dra)
Spurge

Woody, perennial ground cover that may be deciduous or evergreen. It has oval leaves in whorls along the stems. The outer half of the leaf has a toothed margin. Flowers bloom in spikes and are not showy. Zones 4-8.

Selected species and varieties. *P. procumbens,* Alleghany spurge, trails at first and then forms erect clumps 8 to 10 inches high. It spreads to 15 inches across. Fuzzy greenish white to purple flowers appear in early spring. Leaves are 3 inches long and dull green mottled in gray. Deciduous Zones 4-7; evergreen Zone 8. *P. terminalis,* Japanese spurge, is an evergreen growing 9 to 12 inches high and spreading to 3 feet across by underground stems. Leaves are thick, dark green, glossy and 2 to 4 inches long. White flowers bloom in late spring. 'Silver Edge' has narrow silver margins on the leaves. Zones 5-8.

Growing conditions. Grow pachysandra in partial to full shade; leaves will turn yellow in the sun. Soil should be rich, cool, moist and neutral to acid. Pachysandra tolerates drought once established. Protect from winter sun and wind. Pachysandra is susceptible to euonymus scale. Propagate by cuttings or division.

Landscape uses. Plant pachysandra under trees and shrubs, as an edging, on slopes or on flat areas.

Pampas grass see *Cortaderia*
Panic grass see *Panicum*

Panicum (PAN-i-kum)
Panic grass

Annual or perennial, erect or creeping ornamental grass that is grown for its panicles of flowers and seed heads, which are light, open and feathery. Zones 5-10.

Selected species and varieties. *P. virgatum,* switch grass, is a perennial that grows vigorously 5 to 6 feet high. Leaves are green, narrow, 1 to 2 feet long and have rough margins. In autumn, they change to bright yellow or golden orange. Large beige or brown panicles grow on erect stems.

Growing conditions. Grow switch grass in full sun and light, well-drained soil. Dry soil is best, but switch grass tolerates moist soil and poor drainage. Propagate by seeds or division.

Landscape uses. Plant switch grass as a screen, as an accent plant or in a massed planting in a large area.

Parthenocissus
(parth-e-no-SIS-us)

Woody deciduous vine that climbs to 60 feet or more but can be used as a ground cover. Foliage is either three-lobed or made up of three to five leaflets. Small, inconspicuous, greenish white flowers bloom among the leaves and are followed by blue to black berries. Zones 4-9.

Selected species and varieties. *P. tricuspidata,* Boston ivy, climbs to 60 feet on a support, but as a ground cover is 9 inches high, spreading to 8 feet across. Foliage is three-lobed, 8 to 10 inches across, shiny dark green in spring and summer, and bright scarlet in fall. 'Robusta' is a very vigorous grower with waxy leaves. Zones 5-9.

OSTEOSPERMUM FRUTICOSUM

PACHYSANDRA TERMINALIS

PANICUM VIRGATUM

PARTHENOCISSUS TRICUSPIDATA

PASPALUM NOTATUM 'PENSACOLA'

PAXISTIMA CANBYI

PENNISETUM ALOPECUROIDES

Growing conditions. Grow Boston ivy in full sun to light shade in rich, moist soil. Propagate by cuttings, layering or seeds.

Landscape uses. Plant Boston ivy in large areas, either sloped or flat. If it encounters trees, shrubs or walls, it will climb.

—

Partridge berry see *Mitchella*

—

Paspalum (PAS-pa-lum)
Bahiagrass

Warm-season turfgrass that has a very coarse texture and one of the widest leaf blades of any turfgrass. It spreads by short stolons and rhizomes and tends to be tufted in growth habit. Region C.

Selected species and varieties. *P. notatum* is a coarse, tough grass that is medium green in color. It produces numerous tall, fast-growing seed heads that can detract from its appearance. 'Argentine' has an intermediate texture and a softer leaf blade and is the best variety of Bahiagrass for an even, attractive lawn. It is the easiest to mow. 'Paraguay' has a medium-coarse texture and hairy, grayish leaves. 'Pensacola' has a medium-fine texture and a fairly rapid establishment rate, but it tends to yellow.

Growing conditions. Grow Bahiagrass in full sun to partial shade. Soil should be sandy and infertile with a pH of 6.5 to 7.5. Bahiagrass grows best in humid climates. Mow to a height of 1½ to 2½ inches; frequent mowing is necessary to remove the seed heads. Fertilize in spring with ½ to 2½ pounds of nitrogen per 1,000 square feet per year. Bahiagrass has good wear tolerance and excellent drought resistance, although it grows better with frequent rainfall or watering. It is susceptible to few diseases and insects; dollar spot, brown patch and mole cricket are the most common problems. Bahiagrass is grown from seed, although germination and establishment are generally slow.

Landscape uses. Bahiagrass grass is a low-maintenance lawn grass. Its use is limited to the warm, humid Southeast, especially along the Gulf of Mexico, for climatic reasons. It has an extensive root system and is used where erosion control is needed.

Paxistima (pak-SIS-ti-ma)

Neat, compact, fine-textured, shrubby ground cover that has small, shiny, dark green evergreen leaves. Inconspicuous flowers bloom in mid-spring to early summer. Zones 4-9.

Selected species and varieties. *P. canbyi,* Canby paxistima, grows 12 inches high and spreads 3 to 5 feet across. Wiry stems root as they grow. Leaves are narrow, ½ to 1 inch long and turn bronze in winter. Flowers are tiny and may be either greenish white or reddish. *P. myrsinites,* Oregon boxwood, grows 18 to 24 inches high and spreads to 6 feet across. Its flowers are 1½ inches long; otherwise it is similar to Canby paxistima. Zones 6-9.

Growing conditions. Grow paxistima in full sun to partial shade in moist, rich, slightly acid, well-drained soil. It prefers high humidity. Propagate by division or cuttings.

Landscape uses. Plant paxistima under trees, in front of a shrub border or in a rock garden.

—

Pearlwort see *Sagina*

—

Pennisetum (pen-i-SEE-tum)

Annual or perennial ornamental grass that has narrow, flat leaf blades that grow in a graceful, arching habit and nodding seed heads. The seed heads are spiked and slightly plumed. Zones 5-9.

Selected species and varieties. *P. alopecuroides,* fountain grass, is a perennial that grows 2 to 3 feet tall in a mounded form. Leaves are bright green and of fine to medium texture. Seed heads are cylindrical, silvery white and 6 to 8 inches long. 'Hameln' is more compact and 2½ feet high. *P. setaceum,* crimson fountain grass, grows 3 feet high and has graceful, arching, narrow leaves with a fine texture. Seed heads are 6 to 10 inches long and purple to red. 'Rubrum' has red foliage. It is perennial in Zones 8 and 9 but can be grown as an annual in other zones. *P. villosum,* feathertop, grows 2 to 3 feet tall. Seed heads are creamy white and 4 inches long. Feathertop is a perennial in Zone 9 and can be grown as an annual in other areas.

Growing conditions. Grow pennisetum in full sun or light shade in fertile, well-drained soil. Propagate by division or from seeds.

Landscape uses. Grow pennise-tum as a hedge, as a specimen or in a flower border.

—

Periwinkle see *Vinca*

—

Phalaris (fa-LAR-is)

Perennial or annual ornamental grass that has flat leaf blades and narrow spikes of flattened seed heads. Zones 4-10.

Selected species and varieties. *P. arundinacea picta,* ribbon grass, is a perennial that forms a mound of foliage. Leaves are pointed, 12 inches long, and striped in green, creamy white and sometimes pink. Seed heads are white or pale pink and 4 to 6 inches long on 3-foot stems.

Growing conditions. Grow ribbon grass in partial shade; the color will fade in full sun. Ribbon grass tolerates poor, dry or wet soil. It can be untidy by midsummer because the foliage rips from wind and rain and turns brown. It becomes invasive. Propagate by division.

Landscape uses. Grow ribbon grass as a ground cover, a hedge or an accent plant.

—

Phlox (FLOKS)

Upright or low-growing annual or perennial that has lance-shaped or needlelike leaves and five-petaled flowers in clusters that may be either loose or dense. Zones 3-9.

Selected species and varieties. *P. nivalis,* trailing phlox, is a perennial ground cover that grows 6 to 8 inches high and 24 inches across in a loose mat. Leaves are narrow and ¾ inch long. Flowers are white, pink or purple, 1 inch wide with notched petals and bloom in midspring. Zones 6-9. *P. stolonifera,* creeping phlox, is a perennial ground cover that grows 10 to 12 inches high and 18 inches across. Stems are fast-growing and root as they creep along the ground. Leaves are oval and ¾ inch long. Flowers are white, pink, rose, lavender, purple or blue, ¾ inch across and bloom in midspring. Zones 4-9.
  P. subulata, moss pink, ground pink, mountain pink, is a perennial, evergreen ground cover that grows 6 inches high and 24 inches across. Stems are fast-growing and root

as they creep along the ground, forming a dense mat. Leaves are needlelike and 1 inch long. Flowers are white, pink, rose, red, lavender, purple or blue. They are ¾ inch in diameter, have notched petals, and bloom in late spring and early summer.

Growing conditions. Grow trailing phlox and moss pink in full sun and creeping phlox in partial shade. Soil for trailing and creeping phlox should be rich, moist and slightly acidic; soil for moss pink should be poor, dry and neutral to alkaline. All, but particularly moss pink, should be sheared after flowering to keep the plants compact. Mildew can be a problem with phlox. Propagate by cuttings, by division or from seeds.

Landscape uses. Grow phlox on slopes, cascading over walls, as edgings or in rock gardens.

—

Phyla (FY-la)

Creeping, evergreen, perennial ground cover that has toothed or lobed leaves and dense clusters of violet, blue, pink or white flowers. Zones 9 and 10.

Selected species and varieties. *P. nodiflora canescens,* lippia, forms a flat mat 1 to 3 inches high in sun and slightly taller in shade. Stems root as they creep along the ground. Leaves are ¾ inch long, gray in spring and summer, and brown in winter. Lilac or blue flowers with yellow throats and round cloverlike heads bloom in spring. Some gardeners find the flowers objectionable, because they attract bees.

Growing conditions. Grow lippia in full sun and fertile soil. Water deeply but infrequently. Lippia is very heat- and drought-tolerant. Mowing will remove the flower heads—and thus help eliminate bees. Propagate from cuttings or from plugs.

Landscape uses. Because lippia tolerates heavy foot traffic, it is used as a lawn substitute and between stepping-stones. It also tolerates seashore conditions.

—

Piggyback plant see *Tolmiea*

Pinks see *Dianthus*

Plantain lily see *Hosta*

Plume grass see *Erianthus*

PHALARIS ARUNDINACEA PICTA

PHLOX SUBULATA

PHYLA NODIFLORA CANESCENS

POA PRATENSIS

POLYGONUM CUSPIDATUM COMPACTUM

POTENTILLA TABERNAEMONTANI

Poa (PO-a)
Bluegrass

Cool-season turfgrass that may be either bunching or stoloniferous in its habit. Regions A and F; D with irrigation.

Selected species and varieties. *P. pratensis,* Kentucky bluegrass, forms a high-quality turf of medium texture, with medium to dark green color and smooth, soft, shiny blades. It spreads vigorously by rhizomes. 'Adelphi' is very dark green, medium textured and has excellent disease resistance. 'Baron' is dark green, medium to coarse textured and needs frequent fertilizing. 'Bonnieblue' is dark green and medium textured, retains its green color well in cold weather, needs infrequent fertilizing and has excellent disease resistance. 'Bristol' is dark green, medium textured, shade-tolerant and has excellent disease resistance. 'Challenger' is dark green and medium to fine textured, has excellent cold tolerance and disease resistance, and is one of the most drought-resistant Kentucky bluegrasses. 'Eclipse' is dark green, medium textured, very cold-tolerant and somewhat shade-tolerant and has excellent disease resistance. 'Fylking' is dark green and medium to fine textured and needs little fertilizing.

'Merion' is dark green and medium to coarse in texture. It is very resistant to helminthosporium disease but very susceptible to other diseases. It requires heavy fertilization. 'Mystic' is medium to dark green and fine textured. 'Nassau' is dark green and medium to coarse textured and has excellent disease resistance. It turns green earlier in spring than most Kentucky bluegrasses. 'Plush' is medium green and medium textured. 'Rugby' is dark green and medium textured and has good disease resistance. 'Touchdown' is medium green and medium to fine textured, turns green very early in spring and has good to excellent disease resistance.

P. trivialis, rough bluegrass, is a fine-textured, yellowish green, shiny turf. It is the most shade-tolerant cool-season turfgrass.

Growing conditions. Grow Kentucky bluegrass in full sun or light shade; grow rough bluegrass in shade. Soil for both should be moist, fertile, medium textured and have a pH of 6.0 to 7.0. Both bluegrasses prefer humid climates. Mow Kentucky bluegrass to a height of 1 to 2 inches, and rough bluegrass to a height of ½ to 1 inch. Fertilize with 2½ to 6 pounds of nitrogen per 1,000 square feet per year. Kentucky bluegrass has medium to good wear tolerance; rough bluegrass has poor wear tolerance. Propagate Kentucky bluegrass from seed or sod and rough bluegrass from seed. Both kinds of bluegrass are prone to most turf diseases; helminthosporium is the most serious.

Landscape uses. Plant Kentucky bluegrass on lawns receiving average to heavy foot traffic and located in open, sunny areas. Rough bluegrass is used on shady lawns that do not receive foot traffic. Rough bluegrass is also used to overseed dormant warm-season grasses in winter.

—

Polygonum (po-LIG-o-num)
Knotweed

Genus of erect or trailing annual and perennial plants, some of which are used for ground covers. Stems are stiff and wiry, have obvious swollen joints and resemble bamboo. Small flowers bloom in spikes or loose clusters. Zones 3-10.

Selected species and varieties. *P. cuspidatum compactum,* sometimes designated *P. reynoutria,* dwarf Japanese fleeceflower, grows 2 to 3 feet high and spreads by underground stems to 4 feet across. Leaves are oval, 3 to 6 inches long, pale green in spring and summer, and red in fall. Reddish flowers bloom in spikes from the leaf axils in late summer, and are followed by red seeds. Zones 4-10.

Growing conditions. Grow fleeceflower in full sun or light shade in any well-drained, dry garden soil. It can be very invasive but is especially so in poor soil. It can be contained by underground barriers. Propagate by division or from seeds.

Landscape uses. Plant fleeceflower on dry banks or in large areas, especially where soil erosion control is needed.

—

Potentilla (po-ten-TIL-a)
Cinquefoil

Genus of perennials and shrubs, some of which are used for ground cover. Leaves are compound, with three or more hairy leaflets, and resemble the foliage of strawberries. Five-petaled flowers of white, yellow or red with prominent stamens bloom in small, loose clusters. Zones 3-10.

Selected species and varieties.
P. tabernaemontani, sometimes designated *P. verna,* spring cinquefoil, is an evergreen perennial growing 3 to 4 inches high and spreading quickly to form a dense mat 18 to 24 inches across. Branches root as they grow along the ground. Leaves are bright green and have five leaflets each ¾ inch long and toothed. Flowers are yellow, ½ inch across and bloom in late spring. Zones 4-10. *P. tridentata,* wineleaf cinquefoil, three-toothed cinquefoil, is an evergreen perennial that grows 6 to 9 inches high and spreads slowly to 24 inches across. Branches are woody, root as they grow and form a loose mat. Leaves have three leaflets, are shiny dark green in spring and summer, and turn deep red in autumn. Flowers are white, ¼ inch across and bloom in early summer.

Growing conditions. Grow cinquefoil in full sun; partial shade is preferred in areas with hot summers. Soil should be sandy, dry, slightly acid and well drained. Cinquefoil tolerates heat and infertile soil. Spring cinquefoil can be mowed. Propagate by division or cuttings or from seeds.

Landscape uses. Plant cinquefoil where it can grow over rocks or as a border. Spring cinquefoil can be used as a lawn substitute.

—

Prairie cord grass see *Spartina*

Prickly pear see *Opuntia*

—

Pseudosasa (soo-doh-SAS-a)
Bamboo

Evergreen bamboo that has erect stems with obvious joints and long, pointed leaves. Zones 8-10.

Selected species and varieties.
P. japonica, arrow bamboo, metake, grows 6 to 15 feet tall. Stems are ¾ inch across. One branch grows from each joint and has up to 10 leaves. Each leaf is 12 inches long and 1½ inches wide. The upper sides are glossy and dark green, with yellow midribs, and the undersides are patterned in gray and green. The leaves may turn brown during cold winters.

Growing conditions. Bamboo grows in full sun but in hot climates should have afternoon shade. Soil should be rich, moist and well drained. Plant in a location that is protected from drying winds. Arrow bamboo spreads but is not as invasive

as other bamboos. Propagate by division or root cuttings.

Landscape uses. Plant arrow bamboo as a screen, as a hedge or on banks, especially where soil erosion control is needed. It can also be grown in a container.

—

Pulmonaria (pul-mo-NAR-ee-a)
Lungwort

Perennial ground cover that spreads by creeping roots. Leaves are broad to lance-shaped and hairy; they have long stems and form at the base of the plant. Flowers are long and narrow, five-lobed and funnel-shaped. They bloom in nodding clusters at the tops of almost leafless stems in late spring or early summer. Zones 4-8.

Selected species and varieties.
P. angustifolia, blue lungwort, grows 6 to 12 inches high and spreads from 12 to 18 inches across. Foliage is narrow and dark green. Flowers are blue, rose or white, and ¾ to 1 inch long. *P. saccharata,* Bethlehem sage, grows 8 to 18 inches high and spreads to 24 inches across. Leaves are oval, pointed and dark green spotted with white. Flowers are white, blue or purplish red and ¾ to 1 inch across. 'Mrs. Moon' has pink buds that open into large blue flowers.

Growing conditions. Grow lungwort in partial to full shade in cool, moist, well-drained soil. Propagate by division or from seeds.

Landscape uses. Plant lungwort in woodland gardens, under trees or under shrubs.

—

Pussy-toes see *Antennaria*

Quaking grass see *Briza*

Ravenna grass see *Erianthus*

Red fescue see *Festuca*

Redtop see *Agrostis*

—

Rhododendron
(ro-doh-DEN-dron)
Rhododendron, azalea

Large genus of deciduous and evergreen shrubs that vary in plant size and shape, foliage size and flower form. Showy flowers bloom in all colors of the rainbow from early spring to midsummer. Rhododendrons useful as ground covers have small leaves and small clusters of flowers at the

PSEUDOSASA JAPONICA

PULMONARIA ANGUSTIFOLIA

RHODODENDRON INDICUM 'FLAME CREEPER'

ROSMARINUS OFFICINALIS 'PROSTRATUS'

SAGINA SUBULATA 'AUREA'

SARCOCOCCA HOOKERANA HUMILIS

ends of the branches. Azaleas are low-growing and have small leaves and informal clusters of flowers at the ends of the branches. Foliage for both is generally dark green and lustrous.

Azaleas generally have funnel-shaped flowers and rhododendrons generally have bell-shaped blooms. Flowers may be either single or double. Zones 2-10.

Selected species and varieties. *R. impeditum* is an evergreen rhododendron growing 18 inches high. It has ½-inch gray-green leaves. The flowers are blue or purple, ¾ inch across and bloom in midspring. Zones 5-8. *R. indicum* is an evergreen azalea that blooms in early summer. Plants grow 18 inches high and spread to 30 inches across.

There are many hybrids of rhododendrons and azaleas. 'Flame Creeper' is a semievergreen azalea that has orange-red flowers and small leaves, and grows to a height of 10 inches. Zones 6 and 7. 'Gumpo' is a hybrid evergreen azalea that grows 3 feet high and has frilled, 3-inch flowers of white with red spots. It has narrow foliage and blooms in late spring. Zones 7-9. 'Ramapo' is a hybrid evergreen rhododendron that grows 18 to 36 inches high. Foliage is very fine and gray-green; flowers are pale violet and bloom in midspring. Zones 6-8.

Growing conditions. Grow rhododendrons and azaleas in partial shade. Azaleas will tolerate full sun if the soil is constantly moist, and rhododendrons will tolerate full shade. Soil for both should be rich, moist, sandy, acid and well drained. Roots are shallow and should be mulched to keep them cool. Do not plant them where they will be subject to drying winds and winter sun. Propagate by cuttings or from seeds.

Landscape uses. Plant rhododendrons and azaleas in woodland gardens, as borders and under trees.

——

Ribbon grass see *Phalaris*
Rock cress see *Arabis*
Rock rose see *Helianthemum*
Rosemary see *Rosmarinus*

——

Rosmarinus (rose-ma-RY-nus)
Rosemary

Upright or trailing evergreen shrub that has aromatic stems and foliage. Leaves are needlelike, ½ to 1 inch long, glossy green on the upper surfaces and gray on the undersides. Flowers are fragrant, pale blue, tubular, ½ inch long, and appear in upright spikes during winter and spring. Zones 7-10.

Selected species and varieties. *R. officinalis* 'Prostratus', trailing rosemary, grows 6 to 12 inches high and spreads to 6 feet across, rooting as it spreads. Flowers bloom in late spring. Zones 8-10.

Growing conditions. Grow trailing rosemary in full sun in dry, well-drained soil. It tolerates heat, drought and poor soil. Water sparingly and do not fertilize. Propagate by cuttings, division or layering.

Landscape uses. Plant trailing rosemary where it can cascade over rocks and walls. It tolerates seashore conditions.

——

Rupturewort see *Herniaria*
Ruscus-leaved bamboo see *Shibataea*
Rush see *Juncus*
Russian cypress see *Microbiota*
Ryegrass see *Lolium*

——

Sagina (sa-JY-na)
Pearlwort

Tufted or mat-forming annual or perennial ground cover. Leaves are dark green and needlelike; tiny flowers bloom singly or in clusters at the ends of the stems. Zones 5-7.

Selected species and varieties. *S. subulata,* Irish moss, is a perennial evergreen that grows 1 to 4 inches tall and spreads to form a mat or spongy mound 12 or more inches across. Leaves are mosslike and ¼ inch long; white flowers bloom singly atop the foliage during the summer. 'Aurea' has yellow-green leaves.

Growing conditions. Irish moss grows in full sun except in hot climates, where it prefers partial shade. Soil should be moist, rich, fertile and well drained, but Irish moss tolerates dry, sandy soil. It is prone to attack by snails and slugs. Propagate by division or from seeds.

Landscape uses. Plant Irish moss in small areas, wall gardens and rock gardens. Because it takes foot traffic, Irish moss may be grown between stepping-stones.

St. Augustine grass
see *Stenotaphrum*

St.-John's-wort see *Hypericum*

Sand myrtle see *Leiophyllum*

Sandwort see *Arenaria*

Sarcococca (sar-ko-KOK-a)
Sweet box

Erect or spreading multibranched evergreen shrub that constantly sends up new stems from underground. Leaves are thin, leathery and glossy dark green. Small, white, fragrant flowers bloom in racemes among the leaves in late winter and spring. Black or red berries are ¼ inch across. Zones 6-9.

Selected species and varieties. *S. hookerana humilis,* dwarf Himalayan sweet box, grows to a height of 1 to 2 feet and spreads slowly to 8 feet across. It has 2- to 3½-inch narrow leaves.

Growing conditions. Grow dwarf Himalayan sweet box in partial to full shade in rich, fertile, moist, acid, well-drained soil. Protect from winter sun. Propagate by cuttings, by division or from seeds.

Landscape uses. Plant dwarf Himalayan sweet box in woodland gardens or under trees.

Sasa (SAS-a)
Bamboo

Rapid-growing bamboo that has woody stems with obvious joints and spreads by underground runners. Leaves are large and have conspicuous midribs. Zones 6-10.

Selected species and varieties. *S. palmata* has slender stems that grow to 7 feet and bright green, leathery leaves that are arranged at the ends of the branches like fingers. Each leaf grows to 15 inches long and 3½ inches wide. The undersides of the leaves are silvery to blue-green. *S. veitchii,* Kuma bamboo, grows 2 to 3 feet tall when grown in the sun, and taller in the shade. Stems are slender and turn purple as they mature. Foliage is 5 to 8 inches long and 2 inches wide. The upper sides of the leaves are bright green and the undersides are blue-gray. Leaf margins turn tan in fall. Zones 7-10.

Growing conditions. Grow bamboo in full sun to light shade in fertile, moist soil. Foliage may become brown and dry in very cold winters and need to be trimmed. Bamboo is very invasive and should be contained by underground barriers. Propagate by division or root cuttings.

Landscape uses. Plant bamboo as a screen, a hedge or on slopes, especially where soil erosion control is needed.

Satureja (sat-u-REE-a)
Savory

Genus of annuals and perennials, some of which can be used as a ground cover. Stems are square and clothed in aromatic, mint-scented foliage. Small white, pink or purple flowers bloom in whorled spikes. Zones 3-10.

Selected species and varieties. *S. douglasii,* yerba buena, grows to 6 inches high. Its stems root as they spread to 3 feet across. Leaves are oval, 1¼ inches long and 1 inch wide, and have scalloped edges. Flowers are purple or white, ½ inch long and bloom in spikes from spring through fall.

Growing conditions. Grow yerba buena in full sun or in partial shade where summer temperatures are hot. Soil should be moist, rich and well drained. Propagate by division or cuttings or from seeds.

Landscape uses. Because it spreads quickly, yerba buena can be planted in large areas. As it withstands foot traffic, it can be grown between stepping-stones.

Savory see *Satureja*

Saxifraga (saks-IF-ra-ga)

Spreading annual, biennial or perennial ground cover that has foliage that is either soft and mosslike or thick and succulent. Pink, white, purple or yellow flowers bloom in airy, delicate, nodding clusters. Zones 5-9.

Selected species and varieties. *S. stolonifera,* strawberry geranium, mother of thousands, is an evergreen perennial. Foliage is hairy, 4 inches across and round with scalloped edges. It is dark green with pale green veins on the upper surfaces, and red on the undersides. Foliage grows in rosettes 5 inches high; the plant spreads quickly to 18 inches across by runners that form plantlets

SASA VEITCHII

SATUREJA DOUGLASII

SAXIFRAGA STOLONIFERA

143

SEDUM KAMTSCHATICUM

SEDUM SPURIUM 'DRAGON'S BLOOD'

SEMPERVIVUM HYBRID

at their ends. Flowers are white, 1 inch across and bloom in loose clusters on 6- to 12-inch stems in early summer. Zones 7-9. *S.* × *urbium,* London pride, is an evergreen perennial. Foliage is round to oval, 2½ inches across, toothed, yellow-green when young and shiny dark green when mature. The undersides of the leaves are red. The foliage grows in rosettes 6 inches high and the plant spreads slowly to 12 inches across. Flowers are pink, ¼ inch across and bloom in clusters 8 to 10 inches above the foliage.

Growing conditions. Saxifraga grows in full sun, but in hot areas protection from the afternoon sun is beneficial. Soil should be sandy, slightly acidic and well drained. Propagate by division or from seeds. Strawberry geranium is propagated by rooting the plantlets that grow at the ends of the runners.

Landscape uses. Plant saxifraga in small areas, in a rock garden, under trees and shrubs, or as a border.

—

Scotch heather see *Calluna*
Sea oats see *Chasmanthium*
Sea thrift see *Armeria*
Sedge see *Carex*

—

Sedum (SEE-dum)
Stonecrop

Evergreen or deciduous succulent perennial, with some species grown as ground covers. Some spread by trailing branches; others grow upright with rosettes of basal leaves. Flowers are white, yellow, pink, red, blue or purple, five-petaled and star-shaped, and bloom in clusters at the ends of the stems. Zones 3-10.

Selected species and varieties. *S. acre,* goldmoss sedum, is 2 inches high and spreads rapidly by creeping stems to form a mat 2 feet across. Leaves are evergreen, light green, pointed and ⅛ to ¼ inch long. Flowers are ½ inch across and bright yellow, blooming in late spring on short stems. Zones 4-10. *S. anglicum,* English stonecrop, is 2 to 4 inches high and spreads by underground stems to form a mat 12 inches across. Leaves are evergreen, medium green, cylindrical, ¼ inch long and borne densely along the stems. Flowers are pink or white, ½ inch across and bloom in early summer on 6-inch stems. Zones 4-10. *S. brev-*

ifolium, shortleaf stonecrop, grows 2 to 3 inches high and spreads by underground stems to form a clump 12 inches across. Leaves are evergreen, gray to white flushed in red and ⅛ inch long. Flowers are white, ¼ inch wide and bloom on 8-inch upright branches in late spring and early summer. Zones 4-10. *S. cauticola,* shortleaf stonecrop, has deciduous, trailing stems that spread to 16 inches across and form a mat 3 inches tall. Foliage is round, gray-green and ½ inch across. Flowers are ½ inch wide, bright pink to rose and bloom in late summer on 6-inch stems. Zones 5-10.

S. kamtschaticum is deciduous and forms a mound 6 to 9 inches high and 12 to 18 inches across. Leaves are oval, 2 inches long, bright green in spring, summer and fall, and bronze in winter. Flowers are ¾ inch wide and bloom in late summer, but often sparsely. Zones 4-10. *S. lineare,* stringy stonecrop, is a fast-growing evergreen that is 6 inches high and 12 to 24 inches across. Foliage is light green to gray-green, needlelike and 1 inch long. Yellow, ½-inch flowers bloom in early summer. 'Variegatum' has leaves edged in white and is more compact and slower-growing. Zones 5-10. *S. reflexum,* yellow stonecrop, is an evergreen that spreads to 15 inches across. Leaves are gray-green, needlelike and ½ inch long, densely covering 3-inch ascending branches. Flowers are golden yellow and ½ inch wide and bloom in summer on 12-inch stems. Zones 5-10. *S. spurium,* two-row stonecrop, grows quickly by trailing stems to form a mat 3 to 6 inches high and 12 to 24 inches across. Foliage is oval, 1 inch across and semievergreen. Leaves are dark green in spring, summer and fall, and turn red in winter. Flowers are white to pink, ½ inch across and bloom in middle to late summer on 9-inch stems. 'Dragon's Blood' has deep rose to red flowers and foliage edged in reddish purple. 'Splendens' has deep carmine flowers ¾ inch across.

Growing conditions. Stonecrop may be grown in sun to light shade in sandy, poor, dry, well-drained soil. Good drainage is critical in winter. Stonecrop can become invasive but is easy to control as it is very shallow rooted. Propagate from seeds or by division or cuttings. Pieces of stems or leaves tossed on the ground will root quickly with no attention.

Landscape uses. Plant stonecrop in a rock garden, on a rock wall, or under trees or shrubs. Low-growing species are often used between stepping-stones but do not tolerate foot traffic well.

—

Sempervivum
(sem-per-VEE-vum)
Live forever, houseleek

Genus of succulent perennials, some of which are used as ground covers. Leaves are thick and grow in small rosettes; new plants form around the base of the parent plant. Flowers are white, yellow, pink or red, and star-shaped. They bloom in clusters in summer, but often are not showy. Zones 4-10.

Selected species and varieties. *S. tectorum,* hen-and-chickens, grows 6 inches high and 3 to 6 inches across. Foliage is gray-green and the pointed leaf tips are often tinged with purple. Flowers are pink to purplish red, 1 inch across and bloom somewhat unreliably on 12- to 18-inch stems.

Growing conditions. Grow hen-and-chickens in full sun in any well-drained soil. It tolerates poor soil, heat and drought, but should be watered in summer. Propagate from seeds or by removing the offsets from the parent rosette and rooting them.

Landscape uses. Plant hen-and-chickens in small areas, in rock gardens and in rock walls.

—

Sheep fescue see *Festuca*

—

Shibataea (she-BAT-ee-a)
Bamboo

Perennial ornamental grass that has slender, flat stems that grow in a zigzag manner. Zones 6-10.

Selected species and varieties. *S. kumasaca,* ruscus-leaved bamboo, grows 3 to 6 feet tall. Leaves are oval, pointed, 2 to 4 inches long and 1 inch wide, and clothe the upright stem. Foliage is dark green when young and yellow-green when mature.

Growing conditions. Grow ruscus-leaved bamboo in partial shade in rich, moist, acid soil. Foliage may become brown in cold winters. Ruscus-leaved bamboo is not as invasive as other bamboos. Propagate by division or by root cuttings.

Landscape uses. Plant ruscus-leaved bamboo as a hedge or a screen, or in a container.

Siberian carpet cypress
see *Microbiota*

Siberian tea see *Bergenia*

Silver spike grass
see *Spodiopogon*

Snow-in-summer see *Cerastium*

—

Spartina (spar-TEE-na)
Cord grass

Upright, perennial ornamental grass that spreads by rhizomes. Leaf blades are long and coarse. Stems are thin and wiry and topped with one-sided, narrow seed heads in branched clusters. Zones 5-10.

Selected species and varieties. *S. pectinata* 'Aureo-marginata', prairie cord grass, grows 3 to 8 feet tall and has a coarse texture. Leaves are narrow, 2 feet long, arching and shiny green with rough, yellow margins. The leaves turn yellow before dropping from the plant after frost. Seed heads are 6 to 15 inches long on 5- to 8-foot stems and turn yellow in autumn.

Growing conditions. Grow prairie cord grass in full sun or light shade. It will grow in salt and fresh water marshes or in sandy garden soil. It is invasive when grown in water, less so when grown in soil. Propagate by division or from seeds.

Landscape uses. Plant prairie cord grass as a water plant, as a background plant or as a specimen. It has a heavy root system and is useful where soil erosion control is needed.

—

Speedwell see *Veronica*

—

Spodiopogon
(spo-dee-o-PO-gon)

Deciduous, perennial ornamental grass that has arching, stiff foliage and erect stems that carry seed heads in late summer. Zones 5-10.

Selected species and varieties. *S. sibericus,* silver spike grass, grows to a height of 3 feet. Leaves are 12 inches long and 1 inch wide. They are dark green, taking on a red to purple color in midsummer and turning completely red or purple in fall. Silvery seed heads grow 12 inches long on 5-foot stems.

Growing conditions. Grow silver spike grass in full sun or light shade in moist to wet soil. Propagate by division or from seeds.

SHIBATAEA KUMASACA

SPARTINA PECTINATA 'AUREO-MARGINATA'

SPODIOPOGON SIBERICUS

STACHYS BYZANTINA

STENOTAPHRUM SECUNDATUM

STIPA GIGANTEA

Landscape uses. Plant silver spike grass as a specimen at water's edge.

—

Spring heath see *Erica*

Spurge see *Euphorbia; Pachysandra*

—

Stachys (STAK-is)

Annual or perennial ground cover. Oval or lance-shaped leaves clothe square stems. Tubular flowers of purple, scarlet, yellow, white or pink bloom in whorled spikes at the ends of the stems. Zones 4-10.

Selected species and varieties. *S. byzantina,* sometimes designated *S. lanata* or *S. olympica,* lamb's ears, forms a mat of foliage 8 inches high and 36 inches across. Leaves are soft, white, woolly and 4 inches long. Pink or purple flowers that are ½ inch wide and 1 inch long bloom in summer on 18-inch stems. Evergreen Zones 7-10.

Growing conditions. Grow lamb's ears in full sun or light shade in light, sandy, well-drained soil. Good drainage during winter is critical. Propagate by division or from seeds.

Landscape uses. Plant lamb's ears on slopes, under high-branched trees, as edgings or in rock gardens.

—

Stenotaphrum (sten-o-TAF-rum)
St. Augustine grass

Warm-season turfgrass that is low-growing and very coarse textured. It is very aggressive and spreads by thick stolons. Region C; southern parts of B and E.

Selected species and varieties. *S. secundatum* is blue-green in color and spongy in character. 'Bitter Blue' is medium textured and at low temperatures keeps its color better than many other varieties. 'Floratam' is dark green and resistant to chinch bugs and to the virus St. Augustine decline (SAD), which causes mottling of blades, yellowing and general decline in vigor. 'Floratine' is fine textured and keeps its color well in winter. 'Seville' is dark green, very shade-tolerant and resistant to SAD virus and leaf spot.

Growing conditions. Grow St. Augustine grass in full sun to full shade. It is the most shade-tolerant warm-season turfgrass. It has fair drought resistance and good wear tolerance. It prefers humid climate and tolerates seashore conditions. Soil should be rich, moist, fertile, sandy and well drained, with a pH of 6.5. Mow to a height of 1½ to 2½ inches. Fertilize with 3 to 6 pounds of nitrogen per 1,000 square feet per year. The grass discolors in winter when temperatures drop below 55° F. Propagate by plugs or sod. Brown patch, St. Augustine decline (SAD) virus, leaf spot and dollar spot are the most serious diseases; chinch bug is the most serious insect problem.

Landscape uses. Plant St. Augustine grass in warm, humid climates on lawns that will receive average foot traffic.

—

Stipa (STY-pa)
Feather grass

Perennial ornamental grass that has narrow leaves and large, showy, feathery seed heads. Zones 5-10.

Selected species and varieties. *S. gigantea* has a tufted mound of arching foliage 3 feet high at the base of the plant. Leaves are 18 inches long. Seed heads are thin and drooping, 15 inches long and appear in late summer on 6-foot, wide-spreading stems.

Growing conditions. Grow feather grass in full sun to partial shade in light, well-drained, fertile soil. Propagate by division or from seeds.

Landscape uses. Plant feather grass as a specimen or as a background plant.

—

Stonecrop see *Sedum*

Strawberry see *Fragaria*

Strawberry geranium see *Saxifraga*

Sun rose see *Helianthemum*

Sweet box see *Sarcococca*

Sweet fern see *Comptonia*

Sweet grass see *Glyceria*

Sweet woodruff see *Galium*

Switch grass see *Panicum*

—

Symphytum (SIM-fi-tum)
Comfrey

Perennial that may be grown as a ground cover. Large basal leaves and stems are coarse and hairy. Bell-shaped, five-lobed flowers of yellow, blue, white, rose or purple bloom in branching clusters. Zones 4-9.

Selected species and varieties. *S. grandiflorum*, spreading comfrey, grows rapidly to 8 inches high and 24 inches across, spreading by stems that root at their tips. Leaves are dark green, oblong or oval, and semievergreen. Flowers are ¾ inch long, white to pale yellow and bloom in late spring in nodding clusters on 12-inch stems.

Growing conditions. Grow spreading comfrey in partial to full shade in dry, well-drained soil. It can be grown in full sun in cool climates and tolerates poor soil. Propagate by division, by root cuttings or from seeds.

Landscape uses. Plant spreading comfrey on slopes or under trees.

—

Tall fescue see *Festuca*

—

Taxus (TAK-sus)
Yew

Genus of slow-growing, coniferous, evergreen trees and shrubs, some of which grow in a spreading habit and are used as ground cover. Needles are ½ to 1 inch long and very dark green with lighter undersides. Leaves spiral around the branches, lie in a flat plane or form a V. Bark is reddish brown, flaky and thin. Female plants produce red berries; the seed inside the berry, not the pulp, is poisonous, as are the leaves and the bark. Zones 3-8.

Selected species and varieties. *T. baccata*, English yew, has shiny, slightly curved needles that have two pale green lines on the undersides. Needles are usually arranged in flat planes. 'Repandens', spreading English yew, grows 2 to 4 feet high and up to 12 feet wide and has a flat top. Branches spread horizontally and are slightly pendulous at the tips. Needles are 1 inch long. Zones 6-8. *T. cuspidata*, Japanese yew, has soft, dull green needles with two whitish yellow lines on the undersides. Needles are usually arranged in a V shape. 'Densa', cushion Japanese yew, is a dense, rounded shrub 18 inches high and 36 inches across. 'Prostrata' grows 18 to 24 inches high and spreads to 48 inches across with a flat top. Zones 5-8.

Growing conditions. Grow yew in full sun or partial shade. Soil should be fertile, moist, acid to neutral and well drained. Yew will not tolerate constantly wet soil or hot, dry heat. Do not plant it where it will be subject to winter sun and wind. Propagate by cuttings or from seed.

Landscape uses. Plant yews on banks or in hedges. As they respond well to pruning, they are often used in formal gardens.

—

Teucrium (TOO-kree-um)
Germander

Perennial or small evergreen shrub that is used as a ground cover. Stems and foliage are covered with white to silver hairs. Two-lipped, tubular flowers bloom in showy spikes at the ends of the stems. Zones 5-10.

Selected species and varieties. *T. chamaedrys* grows 10 to 12 inches high and spreads to 2 feet across from underground stems. Leaves are shiny, dark green, toothed and ¾ inch long. White, pink or purplish red flowers bloom in summer in loose spikes. 'Prostratum' grows 6 inches high and spreads to 2 feet wide.

Growing conditions. Grow germander in full sun or light shade in any well-drained soil. Water deeply but infrequently. It tolerates poor soil, but does not like drying winds. Propagate by division, by cuttings or from seeds.

Landscape uses. Germander tolerates shearing and is therefore used as a neat edging or a low, formal hedge.

—

Thyme see *Thymus*

—

Thymus (TY-mus)
Thyme

Low-growing woody perennial or small shrub that spreads to form a mat 18 inches across. Leaves are small and aromatic. Lilac or purple flowers bloom in small clusters in summer. Zones 4-10.

Selected species and varieties. *T. praecox arcticus*, mother of thyme, grows 1 to 2 inches high. It has ¼-inch, dark green, leathery evergreen leaves and ½-inch, globe-shaped or hemispherical flower heads. Blooms are white, pink, rose or purple and appear on 4-inch stems. 'Splendens' has red flowers. *T. pseu-*

SYMPHYTUM GRANDIFLORUM

TAXUS BACCATA 'REPANDENS'

TEUCRIUM CHAMAEDRYS 'PROSTRATUM'

THYMUS PRAECOX ARCTICUS

TIARELLA CORDIFOLIA

TOLMIEA MENZIESII

TRIFOLIUM REPENS

VACCINIUM VITIS-IDAEA MINUS

dolanuginosus, woolly thyme, forms a mat ½ to 1 inch tall. Leaves and stems are soft, gray, hairy and ⅛ inch long. It rarely flowers, but when it does, the flowers are pink. *T. serpyllum* is identical in appearance to *T. praecox arcticus* and some horticulturists contend that it is the same plant. *T. vulgaris,* common thyme, is a shrub 6 to 15 inches tall and has ½-inch, evergreen, gray-green leaves and white to lilac flowers in whorls. 'Roseus' has pink flowers. Zones 5-10.

Growing conditions. Thyme may be grown in full sun in dry, poor, well-drained soil. It is very heat-tolerant. Propagate by cuttings or division, or from seeds.

Landscape uses. Plant thyme in a rock garden, between stepping-stones, as a border, as a lawn substitute or on a dry slope. Common thyme is also used as a culinary herb.

—

Tiarella (ty-a-REL-a)

Woody perennial ground cover that spreads by rhizomes to form a clump of basal leaves. Small white or reddish flowers bloom in upright, feathery, cylindrical spikes in spring. Zones 5-10.

Selected species and varieties. *T. cordifolia,* foamflower, has evergreen, heart-shaped, lobed or toothed leaves that are 4 inches across. They form a clump 6 inches high and 24 inches across. White flowers bloom in 4-inch spikes at the ends of slender, 9-inch stems.

Growing conditions. Grow foamflower in partial shade in cool, moist, rich, acid, well-drained soil. Propagate by division or from seeds.

Landscape uses. Plant foamflower under trees, in a rock garden or in a woodland garden.

—

Tolmiea (tol-MEE-a)
Piggyback plant

Perennial ground cover that spreads by rhizomes and forms a clump of basal leaves. Flowers of greenish white or reddish brown bloom in spikes in summer but are not showy. Zones 8-10.

Selected species and varieties. *T. menziesii* has heart-shaped, rich green, hairy leaves that are 4 inches across and may be either toothed or

lobed. The leaves form a mound 9 inches high and 24 inches across. Flowers bloom in 8-inch spikes at the ends of 18-inch stems. New plants grow at the base of the leaf.

Growing conditions. Grow piggyback plant in partial to full shade in cool, moist, rich, acid, well-drained soil. Propagate by division or from seeds. A new plant that grows at the base of a leaf may also be removed and rooted.

Landscape uses. Piggyback plant is grown under trees and in woodland gardens.

—

Trailing African daisy
see *Osteospermum*

Treasure flower see *Gazania*

—

Trifolium (try-FO-lee-um)
Clover

Creeping perennial ground cover that has three round leaflets per leaf and round to oval flower heads of white, pink or yellow. Zones 4-8.

Selected species and varieties. *T. repens,* white clover, is a low-growing perennial less than ½ inch tall that spreads by stolons. Flowers are white and fragrant, and bloom in summer. White clover attracts bees and is considered a weed in high-quality lawns.

Growing conditions. Grow clover in full sun or light shade. Soil should be moist and fine textured and have a pH of 6.0 to 7.0. Climate must be humid. Clover can be mowed from ¼ to 1 inch high. It does not need to be fertilized and has good wear tolerance. Propagate from seeds.

Landscape uses. White clover is sometimes included in turfgrass mixtures for low-quality lawns. It is rarely grown by itself.

—

Vaccinium (vak-SIN-ee-um)

Genus of erect or low-growing shrubs, some of which are used as ground covers. Flowers are urn-shaped, small and generally not showy. They bloom in clusters at the ends of the branches. Showy, edible berries of blue or red follow the flowers. Zones 3-9.

Selected species and varieties. *V. vitis-idaea,* cowberry, is an evergreen that spreads from 15 to 30 inches across by creeping rhizomes. Upright branches grow 6 to 12 inches high, reaching the taller heights in shady locations. Leaves are 1¼ inches long, oval and shiny. Pink flowers bloom in nodding racemes in late spring. Berries are red and edible but sour. Zones 5-9. *V. vitis-idaea minus,* mountain cranberry, is 6 inches tall and has smaller leaves.

Growing conditions. Grow cowberry and mountain cranberry in full sun to partial shade in sandy, rich, moist, acid soil. Propagate by cuttings, division or layering.

Landscape uses. Plant cowberry and mountain cranberry in small areas or as edgings.

Vancouveria
(van-koo-VEER-ee-a)

Perennial ground cover that spreads by creeping rhizomes. Leaves have three leaflets, which are lobed near the tip and dull green. Flowers are small, white or yellow, and bloom in drooping clusters at the ends of the branches. Zones 5-9.

Selected species and varieties. *V. hexandra,* American barrenwort, grows 4 to 18 inches high and 24 inches across, and has wiry stems. Each leaflet is ½ inch to 1½ inches across. Flowers are white, ½ inch across and bloom in late spring in loose, airy panicles.

Growing conditions. Grow American barrenwort in partial to full shade in deep, rich, well-drained, moist soil. Propagate by division.

Landscape uses. Plant American barrenwort under trees or shrubs or as a border plant.

Veronica (ve-RON-i-ka)
Speedwell

Genus of upright and low-growing perennials, some of which are used as ground covers. Tubular flowers appear in spikes at the ends of the branches in late spring or early summer. Zones 4-10.

Selected species and varieties. *V. prostrata,* rock speedwell, is a mat-forming or tufted plant that has ½- to ¾-inch narrow leaves. Showy blue flowers, each ⅓ inch long, bloom at the ends of 8- to 10-inch branches. 'Alba' has white

flowers; 'Rosea' has bright purplish pink flowers. *V. repens,* creeping speedwell, forms a low mat of shiny, ½-inch, mosslike leaves. It can spread to 24 inches across. Blue, pink or white flowers each ¼ inch long bloom in loose clusters at the ends of 4-inch stems. Zones 5-10.

Growing conditions. Grow speedwell in full sun to partial shade in rich, moist, well-drained soil. Creeping speedwell can be very invasive and will become a weed in the lawn if it is not confined with an underground barrier. Propagate by division, by cuttings or from seeds.

Landscape uses. Plant speedwell in a rock garden or as a border plant. Creeping speedwell is used between stepping-stones and as a carpet to spring bulbs.

Vinca (VINK-a)

Genus of erect or trailing evergreen shrubs and vines, some of which are used as ground covers. The trailing types root as they grow along the ground. Single, five-petaled, flat flowers of blue or white bloom in the leaf axils in early spring. Foliage is oval and shiny. Zones 5-10.

Selected species and varieties. *V. major,* big periwinkle, forms an open mound 6 to 18 inches high and 48 inches across. Leaves are oval to heart-shaped, dark green, 3 inches across and formed on wiry stems. Flowers are blue, white, pink or red, and 1 to 2 inches across. 'Variegata' has foliage with creamy white edges. Zones 7-10. *V. minor,* periwinkle, myrtle, forms a dense cover 6 to 10 inches high and 24 inches across. Leaves are leathery, oblong, dark green and 2 inches long, and grow on thin stems. Light blue flowers are ¾ inch across. 'Alba' has white flowers and wider leaves; 'Atropurpurea' has purple flowers. 'Bowlesii', Bowles vinca, is less spreading; it forms a large clump covered with larger leaves. Flowers are deep blue.

Growing conditions. Grow vinca in full sun to partial shade; partial shade is preferred where summers are hot. Soil should be sandy, moist and well drained. Vinca can be mowed. Big periwinkle is more invasive than periwinkle. Propagate by cuttings, division or layering, or from seeds.

Landscape uses. Vinca may be planted on slopes, under trees and under shrubs.

VANCOUVERIA HEXANDRA

VERONICA PROSTRATA 'ROSEA'

VINCA MINOR

VIOLA SORORIA

ZOYSIA JAPONICA 'MEYER'

Viola (VY-o-la)
Violet

Annual or perennial that can be used as a ground cover. It forms spreading tufts of oval or heart-shaped basal leaves. Flowers are five-petaled and violet, blue, red, purple, lilac, yellow or white. Zones 3-10.

Selected species and varieties. *V. odorata,* sweet violet, is a perennial growing 6 to 8 inches high and spreading 18 to 24 inches across. The plant may send out runners that will root at their ends. Leaves are heart-shaped and 3 inches or more across. Flowers are sweet-scented, white or deep violet, and bloom in early spring. Zones 6-10. *V. sororia,* woolly blue violet, is a perennial growing 6 inches high and spreading 18 to 24 inches across by creeping roots. Leaves are heart-shaped, 6 inches across and formed on long stalks. Flowers are blue, ½ inch across and appear in early spring. Zones 5-10.

Growing conditions. Grow violets in full sun to full shade; afternoon shade is necessary where summers are hot. Soil should be rich and moist. Violets can be invasive and sweet violet is prone to spider mite. Propagate by division or from seeds.

Landscape uses. Plant violets under shrubs, in woodland gardens and as a base for spring-flowering bulbs.

—

Violet see *Viola*

Wheatgrass see *Agropyron*

White clover see *Trifolium*

Wild ginger see *Asarum*

Wild lilac see *Ceanothus*

Wintercreeper see *Euonymus*

Wintergreen see *Gaultheria*

Wood millet see *Milium*

Woodruff see *Galium*

Wood rush see *Luzula*

Wood sedge see *Carex*

Wormwood see *Artemisia*

Yarrow see *Achillea*

Yellow archangel see *Lamiastrum*

Yerba buena see *Satureja*

Yew see *Taxus*

Zebra grass see *Miscanthus*

—

Zoysia (ZOY-zee-a)

Warm-season and transitional zone turfgrass that spreads by thick stolons and rhizomes and develops slowly into a uniform, dense, low-growing, high-quality lawn that remains evergreen above 50° F. Stems and leaves are tough and stiff. Regions B, C and E; coastal areas of A and F.

Selected species and varieties. *Z. japonica,* Japanese lawngrass, is dark green and has prostrate leaf blades 3 inches wide. It is the coarsest-textured zoysia. 'Meyer' is medium dark green and medium textured. *Z. matrella,* manilagrass, is light green, has moderately prostrate leaf blades 1½ inches wide, and is medium textured. *Z. tenuifolia,* mascarenegrass, is very light green and has erect leaf blades 1 inch wide. It is the finest-textured zoysia. Zones 9 and 10. 'Emerald' is a hybrid cross of *Z. japonica* and *Z. tenuifolia.* It is medium dark green and fine textured. Zones 8-10.

Growing conditions. Grow zoysia in full sun or partial shade. Mascarenegrass is the most shade-tolerant of the zoysias. All are very tolerant of heat and drought. Soil should be fine textured, fertile, well drained and have a pH of 6.0 to 7.0. Mow to a height of ½ to 1 inch. Zoysia is difficult to mow because of its tough leaf blades. Fertilize minimally with 1 pound of nitrogen per 1,000 square feet in spring, and again in summer and in fall; or ¾ pound of nitrogen per 1,000 square feet monthly throughout the eight-month growing season. All zoysias are very wear-tolerant when growing but have poor wear tolerance during the winter, when they are dormant. Zoysia turns straw brown below 50° F but can be overseeded with cool-season turfgrasses. Propagate by plugs or by sod. Zoysia is relatively free of major insect and disease problems.

Landscape uses. Plant zoysia in lawns that are actively used in the humid warm and transitional regions.

FURTHER READING

Atkinson, Robert E., *The Complete Book of Groundcovers.* New York: David McKay, 1970.

Bennett, Jennifer, ed., *Ground Covers.* Camden East, Ontario: Camden House, 1987.

Brooklyn Botanic Garden:
Ground Covers and Vines. New York: Brooklyn Botanic Garden, 1978.
Home Lawn Handbook. New York: Brooklyn Botanic Garden, 1973.

Cassiday, Bruce, *Home Guide to Lawns and Landscaping.* New York: Harper & Row, 1976.

Dimond, Don, and Michael MacCaskey, *All about Ground Covers.* San Francisco: Ortho Books/Chevron Chemical Company, 1982.

Duble, Richard, and James Carroll Kell, *Southern Lawns and Groundcovers.* Houston, Texas: Pacesetter Press, 1977.

Fish, Margery, *Ground Cover Plants.* Boston: Faber and Faber, 1964.

Foley, Daniel J., *Ground Covers for Easier Gardening.* New York: Dover Publications, 1961.

Franklin, Stuart, *Building a Healthy Lawn.* Pownal, Vermont: Storey Communications, 1988.

Hastings, Don, *Gardening in the South: Trees, Shrubs and Lawns.* Dallas: Taylor Publishing, 1987.

MacCaskey, Michael:
All about Lawns. San Francisco: Ortho Books/Chevron Chemical Company, 1985.
Lawns and Ground Covers. Los Angeles: HP Books, 1982.

Ottesen, Carole, *The New American Gardener.* New York: Macmillan, 1987.

Schenk, George, *The Complete Shade Gardener.* Boston: Houghton Mifflin, 1984.

Sunset Editors, *Lawns and Ground Covers.* Menlo Park, California: Lane Publishing, 1979.

Taylor, Norman, *Taylor's Guide to Ground Covers, Vines and Grasses.* Boston: Houghton Mifflin, 1987.

Thomas, Graham Stuart, *Plants for Ground-Cover.* London: J. M. Dent & Sons, 1970.

Wyman, Donald, *Ground Cover Plants.* New York: Macmillan, 1956.

PICTURE CREDITS

The sources for the illustrations in this book are listed below. Cover photograph by Michael Dirr. Watercolor paintings by Nicholas Fasciano and Yin Yi except pages 96, 97, 98, 99, 100, 101, 106, 107: Lorraine Moseley Epstein. Maps on pages 88, 89, 91, 93, 95: digitized by Richard Furno, inked by John Drummond.

Frontispiece paintings listed by page number: 6: *The Birthplace of Herbert Hoover, West Branch, Iowa,* 1931, by Grant Wood. Purchased jointly by the Des Moines Art Center and the Minneapolis Institute of Arts. Gift of Mrs. Howard Frank of Oskaloosa and the Des Moines Association of Fine Arts, 1982. 36: *Jimmy and Leaf Cart,* c. 1965, by Fairfield Porter, courtesy Mr. and Mrs. E. W. Andrews, Jr. Photo courtesy Hirschl and Adler Modern, New York. 64: Detail, *Ten Thousand Bamboo in Mist and Rain,* Chinese hand scroll, c. 1438, by Jin Wenjin, courtesy Arthur M. Sackler Museum, Harvard University, Cambridge, Massachusetts, gift of Galen L. Stone.

Photographs in Chapters 1 through 3 from the following sources, listed by page number: 8: Bob Grant. 10: John Colwell/Grant Heilman Photography. 14: Allan Armitage. 18: Norm Thomas. 22: Derek Fell. 24: Bob Grant. 26: Ann Reilly. 30, 32: Horticultural Photography, Corvallis, OR. 38: Jim Strawsen/Grant Heilman Photography. 40: Lefever/Grushow/Grant Heilman Photography. 44: Lou Jacobs, Jr./ Grant Heilman Photography. 46: Jerry Pavia. 50: John Colwell/Grant Heilman Photography. 52: Grant Heilman Photography. 54: Jerry Howard/Photo-Nats. 56: Horticultural Photography, Corvallis, OR. 58: Michael Dirr. 60: Horticultural Photography, Corvallis, OR. 62: Larry Albee. 66, 68: Michael Dirr. 72: Bob Grant. 76, 78: Horticultural Photography, Corvallis, OR. 82: Bob Grant.

Photographs in the Dictionary of Lawns and Ground Covers by Pamela Harper, except where listed by page and numbered from top to bottom. Page 110, 3, 4: A. J. Koski. 112, 3: Horticultural Photography, Corvallis, OR. 113, 2: Derek Fell. 114, 3: A. J. Koski; 4: Horticultural Photography, Corvallis, OR. 115, 3: Terrance P. Riordan. 116, 1: Derek Fell. 118, 2: Derek Fell; 4: John L. Smith/ Photo-Nats. 119, 4: Ann Reilly/Photo-Nats. 120, 1: Norm Thomas; 2: Horticultural Photography, Corvallis, OR. 122, 1: David Chalmers. 122, 4: Derek Fell. 123, 2: Tony Avent. 124, 1: Susan Roth; 3: Ann Reilly/Photo-Nats. 125, 1: Jerry Pavia; 2: Horticultural Photography, Corvallis, OR. 126, 3: Robert Lyons/Color Advantage. 127, 1: Ann Reilly/Photo-Nats. 131, 2: Joanne Pavia. 132, 2: A. J. Koski. 135, 4: John L. Smith/Photo-Nats. 136, 2: David M. Stone/Photo-Nats; 3: Derek Fell. 137, 2: Joanne Pavia. 138, 1: Norm Thomas. 139, 2: Horticultural Photography, Corvallis, OR.; 3: Ann Reilly/Photo-Nats. 140, 1: Ann Reilly. 141, 1: Charles Mardin Fitch; 2: Joanne Pavia; 3: Harold Greer/Greer Gardens. 142, 1: Robert Lyons/Color Advantage; 3: Larry Albee. 143, 1: Al Bussewitz/Photo-Nats; 2: Bob Grant. 144, 2 : Horticultual Photography, Corvallis, OR. 145, 1: Daphne Lewis/Bamboo Brokerage; 2, 3: Richard Simon. 146, 2: Norm Thomas. 147, 2: Derek Fell. 148, 2: Derek Fell. 149, 1: Steven Still. 150, 2: Tony Avent.

ACKNOWLEDGMENTS

The index for this book was prepared by Lee McKee. The editors also wish to thank: Joe Borras, Accokeek, Maryland; Sarah Brash, Alexandria, Virginia; Sarah Broley, Washington, D.C.; Rose Crofford, Massapequa, New York; Betsy Frankel, Alexandria, Virginia; John Greenlee, Greenlee Nurseries, Pomona, California; Kenneth E. Hancock, Annandale, Virginia; Mark Hebert, Troy-Bilt Manufacturers Corporation, Troy, New York; Mary Kay Honeycutt, Crofton, Maryland; Dr. Norman Hummel, Cornell University, Ithaca, New York; Tovah Martin, Logee's Greenhouses, Danielson, Connecticut; Ed Moulin, Brooklyn Botanic Garden, Brooklyn, New York; Terry Mulligan, Aspetuck Valley Country Club, Weston, Connecticut; Thanh Huu Nguyen, Alexandria, Virginia; Dr. G. W. Pepin, Pickseed West Inc., Tangent, Oregon; Dr. A. Martin Petrovic, Cornell University, Ithaca, New York; Jayne E. Rohrich, Alexandria, Virginia; Joseph Savage, Nassau County Cooperative Extension, Plainview, New York; Candace H. Scott, College Park, Maryland; Dr. Don Short, University of Florida, Gainesville, Florida; Dr. James Watson, Toro Company, Minneapolis, Minnesota; Stanley Zontek, U.S. Golf Association, West Chester, Pennsylvania.

INDEX

Numerals in italics indicate an illustration of the subject mentioned.

REDEFINITION

Senior Editors	Anne Horan, Robert G. Mason
Design Director	Robert Barkin
Designer	Edwina Smith
Illustration	Nicholas Fasciano
Assistant Designers	Sue Pratt, Monique Strawderman
Picture Editor	Deborah Thornton
Production Editor	Anthony K. Pordes
Editorial Research	Mary Yee (volume coordinator), Gail Prensky, Barbara B. Smith, Elizabeth D. McLean
Picture Research	Caroline N. Tell
Text Editor	Sharon Cygan
Writers	Gerald Jonas, Ann Reilly, David S. Thomson
Administrative Assistant	Margaret M. Higgins
Business Manager	Catherine M. Chase
Finance Director	Vaughn A. Meglan
PRESIDENT	Edward Brash

Time-Life Books Inc.
is a wholly owned subsidiary of

TIME INCORPORATED

FOUNDER	Henry R. Luce 1898-1967
Editor-in-Chief	Jason McManus
Chairman and Chief Executive Officer	J. Richard Munro
President and Chief Operating Officer	N. J. Nicholas Jr.
Editorial Director	Richard B. Stolley
Executive Vice President, Books	Kelso F. Sutton
Vice President, Books	Paul V. McLaughlin

TIME-LIFE BOOKS INC.

EDITOR	George Constable
Executive Editor	Ellen Phillips
Director of Design	Louis Klein
Director of Editorial Resources	Phyllis K. Wise
Editorial Board	Russell B. Adams Jr., Dale M. Brown, Roberta Conlan, Thomas H. Flaherty, Lee Hassig, Donia Ann Steele, Rosalind Stubenberg
Director of Photography and Research	John Conrad Weiser
Assistant Director of Editorial Resources	Elise Ritter Gibson
PRESIDENT	Christopher T. Linen
Chief Operating Officer	John M. Fahey Jr.
Senior Vice Presidents	Robert M. DeSena, James L. Mercer, Paul R. Stewart
Vice Presidents	Stephen L. Bair, Ralph J. Cuomo, Neal Goff, Stephen L. Goldstein, Juanita T. James, Carol Kaplan, Susan J. Maruyama, Robert H. Smith, Joseph J. Ward
Director of Production Services	Robert J. Passantino
Supervisor of Quality Control	James King

Editorial Operations

Copy Chief	Diane Ullius
Production	Celia Beattie
Library	Louise D. Forstall
Correspondents	Elisabeth Kraemer-Singh (Bonn), Maria Vincenza Aloisi (Paris), Ann Natanson (Rome)

THE CONSULTANTS

C. Colston Burrell is the series consultant for The Time-Life Gardener's Guide. He is Curator of Plant Collections at the Minnesota Landscape Arboretum, part of the University of Minnesota.

Wayne Ambler, consultant for *Lawns and Ground Covers,* is a teacher of horticulture. He is a member of the adjunct faculty at J. Sargeant Reynolds Community College and at Patrick Henry High School in Ashland, Virginia.

Library of Congress Cataloging-in-Publication Data
Lawns and ground covers.
    p. cm.—(The Time-Life gardener's guide)
    Bibliography: p.
    Includes index.
    1. Lawns.   2. Ground cover plants
I. Time-Life Books. II. Series.
SB433.L383 1989   635.9'64—dc19   88-37530 CIP
ISBN 0-8094-6632-5
ISBN 0-8094-6633-3 (lib. bdg.)